Early Jazz

SUNY Press Jazz Styles

Early Jazz

A Concise Introduction, from Its Beginnings through 1929

FUMI TOMITA

SUNY PRESS

Top Photo: The Superior Orchestra, 1910. Standing, left to right: Buddy Johnson (trb); Willie "Bunk" Johnson (cornet); "Big Eye" Louis Nelson Delisle (clr); Billy Marrero (b). Seated, left to right: Walter Brundy (drms); Peter Bocage (vln & leader); Richard Payne (gtr).

Bottom photo: Bix's Rhythm Jugglers at the Gennett Recording studios, 1925. From l to r: Don Murray (clarinet), howdy Quicksell (bnjo), TomyY Gargano (drms), Paul Mertz (pno), Bix Beiderbecke (cornet), Tommy Dorsey (trb).

Public Domain/Ben Car Collection

Published by State University of New York Press, Albany

For information, contact State University of New York Press, Albany, NY
www.sunypress.edu

Library of Congress Cataloging-in-Publication Data

Name: Tomita, Fumi, 1971– author.
Title: Early jazz : a concise introduction, from its beginnings through
  1929 / Fumi Tomita.
Description: Albany : State University of New York Press, [2024]. | Series:
  SUNY Press jazz styles | Includes bibliographical references and index.
Identifiers: LCCN 2023022983 | ISBN 9781438496382 (hardcover : alk. paper) |
  ISBN 9781438496399 (ebook) | ISBN 9781438496375 (pbk. : alk. paper)
Subjects: LCSH: Jazz—To 1921—History and criticism. | Jazz—1921–1929—
  History and criticism.
Classification: LCC ML3506 .T64 2024 | DDC 781.6509—dc23/eng/20230515
LC record available at https://lccn.loc.gov/2023022983

10 9 8 7 6 5 4 3 2 1

Contents

Acknowledgments

Although I consider my book an updated version of Schuller's own text, his book provided the basis for my own. I have also drawn on more recent books and articles that explore this music. Some artists have yet to be explored in a full-length book or article, so I have also relied on liner notes from CD compilations and box sets. These includes recent releases from Mosaic, Retrieval, Timeless, Jazz Oracle, and Frog, but also those that are out-of-print such as the *Giants of Jazz* series from the late 1970s and early 1980s. Despite being almost as old as Schuller's book, the research was professional, written by authoritative figures in their respective fields, and, in many cases, still relevant today. Such older materials, including other out-of-print texts, were particularly useful in parsing out certain musicians, like Red Nichols or some of the individual Chicagoans, that have not been explored elsewhere.

Among the other outstanding studies of early jazz that shaped this book are works by Richard Sudhalter, Thomas Brothers, Court Carney, Thomas Hennessey, and Brian Harker's study of Louis Armstrong's Hot Five and Seven. While those recordings are universally agreed upon as being masterful, Harker provides shape to this oeuvre by highlighting six songs that illuminate Armstrong's path to greatness. Mark Berresford's championing of vaudeville-style entertainment on the influence of early jazz was pivotal as well.

I'd like to thank my colleagues at the University of Massachusetts Amherst for their continued support, especially Jeff Holmes, Felipe Salles, Thomas Giampietro, and Cathy Jensen-Hole. Big thank you to everyone at SUNY Press that I've worked with including John Britch and Susan Geraghty; Aimee Harrison and everyone on the design team; and Leonard Rosenbaum for indexing. Special thank you to editor Richard Carlin for his support of my manuscript and his patience through all the revisions. Finally, I'd like to thank my wife, Marianne, for her unending support and love without which I would not have been able to finish the book.

Introduction

A trend in recent jazz history texts has been to focus on the entire history of the genre. While most are excellent, it comes at the expense of the individual eras of jazz history, where the same people, songs, and facts are repeatedly emphasized. There is a need for updated books on individual jazz eras that would allow for a more nuanced reading and detailed understanding of the music. Gunther Schuller's *Early Jazz* is one of the most important books ever written about this topic. But it was published over fifty years ago, and an update has been long overdue. My book fills in the holes left from Schuller's book, while summarizing research from the last fifty years. It is a concise introduction to jazz from its nineteenth-century roots through 1929, when elements of the Swing Era began to emerge.

Schuller's main thesis was to present jazz as an art form, and those who most contributed towards then-modern jazz were highlighted. I define jazz more broadly, as encompassing the artistic and the commercial. This allows for an inclusive reading of jazz history with a diverse spectrum of musicians including not only pioneering African American and white musicians, but also those that are commonly skipped or skimmed over in jazz history textbooks including lesser-known sidemen, prominent musicians by instrument, entertainers or novelty performers, women, vocalists, and American jazz musicians who introduced jazz on their travels around the world.

Schuller's book was part of a larger agenda held forth by Schuller, Martin Williams, and other jazz scholars and critics who successfully posited jazz as an American art form, leading to the institutionalization of jazz, with colleges and universities subsequently offering courses and degrees in jazz studies, the assimilation of jazz within the Smithsonian

Institution and other similar prestigious programs, and the establishment of jazz-centric corporations such as Jazz at Lincoln Center, SF Jazz, and others. The objective was to highlight the outstanding contributions of African Americans to the general American public. White musicians, from Paul Whiteman to Benny Goodman to Dave Brubeck, have always been the face of jazz, and those scholars were successful in redirecting the understanding of jazz and jazz history as an African American art form. It was an important moment and led to the increased visibility of Louis Armstrong, Duke Ellington, Jelly Roll Morton, and scores of other African American jazz musicians who have since been rightfully acknowledged for their work.

Jazz had grown from being a bad word to a prestigious one, but to deny the contributions of whites, or other similarly ignored musicians, is to deny jazz's malleability as an art form. At heart jazz is a flexible art form that is and has always been open and adaptable to different styles of music by musicians of any race or background. Right from the beginning in New Orleans, musicians black, white, Creole, and otherwise were playing nascent forms of jazz and it stayed that way. Everyone played jazz in their own way and in the process injected a little of their own nuances and culture into the music. An African American-based music, jazz is a living and breathing thing that continues to thrive in the hands of its practitioners. This is what makes jazz great yet difficult to define.

∾

Though early jazz sounds foreign to modern ears, in fact, so much of what jazz is and what jazz musicians do was established during the early jazz era and have remained in place, while other characteristics of early jazz have since been reworked, revived, or recast in different contexts. For example, the skill set of jazz musicians has not changed. They balance formal and informal styles of playing: reading or sight-reading music versus playing music by ear or by feel; this unique quality makes jazz musicians versatile, able to play in a wide variety of musical styles and contexts such as orchestras, concert bands, theater bands, circuses, or musicals. Such a skill set lent itself well to studio work; during the early jazz era, Fletcher Henderson, Louis Armstrong, Red Nichols, Eddie Lang, Benny Goodman, and others supplemented their income by working as sidemen in the studios, backing singers and playing a wide range of music. This practice continued throughout jazz history: in the 1960s, Hank Jones, Bob

Brookmeyer, Jim Hall, Jerry Dodgion, and others worked for television network orchestras; in the 1970s and 1980s, the Los Angeles and New York studio scenes were dominated by Michael and Randy Brecker, Larry Carlton, Steve Gadd, and countless others. Many early jazz musicians backed singers (Fletcher Henderson behind Ethel Waters or James P. Johnson recording with Bessie Smith), and this continued with Hampton Hawes playing with Joan Baez, Michael Brecker with Chaka Kahn, and even today with seasoned New York jazz pianist David Cook working as the pianist and musical director for mega-pop star Taylor Swift. J. J. Johnson, Lalo Schifrin, Chico Hamilton, and Dave Grusin are a tiny sampling of jazz musicians who had successful careers as performers as well as composers and arrangers in film and television. The end product is not always jazz, and this may be part of the issue. Still, it demonstrates what jazz musicians can do.

Novelty sounds of the 1920s are often cringe-inducing for modern listeners, but at the time such sounds were popular and a staple on vaudeville where musicians were keen to stand out. Brass players playing with plunger mutes originated from this era and is one of the few holdovers of unusual sounds that included novel instruments such as the comb, kazoo, washboard, slide whistle, and others. Later generations of musicians in the bebop and hard bop eras continued this notion of standing out by developing individual sounds on traditional musical instruments. The philosophy was the same but was recast as expressing one's individuality.

Though such novel sounds are anathema in standard jazz practices, forward-thinking jazz musicians from the 1960s revisited and revived such rejected performance practices in adventurous settings that looked ahead to postbop and free jazz. Eric Dolphy's experimentations with tone recalls forgotten "gaspipe" clarinetists of the 1920s who specialized in playing squeals, honks, laughing sounds, and other such humorous sounds on the clarinet. His duck-imitation sounds on the bass clarinet heard on Ornette Coleman's *Free Jazz* album from 1962 also revives animal-imitation practices that had not been heard since the early days of the Original Dixieland Jazz Band and New Orleans jazz. Played in a "serious" setting, these effects are no longer as humorous and contributed to the vocabulary of free jazz. Multi-reeds player Rahsaan Roland Kirk adopted many unusual instruments (the stritch, manzello, nose flute, etc.) and even played three saxophones simultaneously in the manner of Wilbur Sweatman, who did the same with three clarinets during the early jazz era. But even when he played on one horn, Kirk, like Dolphy, recalled the novelty sounds of the past; he further deepened his ties to early jazz by recording songs and styles from the era. Others who have followed these musicians' lead are members of the Association for the Advancement of Creative Musicians including the Art Ensemble of Chicago. In this light, free jazz's origins are a reflection of a forgotten past.

Finally, there is the reworking of jazz as art. This has been a dominant theme that spurred the bebop movement, whose leading figures rejected the dance and entertainment aesthetic of the Swing Era; Third Stream, with the merging of jazz and classical forms of composition; and the assimilation of jazz as an institution with the founding of jazz education. Yet, Paul Whiteman was already doing this in 1924 with his "Experiment in Modern Music" concert at New York's Aeolian Hall. Why is this issue continually revisited? Perhaps because entertainment played such a strong role in the early days that jazz cannot escape its past with musicians having played for dancers and their resumes including road shows, carnivals, circuses, vaudeville, musicals, and other forms of light entertainment. The same holds true today, though commercial jobs have grown to include film, television, radio, and jingles.

Jazz is unique, as artists, in the traditional meaning of the word, have traditionally focused only on their work and their vision. A select few jazz musicians have done this, but the vast majority are freelancers, with the ability to play different styles including pop, rock, country, soul, R&B, funk, hip hop, electronica, and other styles. Many have applied their skills to other mediums either as teachers, composers, arrangers, managers, producers, engineers, or other roles in the music industry. This is why jazz as art is not the only definition of jazz and certainly not the only kind of music that the jazz musician is capable of playing.

～

Early Jazz serves as an introduction to the great music from this period and is aimed towards those interested in early jazz and/or jazz history. Because Schuller was advocating for jazz as art, his work includes numerous transcriptions and musical analysis. For my book, musical knowledge certainly helps but is not required to understand the content. Song descriptions and tables that outline the details of select performances are included to aid towards better understanding of the music. The material is divided into thirteen chapters.

Chapters 1 and 2 outline the musical roots and beginnings of jazz from its genesis in African American folk songs, blues, and ragtime and include a discussion of the impact of different commercial work on the development of early jazz musicians. Chapter 3 focuses on the development of jazz in New Orleans through the first recorded white bands from the late 1910s and the early 1920s. Chapter 4 centers on King Oliver and Jelly Roll Morton, African American New Orleans musicians in Chicago. Chapters 5 through 7 focuses on different aspects of jazz in New York, including the white studio jazz scene (chapter 5, a continuation of chapter 4), stride piano (chapter 6), and an overview of important dance bands (chapter 7).

Chapters on Louis Armstrong and Bix Beiderbecke (8 and 9 respectively) cover two of the most important soloists in the history of jazz. The Beiderbecke chapter also brings in a discussion of a key group of white musicians known as the "Chicagoans." Chapter 10 acknowledges those who are pioneers and leaders on their individual instruments, while chapter 11 broadens the scope of early jazz beyond New Orleans, Chicago, and New York with an overview of territory bands, particularly those in the Southwest. Chapters 12 and 13 focus on traditionally neglected groups within jazz history including vocalists and pioneers around the world. Though jazz has become globalized, the focus is on pioneering American musicians whose travels around the world helped introduce and popularize jazz.

Early jazz is among the most foreign of jazz styles to modern listeners, a fact Schuller himself acknowledged even in 1968,[1] yet it is perhaps the most fascinating as one can listen song by song to the development of the music. The definition of what jazz was and could be varied tremendously, from Original Dixieland Jazz Band to Paul Whiteman to Louis Armstrong to Duke Ellington, and musicians were quick to adapt to new changes and trends. One could make the argument that all early jazz artists were to some degree experimental. Reviewing the repertoire of artists through the early jazz era, one can notice substantial changes in the music. Even a major star such as Paul Whiteman did not rest on his past success in the early 1920s; he went on and hired the best white jazz musicians, in the process, radically changing his sound.

Early jazz is a dusty road that few have traveled, but one that is well rewarded. I hope that this book provides for the reader a better understanding of jazz and of this wonderful music.

Chapter 1

Ragtime and Traveling Shows

Jazz's roots lie most prominently in ragtime and blues. With ragtime centered around bars and saloons in Midwestern cities and blues being a southern sound connected to the country, there existed from the beginning a "double consciousness" of urban and rural identities that would resonate throughout not only early jazz history but jazz history itself.[1] This dichotomy would reemerge as art and entertainment, high and low culture, and later tradition and modernity and black and white. This chapter discusses the phenomenon of ragtime and provides an overview of work opportunities for African American musicians in the late nineteenth and early twentieth centuries.

Ragtime

Ragtime is jazz's strongest precursor. During ragtime's heyday it was the first significant African American musical style to gain wide acceptance and introduced syncopation to popular music. It was a huge sensation from the late 1890s, peaking in 1912, before giving away to the jazz craze in 1917, the year its most famous composer Scott Joplin died. It is commonly thought of as a style of solo piano music; however the scope of ragtime is wide with strong ties to song and dance with roots in minstrelsy.

Ragtime, which is at heart a merging of African American and European music ideals, has precedent in the music of the American classical composer Louis Moreau Gottschalk (1829–1869). Born into a white Creole family in New Orleans, Gottschalk's music reflects the diverse surroundings in which he grew up in New Orleans (see chapter 3.) Raised in a hotbed of cultural activity with a diverse population, Gottschalk soaked in the music of blacks with echoes of Africa and the Caribbean. Performed in a classical manner, Gottschalk's music predates ragtime. "The Banjo" (1855) includes four key characteristics of ragtime: the oom-pah pattern in the left hand (bass note alternating with a chord); three-against-four polyrhythm; the tresillo rhythm (a Latin rhythm similar to the habanera); and the accent on the fourth beat of every second bar.[2] Other compositions that share the same characteristics include "Responds-moi (Di Que Si)," "Ojos Criollos," "Les Yeux Créoles," and "Pasquinade."

RAGTIME BEGINNINGS

The development of ragtime emerged before the first rags were published. Syncopated banjo and fiddle songs that were performed in minstrel shows were adapted and copied from unknown slave musicians.[3] The practice of syncopating established melodies, known as *ragging* a song, was noted in eyewitness accounts from the 1870s and 1880s; syncopated music, as it became known, was subsequently spread by itinerant pianists who performed mostly in bars, saloons, and brothels all over the country.[4]

From its earliest days, ragtime has been associated with dance beginning with the cakewalk. Originally a plantation dance performed by enslaved people imitating the mannerisms of their white slaveowners, the unsuspecting slaveowners were impressed and awarded a cake to the couple who did the best walk, hence the name. The cakewalk was a popular dance during the 1890s, and the music became increasingly syncopated as rag composers began writing cakewalks. Later, in the 1910s, the connection between ragtime and dance ragtime would deepen with a series of controversial animal dances like the fox trot, the turkey trot, the grizzly bear, and others. Though the syncopations inspired dancers, it also lead to criticism from moral detractors who felt that this music was directly related to a loosening of values in young people. It's hard to imagine today, but ragtime, and later jazz in the 1920s, was at the center of a national debate as many viewed ragtime as detrimental to music and society.

The first public notice of ragtime music was at the World's Columbia Exhibition in Chicago in 1893 which drew many black singers, pianists, and bands hoping for work at nearby cafés and saloons. Among those drawn to perform at or in clubs near the fair were ragtime pioneers Ben Harney, Jesse Picket, and Scott Joplin. The written form of ragtime began with the publication of the first rags which were not instrumentals, but popular vocal songs.

RAGTIME SONGS

Ragtime was first introduced to the public through "coon" songs during the late 1890s and early 1900s. ("Coon" is an offensive term for African Americans.) These songs were performed in a "negro" dialect with frequently demeaning lyrics that made use of racist and stereotypical images of African Americans. Among the first coon songs was African American entertainer Ernest Hogan's "All Coons Look Alike to Me" in 1896, and it was a massive success. The song's syncopation was part of the appeal that led to a craze for coon songs. When the coon genre died out by 1906, ragtime's syncopated rhythms persisted in popular vocal songs. Hogan was heavily criticized for his use of the word "coon" by the African American elite in this song; other African American performers made a point to omit the offensive word whenever they sang it. Although his success ultimately bolstered his career, he regretted the use of the term in his song. Despite the derogatory nature of "coon" songs, they ultimately contributed to the importance of ragtime as a distinctively African American genre.

White pianist and vocalist Ben Harney (1871–1938) is considered the first to adapt ragtime to the piano, when he adapted his own songs. However, the first instrumental rags were published in 1897. The first was "Mississippi Rag" by William H. Krell, while the first African American rag was by Tom Turpin (1873–1922) who published "Harlem Rag" in December 1897. Otherwise, initial ragtime instrumentals were mainly derivative of vocal music, based on the practice of "ragging" unsyncopated music that began during this time through improvisation, arrangements, and published manuals.[5] The publication of Scott Joplin's "Maple Leaf Rag" in 1899 was a turning point and made ragtime a national phenomenon.

SCOTT JOPLIN

Scott Joplin (1867/68–1917) is synonymous with ragtime and its most famous composer. Born to a musical family in northeast Texas, he grew up in Texarkana, Texas. Young Joplin learned to play the violin but was enamored by the piano and took lessons with local teachers including a German teacher, Julius Weiss, who helped shape his aspirations and ambitions towards high artistic goals. Joplin developed a broad repertoire that allowed him to play for various functions. He moved to St. Louis in the mid-1880s, before beginning life as an itinerant pianist, traveling widely including a trip to the Chicago's 1893 World's Columbia Exposition as a cornetist leading an orchestra. He was also a member of the Texarkana minstrels and during 1893–1894, led a vocal group, the Texas Medley Quartette. He sang second tenor, which was the lead voice, and the group made its way as far as away as Syracuse, New York, before settling in Sedalia, Missouri around 1895.

A railroad town with a high percentage of rail workers and a transient population, Sedalia developed a reputation as a city of vice with an ample supply of pool halls, saloons, gambling dens, dance halls, and brothels. Joplin gained employment at such establishments (like the Black 400 Club and the Maple Leaf Club), and ragtime would subsequently become a staple at bordellos and other houses of ill repute all over the country. Once settled in Sedalia, Joplin attended George R. Smith College, a school for African Americans, studying theory, harmony, and composition as he became increasingly studious about his craft with ambitions to become a classical composer and pianist.

Joplin had published his first song in 1895, but he achieved his greatest success with rags starting with "Maple Leaf Rag." Written in 1897 and published in 1899, "Maple Leaf Rag" did not take off until 1900 when its popularity brought Joplin national fame. It features his straightforward approach to composition that would become standard in ragtime including the use of the march form, AABBACCDD, and its variations: there are four sections (ABCD), with the trio section (C) modulating to the subdominant. The main difference between marches and ragtime was the prominent use of syncopation in rags. A comparison with John Philip Sousa's march "Stars and Stripes Forever," written in 1896, illustrates this; Sousa's theme contains virtually no syncopation, the melody always emphasizing beats one and three, likely composed with the notion that the musicians would be marching while playing. By contrast, the opening melody of "Maple Leaf Rag" does not start or end on any downbeat of the song.

"Maple Leaf Rag" is a good example of Joplin's compositional style. Elegant and grand, Joplin had a knack for creating memorable melodies and distinct changes of moods within each section. He achieves this effect

Listening Guide: "Maple Leaf Rag" (1899) by Scott Joplin as played by Joshua Rifkin.[6]

Time	Section	Comments
0:00	A	The melody (played twice) immediately establishes the tonic. It is made up entirely of chord tones that is perhaps a remnant of the banjo's influence. The left hand plays strictly accompaniment figures, bass notes and chords, on the beat that contrast with the syncopated rhythms in the right hand.
0:05		Joplin introduces a new texture and a new chord quality by arpeggiating a diminished chord through four octaves from the left to the right hand.
0:11		A triumphant theme to match the return to the home key as the left hand plays chords on the beat as syncopation in the right hand melody now appears in the form of anticipations, with notes anticipating the downbeat of the measure.
0:16		A repetition of the previous melody (at 0:11), but played an octave lower.
0:22	A	Same as above.
0:43	B	The first half of the B melody is the development of a new theme that begins on the dominant and is based entirely on the first A theme. The left hand maintains an oom-pah-style accompaniment.
0:54		The second half begins like the first before a new texture (same rhythms in both hands) introduces the final gesture.
1:05	B	As above but with a stronger sense of finality on the tonic at the end.
1:26	A	Same as above.
1:48	C	The first half of the trio section begins with a new rhythm as the melody is played twice. As is standard for trio sections, Joplin modulates to the subdominant.
1:58		The second half begins with the melody played a tone higher before reintroducing material from the initial A theme. With exceptions, the oom-pah-style accompaniment dominates the left hand for the remainder of the piece.
2:09	C	Same as above.
2:30	D	The final section introduces yet another rhythm before reintroducing rhythms from the A section's opening and closing themes.
2:41		The second half begins like the first, but this time concludes with a harmonic gesture reminiscent of the A theme.
2:52	D	Same as above.

with his manipulation of harmony. Though his music is centered around a primary key center, he often uses chords outside of the key for contrast before returning to the home key. Yet his choices for the harmonies are logical and are based on common tones or a descending bass line. For example, the first part of the melody from the A section strongly establishes the key center but is offset by a sudden change in harmony, a diminished chord, which is emphasized with a change in texture, before returning to the home key. The phrase ends with a similar but shorter gesture. This manner of harmonic tension and release is a stylistic trait of Joplin's compositions.

In addition to syncopation, rhythm is at the center of "Maple Leaf Rag." Joplin cleverly returns to the rhythm of the A section's first theme throughout the piece which ends up unifying all four sections. Additionally, each new section is distinguished by its own rhythmic character. The B section begins with variations of the first rhythmic idea before introducing new rhythms and textures altogether. Both the C and D sections begin with new rhythmic ideas before returning to the rhythms from the A section. It is a very subtle touch, and Joplin's emphasis on rhythm would continue throughout jazz history.

Publisher John Stark (1841–1927) played an important role in disseminating Joplin's music. The story of how they met, with Stark reportedly "discovering" Joplin playing "Maple Leaf Rag," is a romanticized one because it suggests that Joplin was not motivated by economic concerns. More likely, Joplin sought out Stark. Stark's contract entitled Joplin to one penny for each copy of sheet music sold. While the royalty agreement sounds preposterous today, it was a major advance over the standard practice of paying African American songwriters a flat fee.[7] Fully committed to ragtime, Stark's marketing campaign proclaimed Joplin to be "The King of the Ragtime Writers" and launched his visibility beyond Sedalia to a national level. By 1909, Joplin earned approximately six hundred dollars from "Maple Leaf Rag" alone.[8] Joplin's success led to other rag composers becoming prominent, including James Scott (1885–1938) and Joseph Lamb (1887–1960).

By 1901, Joplin had moved to St. Louis, which had become a center of ragtime concentrated at the Rosebud Café, owned by sometime rag composer Tom Turpin. At the Rosebud, legendary ragtime pianists like Louis Chauvin, Sam Patterson, Joe Jordan, and Scott Hayden congregated, delighting audiences with their performances and engaging in contests, sometimes with visiting pianists, that determined who was the better musician.[9] "Maple Leaf Rag" had become a virtuoso showcase, with pianists playing the rag at breakneck tempos to demonstrate their skills in these battles.[10] For this reason, Joplin, who did not participate in cutting sessions, began to advocate for a more refined version of ragtime indicating on sheet music that "it is never right to play ragtime fast."[11]

In his compositions, Joplin displays a remarkable range writing numerous waltzes including the concert waltz "Bethana" and appropriating Latin American rhythms in "Pineapple Rag" and "Solace," subtitled "A Mexican Serenade." "Magnetic Rag," "Scott Joplin's New Rag," and "Fig Leaf Rag" made use of the minor tonality, its bittersweet and melancholic sound allowing for a deeper emotional palette.[12] Printed sheet music also reveals his compositional sophistication in the programmatic "Wall Street Rag" and the notated foot stomps in "'Stoptime' Rag." But Joplin was increasingly interested in large scale compositions. In 1907, he moved to New York City to focus on getting his second opera, *Treemonisha*, completed and performed. However, he was never taken seriously as a composer and never heard or saw the opera performed properly. He died in obscurity in 1917, although *Treemonisha* would finally receive its premiere in 1972, as part of the ongoing ragtime revival.

WOMEN IN RAGTIME

Ragtime as a solo piano form, known as "classic ragtime," was further invigorated by the popularity of pianos as a status symbol for middle-class Americans. The introduction of the upright piano in the late 1880s made the piano more affordable and adaptable in the living room, and piano production in the U.S. tripled between 1890 and 1909.[13] Women were typically expected to learn to play.[14] Trained in the Western classical tradition, the ability to read music, to sight-read, and to play piano were handy skills during the ragtime boom. The music industry was rapidly expanding with a high demand for salesclerks, demonstrating newly published music for customers, and editors, arranging music for performers, silent films, and piano roll recordings, positions that were often filled by women.[15] Many were passionate enough about the music to compose their own pieces, and during the ragtime era, there were upwards of three hundred women ragtime pianists and composers.

Whitney-Warner was a successful publishing company based in Detroit, who published music by female rag composers including Charlotte Blake (1885–1979) and Louise Gustin (1870–1910). Blake was active composing over thirty-five songs that included ballads and waltzes in addition to rags. Due to sexism, both women had their genders obscured on sheet music and were credited as "C. Blake" and "L. Gustin," though this was later amended.[16] One of the most successful rags by a woman was "Pickles and Peppers" by Adaline Shepherd (1883–1950) from 1906. It was a best seller, part of which became the campaign song for William Jennings Bryan's unsuccessful bid for presidency in 1908. Shepherd composed only a handful of rags and retired when she got married in 1910, a fate that befell many women in ragtime. By contrast, Julia Lee Niebergall (1886–1968) was a fiercely independent woman who supported herself with a career in music throughout her life. Born into a family of musicians, she divorced early and reverted to using her maiden name. She continued to live with her parents and was reportedly one of the first women in Indianapolis to own a car. She composed rags in the late 1900s, the most popular being "Hoosier Rag," and she remained active as a pianist working in theaters and as an accompanist for dance classes.

May Aufderheide (1890–1972) was the most popular and prolific female ragtime composer, and her compositions garnered her critical respect. Born into a middle-class family in Indianapolis, Aufderheide married in 1908 and moved to Richmond, Indiana. She published her first rag, "Dusty Rag," followed by "Richmond Rag" in 1909, both of which got the attention of the press and were later performed by early New Orleans jazz bands.[17] She also played with the Indianapolis Symphony and taught piano. She mentored aspiring women rag composers, such as Gladis Yelvington and Julia Lee Niebergall, encouraging them to publish their own music. Aufderheide wrote rags, songs, and waltzes, but ultimately her career was short and she published her last rags in 1911, likely to concentrate on her marriage although ragtime's decline in popularity may have also been a factor.

Young African American women were also afforded the opportunity to learn piano and study music. With practical experience in church, some looked to the world of show business for careers, a preferable choice over menial labor jobs typically afforded to black women at the time.[18] There were female pianists working at the turn of the twentieth century, but unfortunately, there is little documentation about their activities.

Traveling Shows

With strong roots in blues and ragtime, early jazz developed out of a rich entertainment world that employed many musicians. Although many ragtime and early jazz musicians played popular music for dancing in clubs, cabarets, and saloons, most honed their musical and entertainment skills in traveling shows like minstrel shows, road shows, medicine shows, carnivals, the circus, and vaudeville. To be successful in these shows, jazz musicians had to develop a specific skill set that would be important in their later work in jazz bands.

Minstrel Shows

The minstrel show was the dominant form of entertainment in the United States from the 1840s through the 1890s. Conceived as a theatrical show set on a plantation, minstrelsy emerged with the Virginia Minstrels and contained songs, dances, and skits with white performers performing in blackface. They applied burnt cork on their faces to appear as African American and spoke and sang in a "negro dialect" to imitate black music, humor, and dance. These shows blatantly mocked African American life but were hugely popular among whites, and later African Americans. Although the practice was founded and initially practiced by whites, from as early as the 1840s, African Americans were also active in minstrelsy, also performing in blackface, a tradition that continued into the twentieth century.[19] The first African American minstrel troupes were formed in 1865 and became hugely popular.

Despite the degrading policy of performing in blackface and acting out and perpetuating caricatures of African Americans, minstrelsy ultimately opened doors for African Americans in the entertainment world by making normal and safe the notion of whites watching African Americans on stage. It was also the sole route to a better life for most African Americans, especially those in the South, despite the rigors of traveling and the real threat of racism encountered on the road. The minstrel show set a precedent for musicians and entertainers, who were often one and the same, that continued in traveling shows.

A day's work for a minstrel troupe included a series of promotional activities that announced the coming show to a town's general population. These includes a daytime parade, a concert, another short concert before the show, and the evening performance. Musicians who marched in the daytime parade playing woodwind and brass instruments had to switch to fiddles, guitars, banjos, mandolins, or percussion for the evening show.[20] Many musicians doubled as singers, dancers, actors, or even comedians. The instrumentalist-singer in jazz has a long legacy, including Louis

Armstrong, Jelly Roll Morton, Jack Teagarden, among others. Those who doubled as dancers during their time on vaudeville including Bessie Smith, Ethel Waters, Luckey Roberts, Jo Jones, and Cuba Austin, who was also a talented comedian. Trombonist Jimmy Harrison was also a comedian known for his Bert Williams impersonations. Although such multitasking is not as highly regarded today, the roots of early jazz is clearly in entertainment.

African American Traveling Shows

In the wake of minstrelsy, other opportunities for musicians included road shows, medicine shows, carnivals, circuses, and tented minstrel shows. Although many featured plantation scenes, others featured musicals, plays, and youth bands, known as "pickaninny" bands, an offensive term that refers to young African American children. Minstrels often started in the business as children, and fashionable white female singers in vaudeville were often accompanied by African American children.[21] Examples of musicians who began as a "pick" include Eubie Blake, Luckey Roberts, and Wilbur Sweatman. Perhaps the most celebrated youth band was the Jenkins Orphanage Band. Based out of Charleston, it performed in the inaugural parades of Presidents Theodore Roosevelt and William Taft and its notable jazz alumni includes "Cat" Anderson, Freddie Green, and Jabbo Smith.

Traveling medicine shows also featured entertainers. As quack doctors demonstrated various medicines, potions, and cures, musicians and dancers would attract, or distract, audiences with their performance. Mostly, medicine shows were small enterprises with the alleged doctor working with two or three entertainers; other times there could be a large show or act alternating with the salesmanship.[22]

Carnivals combined the circus with the minstrel show, although the rides were still the main attraction.[23] Noting the popularity of ragtime, circuses, in the late 1890s, opened a sideshow for African American performers. Perry G. Lowery (1869–1942) was a pioneer bandmaster who brought his minstrel band to the circus where he worked for thirty years. A classical cornetist trained at the Boston Conservatory, Lowery began his career in minstrel shows and ran his own vaudeville and concert bands before seizing the opportunity to join a circus sideshow in 1899. Lowery was an enthusiastic educator and a strict disciplinarian who would be a model of excellence for generations of African American musicians who passed through his band.

The circus job resembled the minstrel show with its musicians involved in promotional activities in addition to accompanying sideshow acts.[24] Many African American musicians during this era were employed in the circus including W. C. Handy, Lorenzo Tio Sr., Buddy Petit, Wilbur Sweatman, Charlie Creath, and later Garvin Bushell, Jimmy Harrison, and Lester Young, whose father led a circus band. Several members of McKinney's Cotton Pickers had experience in carnivals or the circus including founder Bill McKinney, John Nesbitt, Cuba Austin, Quentin Jackson, and Doc Cheatham.[25]

Traveling shows provided much-needed professional experience for musicians. Although the upper-crust of African American society deplored minstrelsy and men like Lowery operating in low-entertainment establishments like the circus, this work provided steady employment and reliable pay for musicians during an era when limited opportunities were available to them as both African Americans and musicians. Such work served as training ground for inexperienced musicians who needed to develop their craft.

Vaudeville

Vaudeville was the primary form of entertainment from the 1890s through the dawn of the film industry in the late 1920s. A descendant of minstrel and other traveling shows, it was a variety show featuring a wide range of entertainers including singers, musicians, dancers, actors, comedians, magicians, jugglers, trained animals, ventriloquists, contortionists, and so on. It began in smaller, raunchier venues in the 1870s, but as it grew in popularity vaudeville became family friendly and theaters opened in cities large and small with acts touring along several different circuits. Initially, vaudeville was primarily limited to white performers. African American vaudeville shows began to operate in the 1900s in concert saloons and park pavilions in cities in the southern states: Texas, Florida, Georgia, Kentucky, Louisiana, and Tennessee.[26] Circuits were eventually established in the northeast and by 1921, the Theater Owners' Booking Association (T.O.B.A.) was established as the African American vaudeville circuit with performances catering to African Americans.

Regardless of race, musicians playing in vaudeville developed similar musical skills as in a traveling show. Vaudeville theaters often had a house band, or orchestra as they were referred to, to accompany the show playing background music, cues, and effects in addition to the introductory overture.[27] In the early days, a single pianist was used; although other instruments were added, the drummer emerged as an essential asset. In addition to keeping time, they were responsible for reproducing various sound effects as needed, for example when someone falls, for thunder, or emphasizing the punchline to a joke, among many others.[28] Vaudeville was light entertainment, and such effects were essential to the show.

Other instrumentalists had different responsibilities.[29] They had to be good sight-readers to play music provided by traveling acts. When accompanying singers, they were also expected to transpose songs and to play them in different keys. Popular songs were not written for everyone's vocal range, so to accommodate the singer's voice, songs were often transposed to a different key and musicians were expected to be able to do this on the spot. Ultimately the most prized ability was to play a song by ear or to "fake" one's way through a song as it could easily compensate for one's lack of reading or transposition skills.[30] Much later, popular songs were illegally published as "fake" books (the modern "Real Book" is a reference to this practice).

In this setting, rudimentary improvisational skills were nurtured. This was especially true when playing cues for shows which were sometimes vague, even more so if the actor missed their line. A sample cue sheet from the 1870s/1880s illustrates the range of skills a musician had to possess:[31]

At rise of curtain . . .	(lively music)
Cue . . . It is good Squire Beasley	(jolly music for squire's entrance)
Cue . . . (When comic falls down)	(drum crash)
Cue . . . The villagers are coming	(lively 6-8 time)
Cue . . . (Old man sits down suddenly)	(clarinet squeal)
Cue . . . (While the villagers make merry)	(country dance)

As white vaudeville became more formalized, widespread improvisation was capped in favor of prepared cues, but in African American vaudeville improvisation continued as evidence of "faking" extended into late 1910s and early 1920s.[32] Classified ads in the *Indianapolis Freeman*, a local African American newspaper, from the early 1910s illustrate the necessary skills required of musicians: "Clarinet, piano, saxophone that can read, improvise, transpose, and fake. An experienced showman, vaudeville, stock or road." "Wanted! To strengthen band by Dixie Sere-naders . . . trombone to double, read, and fake."[33]

In 1927, the success of *The Jazz Singer* with vocalist Al Jolson, the first feature-length motion picture with sound, spelled the end of an era for the traveling show and vaudeville that was finalized with the onset of the Great Depression, although the tented minstrel show persisted into the 1950s.[34] However, the musical skills required of the show musician remained in the toolbox of jazz musicians; except for showmanship, in most cases, and "faking," a term no longer used though undeniably still practiced, they continue to be a part of the modern jazz musician's skill set. Traveling shows were ultimately important conduits for musicians who helped spread new trends in music, and this is how ragtime and ultimately the blues spread and developed.

Chapter 2

The Blues

The blues is central to African American music from slavery through the Civil Rights Movement, including jazz, rhythm and blues, soul, and funk. It is hard to imagine early jazz without the blues. Its earliest antecedents are the African American folk songs from slavery times, especially the work song and the field holler.

Work Song

The work song was a song-type that developed during slavery and most obviously stems from Africa, as modern examples of work songs are still practiced in different parts of Africa. As the title implies, the song is sung while working. Some of the earliest and most celebrated examples of African American folk songs were recorded by John and Alan Lomax from the 1930s through the 1950s. A father and son team of ethnologists in search of authentic examples of various forms of American folk music, they found the best practitioners of these songs in prisons where older forms of culture were still practiced. This was not surprising, considering that using prison labor to perform backbreaking work was an extension of practices dating back to slavery. In fact, examples of work songs were recorded through the 1960s and evolved into the prison song.

Recorded in December 1933 at Darrington State Prison Farm in Sandy Point, Texas, "Long John" contains some of the most celebrated examples of the work song and, though it is not a pure example, the performance captures many of the elements heard in this style. The songs feature vocals and percussion only and are dominated by call and response, an essential characteristic of African American music. In this case, the call is delivered by the leader (identified by the Lomaxes as "Lightning") followed by a response from the group. The pulse is very steady and strict and dictated by the percussive sound created by the workers' axes. Videos of work songs from prison show that coordinated movements of the prisoners worked in tandem with the striking of the axes. This is an important aspect of the piece and a trademark of the traditional work song.

Structurally, the song begins with the refrain (or what is known today in pop music as a "chorus") alternating with verses. Each section consists of three-note motives with small varieties on the last note of each phrase. The melodic shape suggests no harmonic movement, but there is a sense of tonality or a key center. As a result, the performance is musically repetitive; it is the sound of a group of prisoners singing and playing time and feeling the music together.

There are also many versions of work songs. Another recorded version of "Long John" from the following year features a completely different verse. The Lomaxes also recorded another performance called "Long Gone" on the same date, which is about the same prisoner and contains the same melodic and formal structure as "Long John." Lyrically, it is the tale of an escaped prisoner; however, lyrical content in work songs expanded to include many topics including songs about work (corn shucking songs, sea shanties, etc.) and other tales.

Field Holler

The field holler, also known as a cornfield holler, is a type of work song but is so different in nature that it warrants its own stylistic category. Instead of a group, the performance features one singer. In contrast to the strict pulse of the work song, the field holler is sung in free rhythm and vocalists can vary their volume, timbre, and pitch. In this setting, the field holler becomes a vehicle of expression as the feeling of the singer takes precedent. Like the work song, there is no harmonic motion, but a sense of tonality exists. The surrounding notes form the basis of a blues scale, especially with an emphasis on the fourth, the flatted third, and the flatted seventh. The Lomaxes recorded prisoners singing field hollers, but country blues musician "Jaybird" Coleman's solo recordings from the 1920s are clear examples of its connection to the blues.

"Mistreatin' Mama"

Born to an impoverished family, Burl C. "Jaybird" Coleman (1896–1950) was from Alabama.[1] He learned to play the harmonica at age twelve and then began singing while in the army. His recordings reveal remarkable similarities to the field holler as he performs solo, singing and accompanying himself on harmonica. "Mistreatin' Mama" from 1927 is a good example of his work. The song consists of two musical phrases and four lines, but the story Coleman is telling lies in the call and response between his vocal and his harmonica.

Listening Guide: "Mistreatin' Mama" by Jaybird Coleman
Jaybird Coleman: vocals and harmonica. Black Patti 8052. Recorded August 13, 1927, in Birmingham, Alabama.

Time	Section	Phrase	Instrument
0:00	Introduction	A	Harmonica
0:13		B	Harmonica
0:23	Section 1	A	Vocal: *I done told you mama, ain't gon' tell you no more*
0:32		A	Harmonica
0:45		B	Harmonica
0:55		A	Harmonica
1:06	Section 2	A	Vocal: *Now, the blues is what's in my mind, 'tween midnight and day*
1:15		A	Harmonica
1:26	Section 3	B	Vocal: *Now the blues been causin' my woman, her to run away*
1:35		B	Harmonica
1:44	Section 4	A	Vocal: *Lord I can't rest continual, don't care what I do*
1:54		A	Harmonica
2:06		B	Harmonica
2:15	Section 5	A	Vocal: *[moaning with yodeling]*
2:26		A	Harmonica
2:37		B	Harmonica
2:48	Coda	A	Harmonica
2:58			Harmonica

The song is based on two phrases. Both resolve on the tonic, while phrase B is distinguished by a clear harmonic move to the dominant, heard in section 3 on the word "woman." Coleman takes advantage of the solo situation to freely alternate phrases A and B between his voice and harmonica. His use of space and held notes are important as well, blurring any sense of pulse.

The subject of the song is suggestive, but the real story is in Coleman's vocal gestures that altered or decorated pitch including melismas, scoops, bent notes, slides, and slurs. They are associated with African American vocal techniques, but his incorporation of yodeling, the process of rapidly alternating between the chest voice and falsetto, or head voice, which is of European origin, is telling of a cross-cultural exchange that prevailed in the South. For Coleman, it is simply another tool to use. Coleman's harmonica playing is noteworthy as he manipulates the instrument to produce many vocal-like sounds to comment on the text. The notion of a musical instrument mimicking the human voice is a powerful theme in African American music and would resonate strongly in early jazz history. On "Mistreatin' Mama," the harmonica and Coleman's voice are one and the same. In essence, we are one step away from applying the formal twelve-bar blues structure, but the *manner* of playing the blues is in place.

Form, Performance Practice, and Genre

In the last decade of the nineteenth century, the blues emerged from the rural South. Early accounts of blues-style singing indicate that the content of the blues was in place, but the twelve-bar form was not. William Christopher Handy (1873–1958) was not the first major composer to publish a blues song, but he popularized the form in 1912 with his hit "Memphis Blues." Known as the first major composer of the blues, Handy was a trained cornetist who wanted to play "respectable" music. On tour with Mahara's Minstrels in 1903, he heard the blues for the first time in Tutwiler, Mississippi, played by a local guitarist. Later at a concert in Cleveland, Mississippi, he allowed a local African American band to play a few songs in a similar style. Handy was not impressed, but the audience's overwhelmingly positive response alerted him to the music's commercial potential. His first published blues songs, "Memphis Blues," and later "St. Louis Blues" and "Beale Street Blues," standardized the twelve-bar form and brought it to a mass audience.

Blues as a performance practice is defined by a strong sense of tonality and its corresponding "blue" notes. In technical terms this primarily refers to the minor third but can refer to other tones, including the flat seventh, that are a part of a group of notes, usually a five-note, or pentatonic, scale. These notes were initiated with scoops, bent notes, slides, and smears that altered the pitch with the intention of enhancing a performance's emotional content. Such notes are best achieved by the human voice, but early musicians achieved the same effect on instruments by applying special techniques. Guitarists used a knife or bottle or similar object across the fretboard (neck) of the guitar to glide to the next pitch. Such innovative methods of playing instruments introduced a vocal-inflected approach to performance that included a wide vocabulary of sounds and gestures. Early African American jazz musicians maintained these gestures even when they were not playing blues songs, and they have remained a part of the jazz tradition.

Concurrent with the developments of early jazz was the blues boom of the 1920s that began with the monumental release of Mamie Smith's "Crazy Blues" in September 1920. It was the first blues recording by an African American, and for many white listeners, it was the first time they heard an African American manner of singing. The recording was a wild success, selling a million copies within a year and setting off a blues craze that would last through the decade. It also set off a steady wave of activity that allowed African American culture to flourish on stage, beginning with 1921's *Shuffle Along* by Eubie Blake and Noble Sissle, and on record as African American artists in blues, jazz, folk, and religious styles began to record. Music executives, however, upheld segregation by marketing such music as *race records* and targeting nonwhite audiences.

During this period, two distinct styles of blues emerged: country or itinerant blues and classic or vaudeville blues. Each style had strong gender implications with men singing, and playing guitar, in country blues and women singing, often accompanied by a band, in classic blues. However, they shared a common language of the blues, one that could not be adequately notated on paper.

Classic Blues Singers

Mamie Smith's success in 1920 prompted record executives to focus on blues and the African American market as they sought out blues singers, specifically female African American singers, to record. It was a golden age for women like Gertrude "Ma" Rainey, Bessie Smith, Clara Smith, Ida Cox, Rosa Henderson, Lucille Hegamin, Bertha "Chippie" Hill, Alberta Hunter, Sara Martin, Victoria Spivey, Sippie Wallace, Ethel Waters, Edith Wilson, and many others who were called "blues queens." However, the blues content varied considerably. While Ida Cox, Ma Rainey, and Bessie Smith were among those well-versed in southern rural blues, other northern singers had varying degrees of blues content in their singing and many sound "citified."[2]

All blues singers, male and female, sang openly about love, sex, and sexuality, but it was particularly pronounced in the work of classic blues singers. By doing so, they challenged mainstream ideological assumptions regarding women and love as well as the notion that the women's "place" was in the domestic sphere.[3] Blues queens rarely sang about marriage, domestic life, mothers, fathers, or children. Instead, they sang candidly about taboo subjects, ranging from extramarital relationships, murderous revenge, homosexuality, lesbianism, domestic violence, and sex. Often projecting a tough image, these topics suggest that the classic blues singers found the mainstream cult of motherhood irrelevant to the realities of their lives.[4]

The exposure also brought opportunity for many singers. Ethel Waters started as a classic blues singer only to break through beyond African American audiences to "white time." Her career continued to thrive as she became a well-known actress on stage and on television, ultimately eclipsing her fabled singing career. Alberta Hunter made her way to Europe in 1927 and became a headliner in shows and cabarets, joining the likes of Josephine Baker, Adelaide Hall, Elizabeth Welch, and other African American non-blues singers who also made careers for themselves overseas.

"Coon" Shouters

Although the recorded history of classic blues singers began in 1920, many of them had already been active on the southern vaudeville circuit for years and were previously known as "coon shouters." The term initially referred to those who sang "coon" songs and included white vaudeville singers May Irwin and Clarice Vance. It was also a reference to the performative aspect, which included physical gestures and extended to using negro dialect, costumes, and cakewalking, a dance that originated from enslaved people mock-imitating their owners (see chapter 1).[5] Songs were transposed to a higher key and singers sang at the top of their range, for thrilling effect. In principle, it was white vocalists imitating the African American manner of singing that would become known as blues.

The "coon song" genre died out by the mid-1900s, but gave away to songs with more discreet references to African Americans, sometimes with words that rhyme with "coon" or, more commonly, the emphasis upon street slang. Sometimes referred to as "up to date coon songs," songs such as African American songwriters Shelton Brooks's "Some of These Days," Joe Jordan's "Lovie Joe," or Chris Smith's "I Got the Blues but I'm Too Mean to Cry" are closer to the blues idiom in language, form, and attitude.[6] Transitional material from ragtime to blues, songs like these provided a platform for the singers to express elements of the blues style. The "coon shouter" label, however, persisted and was extended to African American singers, including early unrecorded stars like Carrie Hall, Bessie Gilliam, and Rosa Scott as well as future classic blues singers of the 1920s, "Ma" Rainey, Bessie Smith, and Clara Smith (no relation).[7] There were, however, African American male singers active on the vaudeville circuit in the 1910s, though they remained tied to the image of the blackface comedian, including Kid Love, Baby Seals, and Charles Anderson.[8]

Although blues songs were sung in vaudeville from at least 1910, the publication and mass appeal of blues songs from 1912 led to their popularity. They became part of the repertoire of African American singers on vaudeville, and soon the "coon shouter" epithet was phased out, and forgotten, in favor of blues. By 1916 both Rainey and Bessie Smith were referred to as blues singers and were stars on the southern vaudeville circuit. They were so popular that classic blues singers are often referred to as "vaudeville" blues singers. Although Mamie Smith was the first to record a blues, she ironically did not sing in an authentic blues manner which is fundamentally a southern style and best heard in the deep voice of Bessie Smith.

Bessie Smith

Bessie Smith (1892/1895–1937) was the most popular blues singer in the 1920s and is known as the "Empress of the Blues." Singing in the pre-microphone era in large auditoriums, theaters, and tents, some singers sang into a megaphone, but others learned to project their voices above the band. Smith's voice was powerful and could be heard without amplification of any kind.

Born in Chattanooga, Tennessee, Smith lived in abject poverty as her mother, father, and brother passed away before she was nine. Raised by her older sister and forced to sing on the streets with her brother for money, she left home early and by 1909 was active on the southern vaudeville circuit.[9] A long-held story states that "Ma" Rainey discovered Smith and nurtured her talents, but in fact, Smith was already on the road when they crossed paths briefly in the fall of 1910, and their association was brief, lasting less than four weeks.[10] They did not perform together again until 1917. In 1912, Smith appeared in a duo with dancer Wayne Burton and was already being labeled as a great coon shouter, singing proto-blues songs like "The Blues (but I'm Too Blamed Mean to Cry)."[11] By 1916 with the press raving about her vocal talents, she was recognized as a blues singer and was a major draw at shows. She signed to Columbia Records in 1923.

"Down Hearted Blues"

Bessie Smith's first record, "Down Hearted Blues," was written by Lovie Austin (1887–1972) and Alberta Hunter (1895–1984). Chicago-based Austin was a respected pianist, bandleader, and arranger. Born in Tennessee, she was formally trained, studying at Roger Williams College in Nashville as well as Knoxville College. Austin was working and touring on the vaudeville circuits when she became the house pianist for Paramount Records, leading recording sessions and backing singers, often accompanied by her own jazz-oriented group, the Blues Serenaders.

Hunter, one of the great classic blues singers, recorded her own version of this song in 1922, but a comparison with Smith's performance reveals the strongly African American character of Smith's voice as compared to Hunter's. Smith's voice is from the church and blues and is untouched by any white influence. Her delivery is straightforward as she eschews gimmicks or tricks of any kind, does not improvise, and does not try to impress her audience with vocal acrobatics. Instead, she captivated audiences with her voice which was rich, full, round, and resonant. While her vocal range was limited, she made up for it with different varieties of pitch and color. On "Down Hearted Blues" she is accompanied only by Clarence Williams on piano as her powerful voice shines through, fully exposed so one can better hear and feel her vocal nuances, like bent notes, slides, or grace notes. Smith uses them sparingly to enhance the emotive qualities of the performance, and they are the windows into her soul. The slow tempo, her favorite, certainly allowed her to decorate the melody in this way. With confident delivery, she demonstrates remarkable control over her voice and projects a powerful image that was and would continue to be a tremendous influence on singers everywhere. Though the song is about rejection and mistreatment from a lover, Smith does not portray a woman who is heartbroken; rather she depicts a woman who is proud and even contemptuous of the man who mistreated her.

"Down Hearted Blues" was a huge success as Smith became the most famous blues singer during the 1920s admired by whites and African Americans. In live performances on the Theater Owners' Booking Association (T.O.B.A.) circuit, she captivated her audiences, but she kept a busy schedule of recording. Some of her best recordings paired her with her equals such as stride pianist James P. Johnson or trumpeter Louis Armstrong. The performances with Armstrong, especially "Reckless Blues" and "St. Louis Blues" from January 1925, are classic as Armstrong's own affinity for the blues matches perfectly with Smith.

Smith was a big enough celebrity to star in her own short film in 1929, entitled, *St. Louis Blues*. Unfortunately, the film is filled with racial stereotypes, but her performance is breathtaking. After the skit that introduces the film, she begins by singing solo, which recalls the field holler. She is then joined by members of the Fletcher Henderson Orchestra with James P. Johnson on piano as well as the Johnson-Handy singers, under the direction of J. Rosamund Johnson. It is a large choir, but Smith can be heard clearly, singing loudly above everyone else. Her voice is rough and sounds strained at times, but combined with her back phrasing (or singing behind the beat) and bluesy gestures, the effect is chilling. It was an astonishing performance, but the onset of the Depression reversed Smith's fortunes though she continued to record until 1933.

Smith's death was almost as legendary as her career. She died on September 26, 1937, from injuries sustained in a car crash in Mississippi, but the exact circumstances remain controversial. For decades, it was believed that she died to due to racist practices from white southern hospitals who chose to care for the white woman in the other car over Smith. The rumor was sparked by an article by impresario John Hammond in the November 1937 issue of *Down Beat* magazine, titled "Did Bessie Smith bleed to death while waiting for medical aid?" At the time, black lives did not matter in the South with prevailing Jim Crow laws so it was a believable story. This myth was immortalized in a 1959 play, *The Death of Bessie Smith* by Edward Albee.

The myth was finally broken in 1972 with the publication of *Bessie*, Chris Albertson's biography of the legendary singer who confirmed that Smith's death was not due to southern hospitals' racist policies. Instead, two ambulances arrived at the scene of the accident and, as was common practice, the white victims were sent to the white hospital while Smith went to the "colored" hospital, since no white hospital would have accepted her. The details were corroborated by Dr. Hugh Smith, no relation, who happened upon the scene as he was returning from a fishing trip. He reported that Smith was already in critical condition with her arm virtually severed from her body when he found her. She was in shock by the time she arrived at the hospital and died some ten hours after being admitted.

Postscript

Though ragtime and blues are important precursors to the development of jazz, it is important to note that the beginnings of jazz occurred almost simultaneously, circa 1900.[12] The practice of "ragging" a tune, or adding syncopation to a preexisting song was still being practiced. Meanwhile, blues was still a manner of performance as the twelve-bar form had yet to be formalized. Yet from these developments jazz emerged from New Orleans.

Chapter 3

New Orleans and Early White Bands

Jazz developed in many places, but its beginnings center around New Orleans with its diverse musical traditions. As the cultural center of the South in the nineteenth century, New Orleans was a hotbed of musical activity enhanced by its rich cultural heritage. A major port city located at the bottom of the Mississippi River and one hundred miles upriver from the Gulf of Mexico, New Orleans allowed easy access into the interior of the United States and was an important link between the U.S. and the rest of the world. Originally inhabited by Native American Indians, the land was coveted by colonialists, discovered by Ponce De Leon in the sixteenth century before the city was founded by the French in 1718. It was ceded to the Spanish in 1763, and aside from a brief period of being under French rule, became U.S. territory as part of the Louisiana Purchase in 1803. Even with three official languages being spoken in a hundred-year span, New Orleans's demographic was further impacted by a successful insurrection in Haiti by slaves against colonial French rule beginning in 1791. With the establishment of a new government, many Haitians, white and free and enslaved blacks, fled the country with many settling in New Orleans, thus doubling its population by 1809.

New Orleans was a haven of diversity, exhibiting a more tolerant attitude towards blacks. From 1817 through the 1840s, enslaved people were allowed to get together every Sunday to sing and dance in a field in New Orleans known as Congo Square. An unusual event in slave history, the sights and sounds were a surprise for white onlookers who wrote accounts about the "exotic" dances and the music that they heard with unusual instruments, singing styles, and sounds. Being a major port, New Orleans ironically had the largest slave market in the U.S., with enslaved people from the interior of the U.S., Africa, and the Caribbean. Brought together in Congo Square, they represented the diverse experiences of the enslaved people.

Amid the comingling of cultures was the emergence of "Creoles," a term that referred to either first generation white European settlers, the black non-slave population of Louisiana, or those of mixed racial descent who were born out of the union of the two. In jazz history, the latter is the most relevant and was applied to both whites and blacks, with those of African descent recognized as "Creoles of color," a separate status from whites and blacks. Creole musicians received a Eurocentric music education, learning to read and write music and to play their instruments with classical technique and tone. While diminishing their own African ancestry, they reveled in their middle-class status and their European heritage, presenting themselves as well-mannered and well-educated. Jelly Roll Morton was Creole, and in interviews he clearly favors his European ancestry while diminishing his own African roots.

Many Creoles looked down upon blacks and shared the prejudice towards darker-skinned people of many whites.[1] But by 1900, Creoles of color were no longer recognized as a separate status in New Orleans; instead all people of African ancestry became black. Creoles were then subject to the increasing ubiquity of Jim Crow laws in the South that enabled segregation and eventually extended to education, housing, employment, and public services. Subsequently, the interactions between Creole and black New Orleans would have a resounding impact on the birth of jazz.

However, the racial makeup of African Americans in New Orleans is far more complex and extended to skin color and tone. Light-skinned blacks were looked upon more highly with access to more lucrative employment opportunities. Creole dance band leaders John Robichaux and Armand J. Piron were able to secure work at prestigious venues in New Orleans, playing for blacks and whites. When Storyville venues began using brass instruments, light-skinned Freddie Keppard was hired to play. Famed vaudeville blues singer "Ma" Rainey would not perform with anyone who was of a lighter skin tone than she.[2] Such a caste system was not unique to New Orleans, and such intraracial prejudice was rampant throughout the United States.

Music in New Orleans

A common denominator among the diverse population of New Orleans was a passion for music that continues through the present day. In the mid-nineteenth century, New Orleans's cultural glory was opera. Despite having a population of only 40,000, New Orleans was the capital of opera in the U.S. During its heyday in the years before the Civil War, there were three major opera companies operating in New Orleans, hosting premieres of the biggest operas of the day, more regularly than any other city in the U.S. Beloved by adults and children alike, opera's popularity cultivated a passion for music-making that eventually became equated with the city.

Music was also nurtured by a passion for dance. Balls, for blacks or whites, were a significant part of the social life in New Orleans that led to a demand for dance orchestras.[3] Such orchestras were primarily the domain of the Creoles of color and typified the "downtown" sound; they demonstrated a refined sound and read stock arrangements. The repertoire consisted of a variety of dances that included older ones like the waltz, polka, and quadrille, set dances like the Scottish Reel or the mazurka, but also newer ones like marches, rags, cakewalks, and one-steps. One of the most popular high society dance orchestras was led by Creole violinist John Robichaux (1866–1939).[4] By 1912 he was the best-known orchestra leader in New Orleans, working in vaudeville theaters and playing for elite African American and white audiences. Many important musicians passed through Robichaux's band including Albert Piron, brothers Lorenzo and Louis Tio, Isidore Barbarin, Manuel Perez, George Baquet, Alphonse Picou, Zutty Singleton, and Edward "Dee Dee" Chandler, among many, many others.[5]

Brass Bands

Among the most popular groups in the United States in the late nineteenth and early twentieth centuries were brass bands. In New Orleans, they were a staple at events and holidays with a similarly broad repertoire. Accounts of brass bands date back to as early as the 1830s with groups by ethnicity including Germans, Italians, Mexicans, African Americans, and Creoles, although later they became mixed white and mixed black Creole bands. They also doubled as parade bands, altering their repertoire to focus on standard marches for ceremonial events and dirges for funerals. New Orleans funeral parades are important events and unique for presenting typically somber music at the beginning of the procession before ending with a happier, joyous selection. The introduction to Jelly Roll Morton's performance of "Dead Man Blues" from 1926 encapsulates such an event beginning at a slow tempo with a quote of Chopin's "Funeral March" followed by the song itself, a joyous, lighthearted blues.

The first generation of jazz musicians began their careers in brass bands with the Olympia Brass Band led by trumpeter Freddie Keppard and the Onward Brass Band led by trumpeter Manuel Perez (1878–1946). Perez was a top parade cornetist with an elegant sound. Although he preferred written arrangements, he was open to improvisation and ear-playing when the practice was becoming popular, hiring young Joe "King" Oliver on cornet.

White New Orleans jazz musicians developed concurrently with African American musicians with the same opportunities afforded blacks and Creoles. The most prominent bandleader was bass drum player "Papa" Jack Laine (1873–1966) who led the Reliance Brass band and the Reliance Orchestra. He was a successful booking agent, sending bands for concerts, parades, parties, and other events. Laine hired musicians from immigrant families, and his bands included German, Irish, English, and Italian musicians, as well as light-skinned Creoles like Achille Baquet. Some of the best musicians included a "crying" clarinet player named Monty Korn and Lawrence Veca (1889–1911), considered one of the great early white cornetists known for his warm tone, sense of rhythm, and creative abilities.[6] But Laine emphasized a collective sound with an emphasis on arrangements that rarely included extended solos. His legacy is vast as just about every significant white New Orleans musician of the 1910s and 1920s worked in his bands including brothers Frank and Emile Christian, brothers Manuel and Leonce Mello, "Chink" Martin Abraham, the Brunies brothers including George and Abbie, Ray Lopez, and others including members of the Original Dixieland Jazz Band, Nick LaRocca, Larry Shields, Eddie Edwards, Henry Ragas, and Tony Sbarbaro.

UPTOWN NEW ORLEANS AND BUDDY BOLDEN

The origin of jazz was long thought to have developed in Storyville, the red-light district in New Orleans; its subsequent closing in 1917 forced its musicians to move, via riverboat, up to Chicago where it flourished.

However, early forms of jazz was being played all over New Orleans at dances, lawn parties, parades, fish fries, and carnival halls. Another avenue of work for musicians were Sundays at the lakefront where resorts had concerts, dance contests, amusement parks, and casinos.[7] Moreover, musicians had already been pursuing new avenues of employment on the road or relocating to new cities since at least 1902 when Charles Elgar came to Chicago. The list includes Bill Johnson, Lizzie Miles, Jelly Roll Morton, Freddie Keppard, Clarence Williams, among many others, as well those who left *after* 1917 such as King Oliver, Kid Ory, and Louis Armstrong.[8] Still, there was a lot of music happening at Storyville with a thriving band culture in saloons and cabarets. Brothels usually hired a single pianist to provide entertainment, most famously Jelly Roll Morton and his mentor and idol Tony Jackson.

Known to locals as "The District," Storyville was established as an area of prostitution and was a rough, poverty-stricken neighborhood, a microcosm of uptown New Orleans, a predominantly black neighborhood. Uptown New Orleans was where African Americans, disgusted with sharecropping and brutal racial terrorism, settled post-reconstruction, part of a larger rural-to-urban migration that occurred throughout the South between 1880 and 1910.[9] During this time, uptown dance halls and honky-tonks opened up to fulfill a demand for music and entertainment. Against a background of illegal gambling, prostitution, and other illicit activities, cornetist Buddy Bolden emerged.

Bolden (1877–1931) was born in the uptown district and is widely acknowledged as the first jazz musician. He was noted for his tone and his emotional delivery, undoubtedly enhanced with the blues. Bolden was self-taught, primarily gaining experience playing in string bands rather than in parade bands; string bands featured guitars, bass, and violin as well as brass and/or woodwind instruments in spite of its name. After 1900, he had established a small band that was gaining popularity playing for dancers all over New Orleans with a diverse repertoire including dances of all kinds, spirituals, hymns, as well as novelty songs and blues.[10] His music was loud and boisterous and especially appealed to black audiences but was quickly gaining popularity with everyone. By 1905, despite their disparate styles, he rivaled Robichaux as the most popular dance band in town. By this time Robichaux was moving with the new trends, adding cornetist Manuel Perez to bolster his sound in band battles with Bolden. However, Bolden's mental health caught up with him, and he was arrested on September 9, 1906, and again on March 13, 1907, for "insanity." He was declared legally insane on April 4 and institutionalized at an asylum where he died on November 4, 1931.

Bolden is representative of a new sound that is described as the "uptown" sound with extensive use of blues gestures that altered pitch such as scoops, bent notes, and slides. At the time, it was new and innovative as blues was far from the mainstream. It existed on the fringes of society, and such sounds, especially in context of a march or ragtime song, would have sounded foreign to the trained ear. Being self-taught, the other "uptown" aspect of Bolden's style was that he was primarily an ear player, an approach that nurtured an interpretive manner of playing or reading music that spells improvisation. Bolden's music thrived as he played for dancers at uptown honky-tonks and meeting halls, including Odd Fellows, Masonic Hall, and most notably Funky Butt Hall, so-called because of the way dancers moved their hips. Bunk Johnson, King Oliver, and Creoles Freddie Keppard, Sidney Bechet, and Kid Ory were among those who were swept away by Bolden's influence, and the music that would become known as jazz was underway.

The new approach created a generation gap with older Creole musicians who favored reading and could not tolerate playing by ear.[11] Despite their Eurocentric approach to playing music, a tradition of singing Creole songs reflected their mixed heritage with call and response (a common musical trait of African American music), Caribbean rhythms (like the tresillo or the habanera), and a flexible performance and storytelling format that encouraged spontaneous composition and improvised lyrics.[12] They were sung during celebrations, parties, and were staples during Carnival season (from January 6 through Mardi Gras, the last Tuesday before Ash Wednesday). Likely a part of the repertoire of jazz bands in the early 1900s, Creole songs were a part of the melting pot of music that also contributed to the birth of jazz.

Of course, the uptown-downtown dichotomy is a simplification of a more complex process. There were musicians who could play in both "styles," like clarinetist Alphonse Picou, and uptown bands that could play sweet music like Jack Carey's or the Tuxedo band.[13] Moreover, Picou's recollection of being invited to a rehearsal in 1894 with a downtown band that did not play from sheet music suggests that improvised bands existed *before* Bolden and among Creoles.[14] While such boundaries would diminish in New Orleans jazz, the uptown-downtown dichotomy would continue to manifest itself in various guises throughout the history of jazz, for example in the opposition between formal-informal, reading-playing by ear, art-entertainment, the street-the classroom, and black-white.

White New Orleans

In context of the development of jazz, the uptown-downtown dichotomy is further informed by the contributions of whites in New Orleans. However, the notion of "white" differed in the late nineteenth and early twentieth century, as many would more likely self-identify as German, Irish, English, Hungarian, or Spanish. Many were recent immigrants from south and central Europe living in integrated neighborhoods that also included blacks and Creoles. Such interactions inevitably led to various forms of transethnic and transcultural exchanges: Louis Armstrong worked for the Karnofskys, a family of Jewish immigrants who lent the young boy money to buy his first trumpet. Similarly, drummer Louis Cottrell Sr. benefited from a Jewish neighbor who gave drum lessons. There were also Jewish musicians (Johnny Stein and the Korn brothers, Montague and Marcus) and bandleaders, but the most prominent white ethnic group in early jazz were Italians.[15]

In 1910, there were more Italians in New Orleans than in any other city in the United States, with an increase from 5,866 to 8,066.[16] However, Italians were regularly discriminated against by white Americans and were already associated with crime and violence with the formation of criminal syndicates known as the "Black Hand." Recent immigrants from Italy did not share the racial prejudices of white southerners, choosing instead to associate with blacks, working in the sugar cane fields or on the docks.[17] Moreover, the common bond was stronger with Sicilians who, along with Jews and Hispanics, were often categorized as nonwhite.

Of course, not all Italians were sympathetic to the plight of blacks. Original Dixieland Jazz Band's Nick LaRocca is an example of one whose racist views clouded his understanding of jazz and African Americans. Despite his unfortunate stance on race within the history of jazz, Italian American involvement during jazz's nascent years was evident among the first generations of New Orleans musicians, including Lawrence Veca, brothers Manuel and Leonce Mello, Tony Sbarbaro, brothers Vincent and Joe Barocco, Manuel Belasco, and later, Henry Vanicelli, Russ Papalia, Charles Scaglioni, Tony Parenti, and Charlie Cordella.

This group also includes Johnny Lala, Tony Schiro, and brothers Arnold, John, and Joe Loyacano, all of whom are Arbëreshë, descendants of Albanian refugees following the Ottoman conquest of the Balkans, who came to Italy from the fifteenth-century onward and retained their language and religion.[18] Comparable to the Creoles of color and blacks, they faced discrimination in New Orleans from Italians, but in jazz bands Sicilians and Arbëreshë played alongside each other. Then there is the presence of Afro-Italians, Manuel Manetta, Natty Dominique, and Ernie Cagnolatti, and the fact that Sicily only became a part of the kingdom of Italy in 1860, all of which reinforces the complex group of peoples who were included under the heading of "Italians."[19]

The Great Migration

Following Reconstruction (1865–1877), new segregationist policies, known as Jim Crow laws, were enacted. Between 1890 and 1910, ten of the former Confederate states passed laws that changed the lives of African Americans in the South, as designated areas for "colored" (or nonwhite) were established. Those who did not follow these laws were punished severely, and by the 1920s, the Ku Klux Klan, a white supremacist hate group that had worked in the underground, began a period of intimidation, violence, and lynching that defined the horrors of the South for African Americans.

Racial tensions in New Orleans reached a nadir in 1900 when an African American man had a run in with the police. Harassed by local police, an altercation resulted in Robert Charles shooting a white policeman. The search for Charles led to a race riot as hundreds of innocent African Americans were the target of violence from the police and fearful whites wary of their black neighbors. The police were eventually tipped off by a member of the African American community as to Charles's whereabouts, and he died in a shootout. He became a folk hero, and a song was written in commemoration of his actions.

Instead of living under such unbearable circumstances, many African Americans chose to leave the South altogether for the larger cities in the North and the West. Thus, the Great Migration of African Americans began, a period that would last until the Civil Rights era. Between 1910 and 1970 over six million African Americans relocated to points north and west, partially to fulfill the demand for industrial workers for World War I and later World War II. As part of the Great Migration, jazz would flourish elsewhere as New Orleans's best musicians sought new opportunities on the road or in different cities, in particular, Chicago with its growing population of African Americans in the South Side of town.

The great cornetist Freddie Keppard (1889–1933) was among those who left New Orleans early. Keppard, who was initially a violinist, began on cornet in the mid-1900s and quickly established a reputation as a powerful cornetist, succeeding Bolden as the king of the cornetists. He played with the Olympia Brass Band, was known for imitating a horse on his cornet, and later became the first cornetist to play in Storyville. The promise of work in Los Angeles by bassist Bill Johnson led to Keppard relocating there in May 1914.[20] Johnson was among the first of the New Orleans musicians to leave when he made his first trip out west in 1904, but he returned a few years later. He subsequently returned to L.A. and was living there when he called for Keppard.

Johnson's group became the Original Creole Orchestra, an important transitional band that traveled around the country, touring on the vaudeville circuit between 1914 and 1918. The band's repertoire consisted of popular songs, blues, and rags, but there was also singing, dancing, and even some skits including one with a live chicken.[21] The skits were set against a backdrop of Southern plantations, log cabins, and master's houses and were not far removed from minstrelsy with the musicians dressed up like field workers with overalls and straw hats and the inclusion of blackface and old minstrel songs.[22] These comic skits were central to the band's success and the manner in which New Orleans music was spread throughout the country.

Keppard's playing was fondly remembered by those who heard him. A famous story states that Keppard turned down an offer to record because he did not want other musicians to steal his music. He was very protective of his playing, reportedly playing cornet with a handkerchief on his hands to hide his fingerings. Whether or not such stories are true, they underscore the competitive atmosphere. Keppard eventually moved to Chicago and did record in the mid-1920s, but by then he was no longer in his prime. A heavy drinker, he contacted tuberculosis in 1928 and died in 1933.

Before he left for California in 1919, trombonist Kid Ory (1886–1973) was an important bandleader during the 1910s in New Orleans.

Having been inspired by Buddy Bolden and later mentoring both King Oliver and Louis Armstrong, Ory represents an important link between the two generations of musicians. Born on a plantation, he came from humble beginnings, singing in vocal quartets and playing in a band on homemade instruments before starting on banjo. He settled on trombone, studying with Zue Robertson, and by 1907 was in the Pickwick brass band. Otherwise, he often led his own dance bands. He heard Bolden play in 1906, and though Ory identified as Creole, he was inspired to play uptown music. Acting as manager, and later as a promoter, his band played dances, lawn parties, parades, fish fries, as well as all kinds of functions from clubs in Storyville to concerts at the lakefront to high society gigs in uptown white circles, competing with John Robichaux on his own turf. Unlike Bolden who mostly played for black audiences, Ory's brand of uptown music was crossing racial and cultural boundaries.

Ory kept a close ear on new trends leading to his hiring of cornetist Joe "King" Oliver for a band they co-led. In 1917, the Original Dixieland Jazz Band made New Orleans jazz a national commodity, and Ory and Oliver took notice. They inserted the word "jazz" into their name, "Ory and Oliver's Greatest Jazz Players," and discarded the violin, eventually bringing the band down to five pieces.[23] When Oliver went to Chicago, his protégé, Louis Armstrong, took his place. Many important musicians passed through his band, including cornetists Thomas C. "Papa Mutt" Carey, King Oliver, and Louis Armstrong; clarinetists Johnny Dodds, and Jimmie Noone; violinists Emile Bigard (uncle of clarinetist Barney Bigard) and Manuel Manetta; banjoists Johnny St. Cyr and Lorenzo Staulz (who played with Bolden); bassist Ed "Montudi" Garland; and drummers "Black" Benny Williams, Ed "Rabbit" Robertson, and Henry Martin.

Early White Bands

By 1910, many white bands formed by former alumni of the Laine groups emerged in New Orleans. As African American musicians began to settle in Chicago, white musicians followed in search of new performance opportunities. The first white band to play in Chicago was Brown's Band of Dixieland, led by trombonist Tom Brown, brother of bassist Steve.

Summoned by dancer and entertainer Joe Frisco, who heard the band in New Orleans, the band opened at Lamb's Café on May 17, 1915, and for the first time the music was introduced as jazz, or *jass*, *jas*, or *jaz*, as it was sometimes spelled.

The origin of the word *jazz* is still unknown with numerous theories and myths about its beginnings, none of which have been verified. The earliest known use of the word *jazz* in print was in context of baseball in the early 1910s, and although there have been allusions to Art Hickman's music being described as jazz in 1913, it next appears in advertisements in Chicago newspapers in 1915.[24] The moniker stuck as other bands in Chicago began advertising themselves playing *jass* or *jazz*; for New Orleans musicians, it was the first they heard of the word *jazz* to describe the music they had been playing, some of whom had been calling it ragtime.[25] Brown's Band of Dixieland played through the summer and never recorded; instead another white band from New Orleans came to Chicago, and they became the first jazz band to record, the Original Dixieland Jazz Band (ODJB).

Original Dixieland Jazz Band (ODJB)

ODJB's recording of "Dixie Jass Band One-Step" and "Livery Stable Blues" was released in the spring of 1917 and marks the beginning of the recorded history of jazz. Their dynamic and energetic performances were a sensation. However, their cornetist Nick LaRocca (1889–1961) has enraged jazz critics, musicians, and fans for negating African Americans and their contributions and his outrageous claims that ODJB "invented" jazz. His racist and ignorant attitude led to many dismissing or diminishing ODJB's position in jazz history. Nonetheless, being the first jazz group on record, they were highly influential with clarinetist Larry Shields exerting considerable influence as well as LaRocca whose driving trumpet lines clearly lead the band.

Nick LaRocca was born in New Orleans and grew up in the Irish Channel neighborhood that was primarily white. His father was adamant his son not become a musician, destroying two of his trumpets before LaRocca relented and settled into a trade. But, demonstrating his strong will, he bounced back to apprentice with the Reliance bands and to form a group with young clarinetist Larry Shields (1893–1953). In 1916, he was asked to join a group in Chicago led by drummer Johnny Stein and trombonist Eddie Edwards with Alcide Nunez on clarinet and Henry Ragas on piano. The band was a success, being one of the only New Orleans bands in town at the time. However, personnel changes led to the band's members leaving Stein, calling up Tony Sbarbaro from New Orleans to play drums, and later replacing Nunez with Shields. Appearing at the Casino Gardens, a recommendation from Al Jolson led to offers to appear in New York, and the group appeared at the Reisenweber Café in New York City in January 1917. They became a huge sensation and recorded "Livery Stable Blues" and "Dixie Jass Band One-Step" for Victor in February.

"Dixie Jass Band One-Step"

Jazz's early roots in marching bands, brass bands, and ragtime are evident on "Dixie Jass Band One-Step," yet the song still contains many defining characteristics of New Orleans jazz. ODJB's sound centered around the front line of cornet, clarinet, and trombone. First, the cornet plays the melody. Then, the clarinet freely plays throughout its range with obbligatos, meaning decorative lines that contrast and complement the melody. Lastly, the trombone plays supportive phrases or tailgate trombone characterized by a glissando, also called slides, smears, or slurs. The term "tailgate trombone" originated when bands were hired to play on the back of a wagon with a large sign on the side announcing whatever was being advertised (an upcoming dance, sale, or event). Slide trombonists sat at the end on the tailgate so that they would not hit anyone else while playing, hence the term. This style of performance is called collective improvisation, but even with the latest recording technology, it can be difficult to identify each instrument. Below the front line is the rhythmic section of piano and drums maintaining a steady pulse while the drummer performs more of a painterly role switching instruments to distinguish the sections.

The form of "Dixie Jass Band One-Step" is ABABCCC and is reminiscent of earlier march forms. Prior to the standardization of the thirty-two-bar song form, this was common throughout early jazz, especially New Orleans music. The song begins with the front line playing rhythmic figures in unison alternating with short bursts of collective improvisation. After a repeat of the A section, the B section features another defining characteristic of New Orleans jazz, the break, which is a brief pause by the band with a short solo feature for a single instrument, in this case, the clarinet. After a repeat of the first two sections, we get to the final C section that is distinguished by cornet and clarinet playing unison

Listening Guide: "Dixie Jass Band One-Step" by the Original Dixieland Jazz Band.
Pete LaRocca: cornet; Larry Shields: clarinet; Eddie Edwards: trombone; Henry Ragas: piano; Tony Sbarbaro: drums. Victor 18255-A. Recorded February 26, 1917, in New York.

Time	Section	Comments
0:00	A	Rhythmic thrusts alternating with collective improvisation.
0:08	A	Same as above.
0:16	B	Clarinet break followed by collective improvisation.
0:24	B'	Same as above.
0:31	A	Rhythmic thrusts alternating with collective improvisation.
0:39	A	Same as above.
0:47	B	Clarinet break followed by collective improvisation.
0:54	B'	Same as above.
1:02	C	Cornet/clarinet unison answered by the trombone. Woodblock sound followed by the syncopated cowbell pattern.
1:33	C	Same as above with occasional bass drum hits.
2:03	C	Same as above.
		At 2:27 for the last phrase, Sbarbaro reverts to snare drum.
2:32	Coda	Final flourish.

melody lines that are answered by the trombone. Sbarbaro moves to the woodblocks, later playing a syncopated pattern on the cowbell. This section is repeated three times, and at the end of the last section, the snare drum is heard signaling the grand finale.

An important aspect of ODJB's music that caught everyone's attention was the raucous timbres of the instruments: growls, scratches, slides, and howls that emanate from the front line, especially Shields's clarinet. It was novel and amusing particularly when the front line mimicked animal sounds as heard on "Livery Stable Blues." It only added to the group's rowdy sound, as the band energetically races through its performances.

Studio recordings from this era, until about 1926, were recorded using an "acoustic" technique that required musicians to play their instruments into a large, conical horn. The fidelity was poor, with drums and bass instruments being particularly difficult to record. For this reason, Sbarbaro used a variety of replacements for a traditional drum set, including woodblocks and cowbell, that could be more easily captured on disc. Furthermore, the placement of the musicians decided who would be the loudest.

The group's stateside success led to an invitation to perform in London, England, in 1919, playing for the Royal Family at Buckingham Palace including King George V and the Prince of Wales. On their trip, they recorded in London, and their music was distributed throughout Europe, helping spread jazz's popularity around the world. New songs like "At the Jazz Band Ball" and "'Lasses Candy" duplicated the group's earlier energetic performances. The London sessions also demonstrate the group's broad musicality, performing very soft passages on "I Lost My Heart in Dixieland" and "Satanic Blues," as well as recording pop songs including two waltzes, "I'm Forever Blowing Bubbles" and "Alice Blue Gown," which display Shields's warmer, lower register.

The band returned to the U.S. in 1920 but began following current trends as their music became increasingly commercial reflecting the new sound of Paul Whiteman and his polite brand of jazz with a focus on arrangements played at relaxed tempos. Otherwise, the breaks and humorous sounds, mostly provided by trombonist Edwards, are still present, but the wild timbres like the growls and shrieks are gone and replaced by generally straight-toned playing. A highlight from this period is Shields's brilliant solo on "St. Louis Blues" from May 1921 with eloquent blues playing full of long slides and simple, off-beat phrases that are vocal-like. It was one of the first jazz solos on record and was copied by countless clarinetists.

By 1923, ODJB struggled onwards before LaRocca suffered a nervous breakdown and the group disbanded. They reunited briefly in 1936, recording contemporary versions of their old hits, but their reunion was short-lived. It was around this time that LaRocca began to promote ODJB's place as the "inventors" of jazz. His diatribes found in magazines and in interviews reveal a bitter man who did not understand why others were being lauded and his group was forgotten. He continued his championing of the ODJB until his death in 1961.

New Orleans Rhythm Kings (NORK)

The NORK were among the most influential of the early New Orleans white bands. Based in Chicago, their relaxed rhythmic conception contrasted effectively with the jerky rhythms of the New York bands while allowing for a greater variety of expression. Unlike the ODJB, NORK openly acknowledged their debt to African Americans like King Oliver, and in turn, they had an important influence on other white musicians in Chicago most notably trumpeter Bix Beiderbecke, members of his band the Wolverines, and Chicagoans such as Jimmy McPartland, Bud Freeman, Dave Tough, and Joe Sullivan, among others.

The band started when cornetist Paul Mares (1900–1949) left New Orleans in 1920 to replace Abbie Brunies in a New Orleans–style group in Chicago where he was later joined by Leon Roppolo (1902–1943) on clarinet. Roppolo, from a musical family, is considered one of the first great white soloists and one of the first to conceive a solo as a statement as heard on three takes of "Tin Roof Blues."[26] By 1921, they were managed by music promoter Husk O'Hare, who booked them at the Friar's Inn where they became a sensation. O'Hare introduced the NORK to Gennett Records executives to record, having already recorded his own band for the label in March 1922.

From their first recording sessions in August 1922, the group had a tight, cohesive sound revolving around the nucleus of New Orleans musicians Mares, Roppolo, George Brunies on trombone, and Steve Brown on bass, augmented with musicians from the Midwest: Jack Pettis on saxophone, Elmer Schoebel on piano, and Frank Snyder on drums. On tracks such as "Eccentric," "Tiger Rag," and others, the band already demonstrates a strong swing feel. Their version of "Maple Leaf Rag," from March 1923, is indicative of their achievement, as they maintain the spirit of ragtime in a New Orleans context while replacing ragtime's stiffer feel with a looser conception that is closer to swing.

The historic sessions from July 1923 are best remembered for the appearance of Jelly Roll Morton on piano in an early interracial recording session that also included his own compositions, "Mr. Jelly Lord," "London Blues," and "Milenburg Joys." Recorded on July 18, 1923, "Milenburg Joys" is representative of NORK's innovative small-group sound with arranged sections, individual solos, and collective improvisation. For this session, the group is augmented with the addition of reeds players Glenn Scoville and Don Murray. Despite the large frontline, a small-group sound is maintained as the other saxophonists are barely audible. The rhythm section consists of Morton on piano, Bob Gillette on banjo, "Chink" Martin Abraham on tuba, and Ben Pollack on drums.

Listening Guide: "Milenburg Joys" by the NORK
Paul Mares: cornet; Leon Roppolo: clarinet; George Brunies: trombone;
Jack Pettis: C-melody saxophone; Glenn Scoville: alto and tenor
saxophones; Don Murray: clarinet and tenor saxophone; Jelly Roll
Morton: piano; Bob Gillette: banjo; "Chink" Martin Abraham: tuba; Ben
Pollack: drums. Gennett 5217-A. Recorded July 18, 1923, in Richmond,
Indiana.

Time	Section	Comments
0:00	Introduction	Four bars played in rhythmic unison.
0:07	A	Eight-bar section featuring call and response between the front line and tuba. Through the A section, Roppolo on clarinet is the only one who veers away from the melody, improvising short riffs and lines. Harmonically, this section moves to the dominant and then back to the tonic.
0:19		Eight bars that temporarily modulate to the subdominant before concluding on the dominant.
0:32	B(a)	Sixteen-bar section that combines material from the introduction and the above AB form. The first section (a) contains the first two measures from the introduction followed by four bars of the melody, as Roppolo freely improvises throughout this entire section; the harmonies move from the tonic to the dominant.
0:41	(b)	The second section (b) begins with a two-bar variation of the first two bars of the introduction, followed by those two bars as played at (a), and followed by two bars of collective improvisation over a chord progression that moves to the subdominant.
0:51	(c)	The third phrase (c) consists of four bars of collective improvisation, that begins on the subdominant before resolving on the tonic.
0:58	Interlude	Four-bar interlude that modulates to the subdominant (as is typical for the trio section).
1:04	CD	Cornet solo by Paul Mares, with a break preceding D at 1:26, accompanied by the rhythm section with drummer Ben Pollack on woodblocks. Morton's counterlines, which outline the harmony, can be faintly heard. The new trio section (C) features the same harmonic progression as the A section but is in the new key.
1:53	C	Clarinet solo by Leon Roppolo with a break at 2:15 as drummer Ben Pollack brings out the backbeat on beats two and four on the cymbal.
2:18	D	Roppolo is joined by Mares and Brunies for collective improvisation as Pollack moves the backbeat to the snare drum.
2:40	Coda	With a short break at 2:42 for Mares before the final chords.

The composition itself is simple and straightforward but the creative arrangement creates three sections that are basically variations of one another. The B section is particularly ingenious with its six-bar phrases. Throughout this half of the performance, the band sticks to the written page except for Roppolo who freely improvises. He stands out, and if not for his part, the band would sound like a well-behaved dance band.

Following a brief interlude, the trio section begins with a typically King Oliver–inspired muted solo by Mares. Behind him is Morton on piano, leading the rhythm section with wonderful counterpoint that brings out the guide tones of the chord (thirds and sevenths). His presence greatly enhances the feel as the rhythm section swings particularly hard behind Roppolo's solo. Pollack, who played woodblocks behind Mares, leads the way by bringing out the backbeat, hitting the cymbal on beats two and four. Tubist Martin creates a nice bounce, balancing his short notes with longer ones and adding syncopated fills. Back-to-back solos on record in 1923 was uncommon, so this certainly stood out at the time. For the last half of Roppolo's chorus, the rest of the band reenters with collective improvisation as Pollack now moves to the snare drum on beats two and four for the finale.

"Milenburg Joys" features a mix of New York (arrangements), Chicago (individual solos), and New Orleans (collective improvisation) styles and points to the future. Ending with collective improvisation as a grand finale following a round of solos was a clever way to maintain the New Orleans manner of performance within the context of written arrangements and individual solos and would become standard practice. Then there is the swing groove which was already alive in Chicago during this time with King Oliver's Creole Jazz Band. Pollack's emphasis of beats two and four is among the first instances in recorded history of such a groove.

The band unfortunately broke up soon afterwards; Mares left music, Brunies joined Ted Lewis's orchestra, Roppolo was soon institutionalized where he spent his last days in an asylum, and Pollack would eventually lead a successful dance band. Although the band was short-lived, their collective vision set the stage for a healthy period of Chicago jazz as NORK's concepts would further materialize in the work of the Chicagoans.[27]

Chapter 4

King Oliver and Jelly Roll Morton

During the early jazz era, Chicago was an underrated center of jazz. Located within a large metropolitan city with a large population of African Americans settling in the south side of town, the music scene was thriving. Some of the greatest artists of early jazz lived, played, and recorded in Chicago, including ex-New Orleanians King Oliver and Jelly Roll Morton, the focus of this chapter.[1] Thus, jazz, born in New Orleans, flourished in Chicago largely as a result of the Great Migration.

King Oliver

Joe "King" Oliver (c. 1881/85–1938) was among the best of the New Orleans cornetists when he left for Chicago around 1918. Later, he became the first of the great New Orleans cornetists to record; his 1923 Creole Jazz Band recordings, for Gennett and Okeh Records, represent a pinnacle of New Orleans jazz. It was an outstanding ensemble that also featured a young Louis Armstrong on second cornet. Additionally, Oliver's solo abilities, reflecting the musical styles of an earlier era, were widely admired and imitated, stemming from a tradition that dated back to Buddy Bolden, Manuel Perez, and Freddie Keppard.

Born outside of New Orleans near plantations where ties to slavery were strong, details of Oliver's early life are obscure including his exact birth date and year, although it is estimated to be May 11, 1881 or 1885. Left blind in his left eye as a child due to an accidental kitchen fire, he was born poor and relegated to manual labor and other menial jobs as a young adult. Oliver reportedly started on trombone before switching to cornet.

By 1900 he was in uptown New Orleans where a rich culture of music proved fruitful for the young cornetist. He played professionally with Henry Allen's Brass Band, the Onward Brass Band, the Original Superior Orchestra, and Frankie Duson's Eagle band and was soon in direct competition with Freddie Keppard, the reigning cornet king, often engaging in band battles.[2] Oliver established himself as a blues player and became admired for his manner of manipulating the cornet's timbre with various objects. Known in New Orleans as "freak music," Oliver was already on his way to creating his famous "wah-wah" sound.[3] By 1916, he had a regular night at Pete Lala's and landed a job in Ory's band, replacing Mutt Carey.

By late 1918 or early 1919, Oliver relocated to Chicago, where other New Orleans jazz musicians had already settled, including Keppard, Johnny Dodds, Ed Garland, and Kid Ory. With a bustling music scene, he settled right in joining two bands, one led by drummer Paul Barbarin at the Royal Gardens and another by clarinetist Lawrence Duhé at Dreamland Café; he would eventually take over the latter band. Away from New Orleans, the old caste system of blacks and Creoles no longer existed as African Americans tended to band together. Though Jim Crow laws were no longer relevant, racism continued to permeate the cities in all manners and forms. As Oliver's reputation grew, he reportedly gained his nickname "King" while he was in Chicago where he formed the Creole Jazz Band. The irony of calling his band "Creole" could only happen outside New Orleans and was so named to help promote his music. He took the first edition of the group to California where they played for a year. But by 1922, he returned to Chicago and secured an engagement at the Lincoln Gardens Café with a new band and one that would make history.

CREOLE JAZZ BAND

The band, included Oliver on cornet, Dodds on clarinet, Honoré Dutrey on trombone, Lil Hardin Armstrong on piano, Bill Johnson or Bud Scott on banjo and/or bass, and Dodds's little brother, Warren "Baby" Dodds, on drums. The entire group was from New Orleans, except for the Memphis-born Armstrong, who by this time had been active in Chicago for a number of years. Louis Armstrong, Oliver's protégé from New Orleans, was summoned in July to join the band on second cornet. It has been widely speculated that Oliver, who was not at his prime at this time, brought in Armstrong to hide this fact. Still, Armstrong was delighted to play with his idol and mentor, whom he referred to as "Papa Joe."

A 1921 publicity photo of King Oliver on the West Coast shows Oliver and his band dressed in farm clothes (straw hats and overalls, with Lil Hardin Armstrong in a gingham dress), but at the Lincoln Gardens, the Creole Jazz Band dressed for success and wore tuxedoes. Still, they were part of the evening's entertainment with Oliver imitating a baby crying and Dodds playing his "shimmy beat," dancing while playing drums. But the centerpiece was the floor show whom the band accompanied. In Chicago, tempos were generally faster than in New Orleans, which had a tremendous influence on the dancing and the music.

Word spread quickly as the public was awed by the group's chemistry and musicianship. Not only were dancers impressed, but late-night sets often had both African American and white musicians sitting in front of the band. Aspiring young white musicians like Frankie Teschmacher, Jimmy McPartland, Eddie Condon, Dave Tough, and others came to observe and study the group. The Creole Jazz Band created enough of a sensation to gain an invitation from Gennett Records to record, eventually cutting thirty-seven different tracks for four different record companies between April and December 1923.

An original by Oliver, "Snake Rag" is an excellent example of the group's performances. The form, ABBACCC, is difficult to follow because the texture never deviates from collective improvisation, except for the breaks. Furthermore, there are hardly any distinctive changes in melody, harmony, or texture to determine the form; while drummer "Baby" Dodds was known to change the percussion texture for certain soloists, he does not play any fills to mark the form as it was not yet standard practice. The song was recorded in April for Gennett Records, but was rerecorded in June for Okeh. Both versions are strong for different reasons, but the sound quality on the Okeh release is far superior with better separation of the instruments.

The breaks heard at the beginning of the performance feature snake-imitation sounds from the cornets and then the trombone. During the C section, the breaks happen in the middle of the section; this can be confusing for fans of modern jazz because breaks today normally happen at the end of the form. Johnny Dodds's break is aggressive and strong, but it is the Oliver-Armstrong muted two-cornet breaks during the last

Listening Guide: "Snake Rag" (Okeh version) by King Oliver's Creole Jazz Band
King Oliver and Louis Armstrong: cornets; Johnny Dodds: clarinet; Honoré Dutrey: trombone; Lil Hardin Armstrong: piano; Bud Scott: banjo and vocal break; Baby Dodds: drums. Okeh 4933-B. Recorded June 22, 1923, in Chicago.

Time	Section	Comments
0:00	Introduction	The last part of the A section: collective improvisation followed by the snake-imitation break: downward flourish by the two cornets and the trombone slide.
0:09	A	Collective improvisation ending with the "Snake Rag" break.
0:27	B	Collective improvisation with a trombone break in the middle of the form at 0:33. Ends with the "Snake Rag" break.
0:45	B	Same as above with the trombone break in the middle of the form at 0:52.
1:03	A	Collective improvisation ending with the "Snake Rag" break.
1:21	C	Trio section and a modulation to the subdominant. Collective improvisation continues with a stronger quarter-note-driven feel. Trombone figures are based on the Afro-Cuban clave. Clarinet break in the middle of the form at 1:37.
1:57	C	Preceded by a strong quarter-note rhythm windup from 1:55. Two-cornet break in the middle of the form at 2:13.
2:34	C	This section is preceded by Bud Scott's "Oh Sweet Mama!" Blues-driven two-cornet break in the middle of the form at 2:50.
3:08	Ending	Final phrase is repeated twice at 3:10.

third of the performance that contributed to the mystique behind the band's popularity. At the Lincoln Gardens, audiences marveled at their ability to play such improvised unison riffs seemingly out of nowhere. In practice, these lines were worked out in advance, and Armstrong would get a cue from Oliver a few measures before the break letting him know which line to play.

Dodds excelled in his role, and his rich sound with a strong vibrato that was common to New Orleans musicians of his era made him one of the best clarinetists of his generation. Since recording engineers did not allow for drums to play too loud (if at all) on records, the younger Dodds's contributions on "Snake Rag" are limited to breaks. Ironically, he missed one at the end and was covered by banjoist Bud Scott's yelling "Oh Sweet Mama!," whose line subsequently became part of the performance.

"Snake Rag" also points the way towards the modern swing feel with a strong groove based in quarter notes or a 4/4 feel. It is first heard at the first C section at 1:21 with banjoist Bud Scott playing insistent quarter notes. Meanwhile the trombone is playing a short, repeated rhythm reminiscent of the 2:3 clave (a two-bar recurring rhythm common to Cuban music) that helps lock in the groove with the banjo, and from this point forward, the entire band is rhythmically in sync. Later, at the end of the first C section (approximately 1:55), the two cornets along with piano can be heard accenting quarter notes as a windup back to the beginning of the section, creating a tremendous sense of forward motion.

Groove is a key element of the group's cohesive sound as each member of the group relates strongly to the other with the pieces fitting together like a mosaic. Other excellent examples of their cohesive performances can be heard on "Canal Street Blues," "High Society Rag" (with its famous clarinet part by Alphonse Picou, in fact a transcription of a piccolo solo), and "Jazzin' Babies' Blues." Recordings from October and December of 1923 feature new musicians, yet the same collective ethic is still present.

PAPA JOE THE CORNETIST

King Oliver is considered one of the great cornetists. An ensemble player first, he favored the low and middle register of the instrument and took a theme-based approach to improvisation. Attracted to expressive sounds on the instrument, Oliver experimented with different ways to mute his cornet using his derby hat and a plunger mute, among other items that are still used today. In live performance with the Creole Jazz Band, he used to imitate the sounds of a crying baby as he was being "nursed" by Bill Johnson's horn, part of a skit that the band used to entertain audiences.

Listening Guide: "Dipper Mouth Blues" by King Oliver's Creole Jazz Band
King Oliver and Louis Armstrong: cornets; Johnny Dodds: clarinet; Honoré Dutrey: trombone; Lil Hardin Armstrong: piano; Bud Scott: banjo and vocal break; Baby Dodds: drums. Okeh 4918-A. Recorded June 23, 1923, in Chicago.

Time	Section	Comments
0:00	Introduction	
0:05	Chorus 1	Collective improvisation.
0:21	Chorus 2	Same as above.
0:36	Chorus 3	Clarinet solo by Johnny Dodds with rhythmic hits played by the entire band.
0:51	Chorus 4	Same as above.
1:07	Chorus 5	Three-horn collective improvisation minus Oliver.
1:22	Chorus 6	King Oliver wah-wah cornet solo with piano, banjo, and drums with light collective improvisation from clarinet and trombone.
1:37	Chorus 7	Same as above.
1:53	Chorus 8	Same as above. Ending with Bud Scott exclaiming: "Oh, Play That Thing!"
2:08	Chorus 9	Collective improvisation minus Oliver.
2:20	Ending	Final phrase is repeated at 2:23.

"Dipper Mouth Blues" features excellent ensemble work and three choruses of Oliver playing with his famed wah-wah sound with melodically driven lines that evoke blues phrasing and that accentuate his vocal-like approach. He creates momentum in his solo without ever leaving the framework from which he is improvising. The solo was widely admired in its day and was copied and emulated by cornetists. Oliver is preceded by Dodds's blues-drenched solo with his deep tone and wide vibrato, a sound prized by musicians of his generation.

A note on improvisation: the group recorded a slower version of "Dipper Mouth Blues" in April for Gennett with Oliver playing the same solo. For the most part, musicians of this era did not always reproduce new solos with every performance or take, playing the same solo if they arrived at a model they were pleased with. But this is not always the case as is evident on the band's three different versions of "Mabel's Dream," where Oliver can be heard improvising from a sketch, moving further and further away from the melody with each subsequent take.

Oliver was also active as a freelancer, playing on dozens of recording sessions mostly backing blues singers. "Morning Dove Blues" by Sippie Wallace from February 1925 features Oliver performing some of his most memorable blues playing with slow bends and slides commonly associated with vocalists and slide guitarists. Although he does not take a solo, his response phrases and backing lines create a wonderful synergy with the other musicians while demonstrating an even deeper understanding of the blues not heard on his own recordings. A pair of duets with pianist Jelly Roll Morton were recorded in 1925, but unfortunately, the sound quality is rather poor, diminishing the quality of the music. Still, it is a marvel to listen to as the two great New Orleans musicians, roughly the same age, seem to be in competition with each other. "Tom Cat Blues" is the stronger performance where despite a surprise break that caught Oliver off guard, his playing shines through with assertiveness and strength of tone.

POST–CREOLE JAZZ BAND

One by one the members of the Creole Jazz Band left Oliver, with his protégé Armstrong being the last to leave in June 1924. Unfortunately, it was the beginning of a long decline for Oliver as uneven performances, bad business decisions, and changing public tastes led him away from the spotlight as his remaining recordings were not nearly as innovative or influential. He was also not considered to be in great playing shape in the 1920s as he suffered from bad gums, a condition that would only worsen during the decade.

By the end of 1924, the Creole Jazz Band's run at the Lincoln Gardens ended when the venue caught on fire on Christmas Eve. Taking a temporary job with pianist and dance bandleader Dave Peyton at the Plantation Club, Oliver eventually became the leader summoning musicians from New Orleans including pianist and bandleader Luis Russell, who became the group's musical director. The group became known as King Oliver's Dixie Syncopators and featured at various times clarinetists Albert Nicholas, Omer Simeon or Barney Bigard (a future Ellingtonian), trombonists Kid Ory and J. C. Higginbotham, and drummer Paul Barbarin, among others. Yet despite the strong musicianship, the performances, recorded between 1926 and 1928, vary in quality.

The music also moved away from Oliver's New Orleans roots and reflects the influence of Fletcher Henderson and the New York dance band sound. With a larger group expanded to include three clarinet-saxophone players, the music now consisted primarily of written arrangements that mix solo and collective improvisation with features for either brass or clarinets. Oliver even went as far as to record Henderson's version of Oliver's own "Dipper Mouth Blues," retitled "Sugar Foot Stomp." The Dixie Syncopators's version is spirited, with clarinetist Albert Nichols playing Dodds's original solo, but gone were the cohesive collective ensembles that Oliver was famous for, and the music was not as well received.

Retrospectively, some of the performances are quite strong boasting excellent solos by Oliver and his musicians. The up-tempo numbers "Deep Henderson" and "Wa Wa Wa" and the slow "Aunt Hagar's Blues" are well played with excellent solos, the latter featuring Bigard, Simeon, Higginbotham, and Oliver. Perhaps his most famous moment was his eight-bar break on "Snag It" that would be quoted countless times in solos and big band charts.

A successful run at the New York's Savoy Ballroom in 1927 led to an invitation to perform at the Cotton Club later that year. But Oliver turned it down feeling that he would not be properly compensated and instead a young Duke Ellington headlined, and Oliver's chance at even greater fame was lost. Continuing to play in larger dance bands, Oliver made his last set of significant recordings for Victor in 1929 and 1930, but the quality is again inconsistent and at times more directed by the record company than Oliver himself. Ironically, some of the best tracks were arranged by Luis Russell ("Call of the Freaks," "The Trumpet's Prayer," and "Freakish Light Blues") who later rerecorded these tracks under his own name to greater success, becoming the leader of an important proto-swing dance band in the process.

Oliver's run of bad luck continued when he discovered that Ellington's "Creole Love Call" was in fact his own composition "Camp Meeting Blues" from 1923. The song was credited to Ellington, trumpeter Bubber Miley, and clarinetist Rudy Jackson, who played with Oliver and responsible for the plagiarism. Unfortunately, the song was originally copyrighted as "Temptation Blues" before its name was changed at the recording session, and therefore, Oliver could not collect royalties on Ellington's performance. Oliver made his last recordings in 1931 but continued to tour in the South and Southwest with younger musicians. Working during the lean

Depression era and with rapidly declining health, these were difficult years for Oliver. He managed to keep a band together until 1937, but by then he was living in poverty in Savannah, Georgia, where he died of a cerebral hemorrhage on April 8, 1938.

Jelly Roll Morton

Jelly Roll Morton (1890–1941) is jazz's first great composer and arranger. Although the exact years of when his compositions were written is difficult to pinpoint and assess, he wrote many jazz standards that were later recorded by himself and others. He is celebrated for his pioneering arrangements with his group the Red Hot Peppers from 1926 to 1927 that demonstrate a high range of skill and thought with the intent of orchestrating the New Orleans sound. Although his writing has gained him acclaim and a strong position in jazz history, he was also an excellent pianist and an underrated singer. Yet he was so much more than a great musician, for Morton was also one of jazz's most colorful characters. A sharp-dressed, flamboyant man with a diamond in his tooth, he was also a pimp, a gambler, and a hustler. He was a big talker and had a tremendous sense of self (claiming to be "the world's greatest hot tune writer") with a penchant for telling tall tales including claims that *he* invented jazz. However, his story is more complicated with his last years spent trying to recreate himself amid failing health and complete apathy for his music by the entertainment industry.

Early Life

Born Ferdinand Joseph Lamothe on October 20, 1890, Morton was an only child and the descendant of Creoles of color. He began playing piano at seven and soon aspired to be a musician. By age twelve, he was inspired by the honky-tonk ragtime that emanated from the brothels in Storyville. However, his family and especially his grandmother fervently clung to their European ancestry, and the thought of the young Lamothe playing such low-brow music was out of the question. But Morton was adamant and snuck out of his house to become an in-demand pianist in Storyville's brothels and after-hours saloons. During this time, he met and heard the Storyville pianist-singer Tony Jackson (1884–1921), whom

Morton greatly admired. When his grandmother found about his late-night whereabouts, she kicked him out of the house.

Subsequently disowned by his family, Morton struck out on his own, becoming an itinerant pianist traveling and living all around the country. Few others were familiar with New Orleans blues and rags, so he easily outclassed and bested any pianist wherever he went. During these early years, he developed a flashy appearance with expensive clothing, sporting diamonds in his teeth and adopting the sobriquet "Jelly Roll." He worked in traveling shows as an entertainer, singing and dancing, but was also involved in hustling, becoming an adept card and pool shark, a womanizer, and later a pimp. He met numerous musicians along the way, W. C. Handy in Memphis in 1908, James P. Johnson in New York in 1911, and Count Basie on his own travels in Los Angeles in 1921. Along the way Morton developed compositions that would make him famous including "King Porter Stomp," "New Orleans Blues," and "Jelly Roll Blues," which he published in 1915. Living in Chicago at the time, he continued his travels with sightings of the great composer in New York, St. Louis, Detroit, and Los Angeles, where he relocated in 1917, managing a dance hall and playing with his old friend King Oliver as a guest who was playing on the West Coast at the time.

By 1923, Morton ended up back in Chicago, primarily to sort out copyright problems he had with his song "The Wolverines." He was outraged because the Spikes brothers, prominent music publishers in the Los Angeles nascent jazz scene, wrote lyrics to the piece, adding their names to the songwriting credit. Later, the song was bought by Chicago music publishers Walter and Lester Melrose who renamed the song "Wolverine Blues" and credited it to "Fred" Morton. It had already been recorded by the New Orleans Rhythm Kings and King Oliver, and it became a huge hit. Morton received second billing and was furious. Happy with their hit song, the brothers agreed to give Morton first billing on the song and arranged for him to record for Gennett Records.

In fact, Morton had already made his first recording session for Paramount in June 1923, but his first significant dates were for Gennett, as a guest with the New Orleans Rhythm Kings and then his own solo piano recordings in July. His solo work represents an important bridge from ragtime, as he freely mixes his ragtime pieces with blues and stomps. The result is a relaxed conception of rhythm; ragtime's syncopation figures are still there, but now there is a sense of swing and forward momentum in the way Morton executes his lines. Nevertheless, Morton maintains the multistructure form that characterizes marches and ragtime songs as well as the intrinsic harmonies and customs that are trademarks of the style. Highlights include early versions of "Grandpa's Spells," "King Porter Stomp," and "New Orleans Joys."

Morton's famous quote that jazz required the "Spanish tinge" is evident on "New Orleans Joys," which features a prominent habanera, or tango, rhythm. Consisting of four sections, each repeated twice except for the last, both takes reveal Morton's skill at improvisation as he varies the theme during each repeated section. His creativity at adapting the blues language to the piano is on display including semitone double stops on the flatted and natural third (heard in the first section), an excerpt of a famous boogie-woogie bass line in the second variation, and a liberal sense of around-the-beat phrasing that permeates the third section before climaxing with a brilliantly swinging chorus.

JELLY ROLL MORTON AND HIS RED HOT PEPPERS

Morton's recordings with the Red Hot Peppers are considered some of the finest examples of New Orleans jazz and cemented his reputation as jazz's first arranger and orchestrator. By 1926, he had secured a contract with Victor Records along with a budget to pay musicians to rehearse and record his music. Morton took advantage of the opportunity to craft his music down to the smallest detail, meticulously planning written and improvised passages, breaks, and solos. Except for cornetist George Mitchell, the sidemen hail from New Orleans, a calculated move on Morton's part to ensure his music was played authentically. In addition to Andrew Hilaire on drums, the group included journeyman Omer Simeon (1902–1959) on clarinet and veterans Kid Ory (1886–1973) on trombone and Johnny St. Cyr (1890–1966) on banjo from Louis Armstrong's Hot Five recording sessions. John Lindsay (1894–1950), who also doubled on trombone, was a pioneering jazz bassist, carrying the rhythm with his full bass sound and driving quarter notes. Morton's preference for New Orleans musicians to play his music would continue throughout his period for Victor.

Right from the first song from the first session in Chicago on September 15, 1926, "Black Bottom Stomp," Morton announces his arrival as an orchestrator with six timbral combinations. Each instrument is featured at some point, but they do not necessarily play together all the time. Examples of frequent contrasts in timbre include open versus muted trumpet solos, high or low registers in the clarinet during solos, and the bass alternating between one-, two-, and four-feels. Each instrument of the early drum set was featured at various points: woodblocks, choked cymbal, hi-hat, and tom-tom drums. Finally, the breaks are varied with some lasting two measures, others one, while also including a displaced hemiola beat.

The group returned to the studio six days later, this time recording songs in the then-popular hokum-style creating the allusion of a vaudeville skit with spoken monologues as introductions and a range of sound effects including car horns, whistles, and church bells. "Dead Man Blues" from this session is a highlight, beginning with a dialogue between Morton and St. Cyr followed by a quote from "Flee as a Bird to the Mountain," a staple song at New Orleans' funerals. Then in the same way that such funerals suddenly burst into joyous song to celebrate the deceased, the band suddenly reverts to collective improvisation over a medium tempo blues. After solos by Simeon and Mitchell comes a light three-clarinet theme with an aggressive response from the cymbal that is augmented the second time with a lovely trombone line. The performance ends with collective improvisation before a reprise of the three-clarinet theme. It is one of the highlights of Morton's writing.

"Grandpa's Spells" (1926)

Recorded on the third session from December 16, "Grandpa's Spells" finds Morton expanding upon the textural changes heard on "Black Bottom Stomp," with trading, more frequent and faster changes in texture including a different instrument playing the break than what was previously heard. All in all, the listener is treated to *twelve* changes in texture in three minutes. That he achieved so much timbral variety is an indicative of his creative abilities as an orchestrator. Compared to his solo version from 1923, Morton added more breaks, but much of the melodic material is the same although he rearranged the form. Furthermore, listening to the two versions, one gets a strong sense of the connections between ragtime and New Orleans jazz.

Morton's recordings were successful and sold well, and he continued recording. A trio with the Dodds brothers, Johnny on clarinet and Baby on drums on "Wolverine Blues" and "Mr. Jelly Lord," are particularly

Listening Guide: "Grandpa Spells" by Jelly Roll Morton's Red Hot Peppers
Jelly Roll Morton: piano, arranger; George Mitchell: cornet; Omer Simeon: clarinet; Kid Ory: trombone; Johnny St. Cyr: banjo; John Lindsay: bass; Andrew Hilaire, drums. Victor 20431-A. Recorded December 16, 1926, in Chicago.

Time	Section	Comments
0:00	Introduction	Full Band
0:05	A	Guitar breaks followed by collective improvisation.
0:14	A'	Same as above.
0:23	A	Trumpet breaks followed by collective improvisation.
0:32	A'	Same as above.
0:41	B	Trumpet melody with drum responses and collective improvisation and piano break at 0:48.
0:50	B'	Trumpet melody again with high trombone countermelody.
1:00	B	Low clarinet accompanied by guitar and bass with break at 1:07.
1:09	B'	Same as above.
1:18	A	Trombone/bass, bass break, then collective improvisation.
1:27	A'	Same as above.
1:36	C	Muted trumpet with guitar and bass.
1:46	C'	Same as above.
1:55	C	High clarinet with drum "hits."
2:04	C'	Same as above.
2:14	C	Piano with guitar.
2:23	C'	Low clarinet with guitar (no bass).
2:32	C	Collective improvisation with full band.
2:41	C'	Same as above.
2:50	Ending	Guitar break and final band hit.

strong. However, in spite of his successes, Chicago police were doubling down on illicit nightclubs, and work became scarce with musicians struggling to find gigs. Given the circumstances, Morton took advantage of a tour to relocate to New York in early 1928.

Unfortunately, Morton's stay in New York did not expand on his previous success and instead his career began to slowly slip away. Modern sounds of the New York bands rendered Morton's music out of date. Additionally, his elegant piano playing paled in comparison to the new innovations of the Harlem stride pianists, who were relying increasingly on advanced technique and speed. Morton recorded again in June 1928, but the results were not as strong. Simeon was the only New Orleans musician on the date; otherwise the rest of the band simply did not understand his music, and the performances are mixed. A November 1929 session—producing "Sweet Peter," "Jersey Joe," "Mississippi Mildred," and "Mint Julep"—feature an updated New Orleans sound as the musicians, especially Henry "Red" Allen on cornet, are informed by the innovations of Louis Armstrong. It was a stellar New Orleans group with Allen, J. C. Higginbotham on trombone, and Albert Nicholas on clarinet. Still, despite composing the songs for the session, Morton the arranger is missing.

By 1930, Morton found himself without a record contract and went unrecorded for nine years. His music however was making a comeback as Fletcher Henderson and later Benny Goodman would revive "King Porter Stomp," which became an anthem for the Swing Era. However, Morton's publisher, Walter Melrose, had illegally cut him off from his portion of the royalties a few years back, and Morton never reaped the financial benefits. An attempt to join the American Society of Composers, Authors, and Publishers (ASCAP) was rejected as nearly all African Americans were kept out of the organization.

By 1935, completely washed up and ignored in New York, Morton ended up in Washington, D.C., running a seedy bar and playing piano. A chance meeting with an old friend, Roy Carew, from his days before he left New Orleans inspired Morton to pick up the pieces of his life, and he began a crusade to undo the many wrongs in his life. In 1938, incensed that W. C. Handy was known as the creator of jazz and blues, he began a letter-writing campaign reminding readers that he had invented jazz, resulting in a public feud between the two men in the pages of *Down Beat* magazine. 1938 was also when Morton was interviewed by Alan Lomax. The resulting recordings were released commercially and detail the ups and downs in his life, his many tall tales, and a rich description of life and music in New Orleans at the turn of the century. Though the veracity of his narrative is at times doubtful, he is a charming orator and had not lost his touch as a pianist and vocalist. Later, the recordings were released after his death as was Lomax's book, *Mr. Jelly Lord*, based on the interviews.

Morton returned to New York in 1939 with a mission to claim his profits from Melrose, to continue his campaign to join ASCAP, and to attempt a comeback. Although his health was failing, he was still a bold man and intent on regaining the respect and money he deserved, but he ultimately failed on all three counts. While he had written new compositions, his final recordings which included Sidney Bechet, Sidney de Paris, Albert Nicholas, and Zutty Singleton, among others, failed to make any impact. Hearing that his godparents died in Los Angeles, Morton made an ill-fated choice to drive across the country to claim either his share of the fortune or anything he could gather. He also saw an opportunity to again restart his life and career over again in a more temperate climate. He had been writing new material and had gathered old New Orleans friends in Los Angeles to play and ultimately record his music, but unfortunately, Morton passed away on July 10, 1941.

Chapter 5

The New York Scene

The Small Groups

During the early jazz era, New York was central to jazz's development with a thriving music industry, prominent large dance bands, both white and African American, and the development of Harlem stride piano at cutting sessions. Another important element was the white New York scene that consisted of small-group bands that featured some of the best white jazz musicians of the era. The pinnacle was in the mid- to late 1920s with trumpeter Red Nichols's innovative small-groups. Responsible for organizing and leading countless recordings sessions, Nichols was the most popular and prolific trumpeter of the early jazz era. Forerunners to this scene were the scores of bands that formed in the wake of the Original Dixieland Jazz Band (ODJB).

Original Memphis Five

ODJB's impact in 1917 was enormous, and their success led to many similar-sounding five-piece groups forming in New York like the Original New Orleans Jazz Band, the Louisiana Five, and Earl Fuller's Famous Band, one of ODJB's biggest competitors, that included Ted Lewis (1890–1971) on clarinet. Clarinetist Wilbur Sweatman was Columbia's answer to ODJB during 1918–1920. However, none matched the success or longevity of the Original Memphis Five (OM5) who recorded hundreds of songs during their prime from 1922 through 1925.

Inspired by live performances of the ODJB at Reisenweber's in 1917, an early version of the group was formed and led by Phil Napoleon (1901–1990) on cornet, Miff Mole (1898–1961) on trombone, and Frank Signorelli (1901–1975) on piano. They landed a vaudeville tour but temporarily disbanded before coming back together in 1921 under the guidance of bandleader and contractor Sam Lanin (1891–1977).

The group's first recordings, as Ladd's Black Aces for Gennett Records, "Aunt Hagar's Blues" and "Shake It and Break It," were big hits. Recorded in August 1921, the band emulates ODJB's circa 1920 style, with a straight-toned sound, a stiff rhythmic feel, and a focus on arrangements as well as collective sections. Under Lanin, the group stayed busy recording for multiple record companies, often cutting the same songs with the same arrangements under a series of aliases like the Black Dominoes, Napoleon's Emperors, the Cotton Pickers, and finally the Original Memphis Five, although none of the members were actually from Memphis. Gennett Records was involved in similarly deceptive practices positioning Ladd's Black Aces as an African American group, inserting the band in the company race catalog, and billing them as "Snappy Dance Hits on Gennett Records by Exclusive Gennett Colored Artists."[1]

Despite the OM5's huge output, there is not a lot of stylistic diversity, with most of the songs being medium- to up-tempo versions of current popular hits, few of which are remembered today. However, their records for the smaller Pathé label captured the band at its best. "Memphis Glide" from 1923 is an excellent example of their music with breaks by everyone. The band's sound revolves around Napoleon and Mole, who is already displaying some of his pioneering work on trombone with extended range and strong technique. Even in a collective situation, like on "Struttin' Jim" or "Shufflin' Mose," Mole's articulate lines shine through as he guides the trombone away from the tailgate tradition, something he would further develop with his work with Red Nichols. Napoleon is a devotee of Nick LaRocca with a similarly straightforward approach, but he could also play muted cornet similar to King Oliver. Signorelli is influenced by the Harlem stride style, playing with a percussive attack that dominates the groove. His is a forceful personality that comes through on collective sections, especially those with Napoleon on "That Big Blond Mama" or "Ji Ji Boo." Legendary alto saxophonist Loren McMurray was in New York at the time working with Lanin and guested on recordings with OM5, but he is mostly playing written parts, so his actual style is not heard.

The Georgians

The Georgians were another excellent New York small group during the early 1920s. Based on Paul Whiteman's Virginians, a small group led by Ross Gorman within the Whiteman Orchestra, the Georgians were the small group within the Paul Specht Orchestra, a society band that originated from Pennsylvania that was in residence at New York's Hotel Alamac. Their style is similar to the OM5, using arrangements, with smooth playing, a mostly clean sound, and a repertoire of current popular songs and novelties. Leader Frank Guarente's King Oliver–informed trumpet playing stands out. Born Francesco Saverio Guarente in Italy in 1893, Guarente's family emigrated to Pennsylvania in 1910 before settling in New Orleans. He assimilated himself in the music scene, meeting and befriending King Oliver, who became an influence. Leaving New Orleans in 1916, Guarente freelanced before joining the U.S. Army during the Great War and ended up with Specht's Orchestra in Atlantic City in 1921.

On record with the Georgians, Guarente is often muted when soloing, as on "Somebody's Wrong," "Hometown Blues," or "Barney Google," whose introduction begins with his horse impression on cornet. The Georgians were often creative, making frequent use of Johnny O'Donnell's bass clarinet, including an early solo on "I'm Sittin' Pretty in a Pretty Little City" and giving drummer Chauncey Morehouse an early brush solo on "Land of Cotton Blues." In 1923, Guarente led a version of the Georgians in England and returned the following year for another engagement and played all over Europe through 1928.

It is also noteworthy that many of these early bands featured many northeastern Italian Americans. Besides Guarente, Signorelli, and Phil Napoleon, born Filipo Napoli, the list also includes Jimmy Durante, Tony Colucci, Pete Pellizzi, Nick Vitalo, and Charlie Panelli.

The California Ramblers and Adrian Rollini

One of the most popular new bands to emerge from New York were the California Ramblers who recorded hundreds of records under various aliases from 1922 through 1929. A hugely successful band, they were firmly entrenched in high-society circles, a ubiquitous presence at proms and dance halls, and a fixture on radio, then a new medium for promoting music. Their success was the work of manager Wallace T. "Ed" Kirkeby, who would later become Fats Waller's manager. He took over the band in 1922, booking them for a series of dates in New York. The band was formed the previous year in Ohio as the Ramblers. The deceptive "California" moniker was added later to associate themselves with the emerging West Coast bands, namely those of Art Hickman and Paul Whiteman, that were dominating the popular music scene.

Their buoyant performances featured cleanly executed arrangements with solos that are primarily melodic statements. "On the Oregon Trail" from April 2, 1925, for Edison is a good example, but on "Ev'rything is Hotsy-Totsy Now," recorded a few weeks later, the influence of Don Redman and Fletcher Henderson can be felt with a three-clarinet soli section and extended solos by Red Nichols on trumpet, either Arnold Brilhart or Jimmy Dorsey on alto saxophone, Tommy Dorsey on trombone, and a duet between pianist Irving Brodsky and the Ramblers' most important musician, bass saxophonist Adrian Rollini (1903–1956).

Rollini is one of the great unsung heroes of the early jazz era. His considerable skills as a soloist were monumental for the time, displaying a relaxed feel, a keen melodic sense, and a strong command of rhythm and swing even, which set him aside from his bandmates and contemporaries making him one of the first important white jazz musicians. That he accomplished this on such an unwieldy instrument as the bass saxophone is all the more astonishing and a testament to his musicianship. A rare instrument even in the 1920s, Rollini developed a distinctive voice and a fluid technique partially through his own tinkering, such as using a baritone saxophone mouthpiece to improve the playability of the instrument. He developed a warm, light sound that predated the efforts of baritone saxophonists Serge Chaloff and Gerry Mulligan.

A native New Yorker, Rollini was a child prodigy on piano, giving a recital at the Waldorf-Astoria Hotel at the age of four. Later, he learned the xylophone and embarked on a career in music while in high school, cutting some piano rolls for the Republic Company during 1920 and 1921 before joining the California Ramblers at age eighteen in 1922 on both instruments. He settled on the bass saxophone that anchored the group while also helping them stand out because they did not employ an arranger and relied on stock arrangements. His penchant for the unusual led to the adoption of other novel instruments like the "hot fountain pen," a miniature clarinet, and the "goofus," a type of harmonica in the shape of a toy saxophone known as the couesnophone.

The demand for jazz content in the California Ramblers' repertoire ramped up in 1924 with the popularity of the Wolverines and its trumpeter Bix Beiderbecke, so Kirkeby adjusted and adopted the popular band-within-a-band concept, forming the University Six and Varsity Eight to appeal to college audiences. With small groups gaining popularity, he increased their recording schedule at the end of the year and recorded small-group editions of the Ramblers using different names including the Little Ramblers, Five Birmingham Babies, Bailey's Dixie Dudes, the Kentucky Blowers, and the Goofus Five. Rollini was by far the groups' best soloist, and to bolster the jazz content, "hot" jazz musicians like Jimmy and Tommy Dorsey and Red Nichols were added, laying down the foundation for the New York sound that Nichols would expand upon in his own groups.

By 1925, Rollini was directing the California Ramblers, but their recorded output consisted of mostly popular songs of the day and are mostly period pieces. He also began to freelance heavily, and his bass saxophone would grace the records of Red Nichols, Bix Beiderbecke, Frankie Trumbauer, the Joe Venuti Four with Eddie Lang, and vocalists Jay C. Flippen and Annette Hanshaw. He led a stellar group at the Club New Yorker, but the engagement was not a success, and he subsequently moved to England to join Fred Elizalde's dance orchestra in London. When he returned to the U.S., Rollini resumed leading his own bands through the Swing Era, gradually discarding his outdated bass saxophone in favor of the vibraphone.

Red Nichols

Arguably the face of the New York scene was trumpeter Red Nichols (1905–1965). With his frequent sidekick, Miff Mole on trombone, he recorded numerous small-group sessions that featured group arrangements as well as solos. His body of work is among the most progressive white jazz of the era with the merging of improvisation and arranging within a small-group setting. Nichols recorded with some of the best white jazz musicians of New York including Jimmy Dorsey, Pee Wee Russell, Fud Livingston, and Benny Goodman on reeds; Tommy Dorsey, Jack Teagarden, and Glenn Miller on trombone; Lennie Hayton on piano; Eddie Lang, Carl Kress, and Dick McDonough on guitar or banjo; and numerous Chicagoans including Eddie Condon, Frank Teschemacher, Joe Sullivan, and Gene Krupa, among countless others.

Ernest Loring Nichols was born to a musical family in Ogden, Utah, his father being a professor and bandleader. "Red," named after his hair color, picked up the bugle first before moving to cornet playing in family bands and brass bands in his teens. After a short spell studying music at the Culver Military Academy, he returned to Utah where he later joined the Syncopating Five, a seven-piece group that played in the style of the ODJB. They toured around the country, and Nichols found himself in Atlantic City in 1923. A popular summer resort, Atlantic City with its hotels and nightclubs was fertile ground for bands where many future musicians of the New York jazz scene were active, including Nichols, the Dorsey Brothers, Joe Venuti, Eddie Lang, and Miff Mole. In 1924, Nichols moved on to New York to join the Sam Lanin orchestra, a popular society band that headlined at the Roseland Ballroom, where they played opposite Fletcher Henderson. Lanin was an important bandleader and talent scout and, through his connections, Nichols immersed himself in the busy dance band scene becoming a sought-after sideman and freelancing with different bands including the California Ramblers.

RED NICHOLS AND HIS FIVE PENNIES

1925 was the year Nichols began recording under his own name, and he became widely popular, his records selling in the hundreds of thousands. He formed his groups from the orchestras of Ross Gorman and Sam Lanin, recording as Lanin's Red Heads in 1925 before using a series of other aliases, most notably Red Nichols and His Five Pennies, but also the Charleston Chasers, the Arkansas Travellers, the Six Hottentots, and many others. The groups' peak was from 1926 through 1928, when the Five Pennies began to swell to upwards of more than ten musicians. The arrangements were well-rehearsed and played with finesse and polish. But there was also plenty of room for collective improvisation and individual solos that are marked by a light drive and thoughtfulness that often lent a cool air to the music.

As a trumpeter, Nichols was technically fluid and flexible enough to absorb the nuances of his contemporaries. A great admirer of Bix Beiderbecke, he has been criticized for sounding too much like him, but he was overall a solid player and a good soloist. His solos on "That's No Bargain" (with its advanced harmonic progression) from 1926 or "Crazy Rhythm" from 1928 are good examples of his style: terse, simple, and understated. But ultimately, Nichols's importance lies more in the conception of his music and as an organizer and leader of sessions. He was successful enough that he could record his instrumental small groups without conceding to commercial tastes.

Nichols's main partner in his groups was trombonist Miff Mole (1898–1961), an outstanding pioneer on the trombone who moved away from the New Orleans tailgate tradition to position the instrument as a true solo voice. Originally from New York, he played violin, piano, and alto horn before settling on trombone. He did not solo when playing with the Original Memphis Five, but his break on Ladd's Black Aces' "Muscle Shoal Blues" from 1922 is ample evidence of his advanced technique. Mole had extraordinary command of the instrument, playing with good intonation and a broad range that facilitated a linear approach. "Slippin' Around" by Red & Miff's Stompers is an original by Mole and a good example of his dexterous playing, as is his break on the Arkansas Travellers' "Sensation," written by ODJB's trombonist Eddie Edwards, an early influence. Other highlights of his work include his solo on the Arkansas Travellers' "Boneyard Shuffle," with excellent trading between Mole and the rest of the band, and his stunning break on the "Original Dixieland One-Step" by Miff Mole and his Little Molers.

Nichols often worked with a solid rhythm section of Arthur Schutt (1902–1965) on piano, Joe Tarto (1902–1986), and Vic Berton (1896–1951) on drums.[2] Schutt was a member of Paul Specht's orchestra and the arranger for the Georgians. His playing was a mixture of ragtime, stride, and classical, but he was also active in the popular "novelty-piano" style, an offshoot of ragtime and player piano music of the 1910s. On his best solos, he can be creative whether playing advanced harmonic material on his own composition "Delirium" by the Charleston Chasers or off-beat phrases on "Hurricane" by the Six Hottentots.

Tarto, who also played with Specht, doubled on tuba and bass and was an extremely flexible musician, well-suited to studio work. Besides his work with Nichols, he would remain active in the studios through the 1980s. Berton was a pioneering drummer. He varied his accompaniment, whether playing syncopated rhythms on his hi-hat, backing soloists with his toms, or accompanying collective improvisation sections on woodblocks or the cowbell. His pioneering use of the timpani suited his tendency for accenting the different colors of his kit.

Jimmy Dorsey (1904–1957) was another standby on Nichols's recording and the first notable jazz alto saxophonist, predating Johnny Hodges by a couple of years. He was influenced by the rapid articulation of saxophone virtuoso Rudy Wiedoeft, whose music was not jazz and mostly derived from ragtime. Born in Pennsylvania, Dorsey played with the Scranton Sirens and the California Ramblers with his brother Tommy, who played trombone and trumpet, before working with Nichols.

He was at his best when he was more vocal-like as his solos somehow had a dreamy quality despite his technical approach.

RED NICHOLS'S "ALABAMA STOMP," ACTUELLE AND EDISON VERSIONS

Nichols often recorded the same song under different aliases, but he freely altered the arrangement depending upon the situation. A comparison of several takes of "Alabama Stomp" recorded in a four-month period demonstrates his creativity. The first version was recorded as the Red Heads for the Actuelle label on September 14, 1926. To the thirty-two bar AABA song form, Nichols adds a written introduction, interlude, and coda. The interlude material on the bridge of the third chorus is tricky but well executed. The tempo is brisk as Berton plays time on the hi-hat throughout the performance, but the ensemble is energetic as they romp through the collective improvisation sections with solos by Mole, Nichols, and Schutt. Mole's solo is typically fluid, but solos by Nichols and Schutt are considerably more rhythmic in nature with Nichols driving his solo with rhythmic permutations on one note while Schutt begins his with a rapid whole-tone run before settling into a similarly syncopated romp, augmented by hitting the other parts of the piano with his hands.

The second version of "Alabama Stomp" was recorded a month later as Red & Miff's Stompers on October 13, 1926, for Edison, a premiere record label whose thicker discs allowed for high-quality fidelity and longer performances. Nichols expands upon the basic arrangement to include another chorus, another statement of the interlude, and a new solo order. The performance is filled with numerous details including Berton's various instruments, the horn backgrounds behind Dorsey's solo, variations on the two-bar break, and the introductory figure which returns at the end of every chorus. Only Mole and Dorsey on alto take full chorus solos; otherwise Nichols, Berton, and Schutt on the interlude get short features. Dorsey's solo is particularly excellent, playing with grace and a light-hearted touch. Nichols's blend of composition and improvisation and his numerous changes in instrumental texture are reminiscent of Jelly Roll Morton's "Black Bottom Stomp," recorded one month earlier on September 15 (a song, incidentally, that Nichols would record twice in late 1926).

Listening Guide: "Alabama Stomp" by Red and Miff's Stompers (Edison version)
Red Nichols: trumpet; Miff Mole: trombone; Jimmy Dorsey: alto saxophone and clarinet; Alfie Evans: alto saxophone; Arthur Schutt: piano; Joe Tarto: tuba; Vic Berton: drums. Edison 51854 (11245-A). Recorded October 13, 1926, in New York.

Time	Section	Description
0:00	Introduction	Triple meter
0:07	Chorus 1	AABA: Collective improvisation, with a two-bar recurring break by the group (at 0:40).
0:42	Chorus 2	AABA: Trombone solo by Miff Mole with Vic Berton playing fills on the hi-hat. Ends with a two-bar recurring break by the group (at 1:16).
1:18	Interlude	Sixteen-bar form that is scored with written parts and collective improvisation.
1:36	Chorus 3	AA: Brushes solo on the snare drum by Vic Berton with hits from the band, ending with a far more complex two-bar break leading into a second interlude scored over the bridge.
1:54		B: Interlude material on the bridge with Berton on woodblocks.
2:03		A: Trumpet solo by Red Nichols with the two-bar tag at the end of the chorus (at 2:10).
2:12	Interlude	Same as above but played solo piano by Arthur Schutt.
2:29	Chorus 4	AA: Clarinet solo with backgrounds by trumpet, alto sax, and trombone, ending with a two-bar break.
2:47		B: Clarinet solo continues but the backgrounds stop.
2:56		A: Backgrounds resume behind the clarinet solo, two-bar break for Berton on hi-hat (at 3:03).
3:05	Chorus 5	A: Collective improvisation.
3:14		A: Same as above with emphasis on Berton on tom-toms who takes the two-bar break at the end of the section (at 3:20).
3:23		B: Same as above with Berton on tom-toms.
3:32		A: Same as above with Berton on woodblocks.
3:32	Coda	Based on the introduction.

"ALABAMA STOMP," BRUNSWICK VERSION

Nichols recorded "Alabama Stomp" one more time on January 12, 1927, for Brunswick as Red Nichols and His Five Pennies, adding Dick McDonough on guitar. Otherwise, the performance is completely different with its emphasis now on solos. While Nichols's solo contains elements from previous recordings, his transposition of a motive through the chords on the bridge, likely worked out ahead of time, is distinctive. Dorsey is more fluid here, as is Mole, but McDonough's solo is noteworthy for his blues-like gestures and phrasing.

The arranging component is still present with a new introduction and distinctive tone colors behind each soloist: trombone and hi-hat; trumpet and guitar; alto saxophone and timpani; and guitar and light backgrounds from the front line. Other small details include the two-bar breaks at the end of each soloist's chorus, Schutt's descending figure at the end of the different sections behind Mole's solo, Dorsey switching to

Listening Guide: "Alabama Stomp" by Red Nichols and His Five Pennies (Brunswick version)
Red Nichols: trumpet; Miff Mole: trombone; Jimmy Dorsey: alto saxophone and clarinet; Arthur Schutt: piano; Eddie Lang: guitar; Vic Berton: drums. Brunswick 3550 (E 4382; E 22981). Recorded January 12, 1927, in New York.

Time	Section	Description
0:00	Introduction	Call and response between the front line and Berton on timpani before ending with a flourish by Schutt on piano.
0:09	Chorus 1	AABA: Trombone solo by Miff Mole with Berton on hi-hat and a two-bar recurring phrase played on piano (0:18, 0:24, and 0:42) and a break for trombone at 0:44.
0:46	Chorus 2	AABA: Trumpet solo by Red Nichols with a strong quarter-note pulse accompaniment by Dick McDonough on guitar with a two-bar break for trumpet at 1:20.
1:22	Interlude	Sixteen-bar form that is scored with collective improvisation with Berton on woodblocks.
1:40	Chorus 3:	AABA: Alto sax solo by Dorsey accompanied by Berton on timpani and a two-bar break for alto sax at 2:15.
2:17	Chorus 4	AA: Guitar solo by Carl Kress with backgrounds.
2:35		BA: Collective improvisation with Berton on woodblocks.
2:51	Coda	Short timpani flourish.

alto saxophone from clarinet at the end of the collective improvisation section, and Berton's use of the timpani to "comp" behind the soloist. By accenting each solo chorus with a new instrumental texture, Nichols's work looks ahead to future developments in jazz performance, arranging, and composition.

NICHOLS'S LARGER BANDS: 1927–1929

Nichols's sessions from August through September 1927 produced brilliant material and featured expanded ensembles with new artists including tenor saxophonist Fud Livingston (1906–1957) who contributed brilliant arrangements to the Nichols canon. "Feeling No Pain" from August 15 is straightforward, but the version credited to Miff Mole and his Molers from August 30 is rearranged with an introduction, a shout chorus, and a new coda. For the ending, Schutt plays solo piano for the first half before the band returns roaring back at full volume for the final ending. The coda on the earlier version is also magnificent, ending on a rich dominant thirteenth chord. Livingston's original composition "Imagination," from September 8, is aptly titled and effectively a through-composed piece with numerous sections, chromatic harmonies, multiple key centers, as well as various themes, motives, and moods.

A most distinctive voice on the clarinet throughout his career, Pee Wee Russell (1906–1967) made his recording debut on August 15. His early solos demonstrate the influence of Beiderbecke, but his sound is strong and impassioned taking excellent solos on "Riverboat Shuffle," "Feelin' No Pain," and "Ida (Sweet as Apple Cider)," the latter a major hit for Nichols. Russell's iconoclastic style came into focus on 1929's "That Da-Da Strain" with a motive-based solo filled with unexpected twists, unusual notes, and asymmetrical phrasing.

The arrival of the Chicagoans in New York in the summer of 1928 shifted the sound of the New York scene.[3] On "Windy City Stomp" and "Shim-me-sha-wabble" from July 6, Nichols and Mole are joined by Eddie Condon on banjo, Frank Teschemacher on clarinet, Joe Sullivan on piano, and Gene Krupa on drums. Their aggressive energy, drive, and swing dominate the recordings as Krupa's four-on-the-floor bass drum pioneered the new quarter-note-driven sound that would soon dominate jazz. Despite the mutual loathing between Nichols and the Chicagoans, Nichols needed their advanced sense of swing as they needed the work. This combination of styles was already noticeable on Nichols-led recordings for the Wabash Dance Orchestra from September and, especially, the Five

Pennies' "A Pretty Girl Is Like a Melody" from October 2, which also features an excellent mellophone solo by Dudley Fosdick.

On Five Pennies' recordings from early 1929, the swing feel became stronger with the elimination of the tuba and the addition of string bass. Plus, Berton adopted Krupa's new drum sound, dispensing with his timpani, woodblocks, and other novel sounds, and focused instead on keeping time and maintaining a subtle rather than obvious presence. Even Nichols sounds looser, taking a fine solo on "I Never Knew." However, it was also the addition of future Swing Era stars Benny Goodman (1909–1986) on clarinet and Glenn Miller (1904–1944) on trombone that further predicted a new future for Nichols and jazz.

Along with Fud Livingston, Goodman and Miller had already gained important professional experience with popular dance bandleader Ben Pollack (1903–1971). A pioneering drummer and a former member of the New Orleans Rhythm Kings, Pollack started in Chicago before moving on to engagements in New York in March 1928. Goodman, originally from Chicago, learned from records and the Chicagoans. He was a precocious talent, and he joined Pollack at the age of sixteen in 1926. Miller, originally from Iowa, played trombone and wrote arrangements for the band. Pollack's "Waitin' for Katie" from December 7, 1927, features a full chorus of Goodman full of vitality and drive. Following a vocal trio, he switches to cornet to join the brass in a series of exchanges with Miller on trombone. Although Pollack had a strong cohort of jazz musicians in the band including Jimmy McPartland on cornet and Jack Teagarden on trombone, his recordings show an uneasy compromise between jazz and commercial dance band music, with good solos juxtaposed against sometimes uninspired ensemble passages, dated vocals, and long-forgotten pop material.[4]

With Nichols's group Miller did not solo much; instead he wrote arrangements. "Indiana," from April 1929, showcases his straightforward style with subtle changes in texture. The song also features an excellent solo by trombonist Jack Teagarden who would also be a continued presence on Nichols's recordings, his blues-inspired playing helped him displace Mole as the leading trombonist of the era. Goodman's solo is excellent as well although he is even better on Miller's "Shim-me-sha-wabble." Recorded in July 1930 by a twelve-piece band with Krupa on board, Goodman seems more inspired digging in more forcefully as the Swing Era begins to assert itself.

The Dorsey Brothers formed their own studio band in 1928. Their music was sweet and commercial in the vein of Guy Lombardo with a pervasive two-beat feel and little jazz or even solo content. Tommy opted for melodic statements that sometimes showed off his gorgeous tone, but Jimmy on clarinet was the main soloist. Otherwise, the band relied on Miller's no-nonsense arrangements for various brass, woodwinds, strings, and a parade of anonymous vocalists, with the notable exception of Bing Crosby (1903–1977) who sings well on "Let's Do It" and especially "My Kinda Love" from January 1929.

Ultimately, Nichols's new music was more suited to Krupa, Goodman, and Miller as his influence and innovations quickly diminished. The stock market crash of 1929 decimated the music business; while the Dorsey brothers managed to attain continued success together and then on their own after a falling out, other musicians from the New York scene were suddenly less visible, languishing in anonymous roles in dance bands, pit orchestras, and studio groups.

Chapter 6

Stride Piano

Stride piano is a descendant of ragtime that emerged in Harlem cutting sessions during the 1910s and 1920s. A highly virtuosic style of performance, stride required advanced technique, range, and tempo than what was previously heard in ragtime; its name is derived from the speed of the left hand alternating between bass note and chord. While ragtime's rhythms were stiff, stride piano's feel was looser and introduced a rolling swing feel that would be influential. Stride pianists were ambitious, and all were composers, writing original stride pieces, songs, and in some cases classical works. Like the blues, stride piano has multiple meanings, being a manner of playing the piano and a separate genre unto itself. This chapter outlines the development of the stride piano style and gives an overview of its key practitioners: Luckey Roberts and the big three of stride, James P. Johnson, Willie "the Lion" Smith," and Fats Waller.

Luckey Roberts

The first major Harlem pianist was Charles Luckeyth "Luckey" Roberts (1887–1968), an important transitional figure from ragtime to stride. A powerhouse pianist, his published rags from the 1910s display the speed and technique that would dominate stride piano. But by the time the stride movement was on its way in the late teens through the 1920s, Roberts had moved on to writing popular songs and was an in-demand high society pianist. He did not record until 1946 when he was fifty-nine years old, and although he was no longer in his prime, his recordings still demonstrate his prowess on the piano.

Roberts was born in Philadelphia in 1887 and spent his youth singing, dancing, and performing in minstrel shows and on the vaudeville circuit. He started young at age five performing in Gus Seeke's Pickaninnies before moving on to Mayme Remington and Her Black Buster Brownie Ethiopian Prodigies, a so-called "pick act." Along the way, Roberts learned the piano and eventually accompanied singers in Philadelphia saloons, reportedly only playing with the black keys, before making his way to New York. He immersed himself in the scene, hearing his contemporary fellow pianist Eubie Blake, and was encouraged by friends to learn piano formally and began taking lessons.

By 1910 Roberts was house pianist at Barron Wilkins's club in New York and had developed a reputation as a strong pianist while beginning to shine as a composer. He wrote "Nothin'" around 1908, a virtuosic piece written to win contests and amaze listeners. It was never published or recorded until 1958 when he was seventy-one years old. In 1913, he became the first Harlem pianist to publish with "Junk Man Rag," followed by his best one, "Pork and Beans." He ended up only publishing five rags because the rest were deemed unplayable for amateurs including the fast "Ripples of the Nile," a personal favorite of George Gershwin who briefly studied with Roberts. With an aggressive attack, Roberts was famous for his rapid-fire tremolos, fast chromatic playing, and most significantly his rhythmic approach to playing the piano including his technique of rapidly playing a single note with different fingers creating a remarkable machine-gun effect. His virtuosity set the stage for stride piano.

James P. Johnson

James P. Johnson (1894–1956) is considered to be the founder of stride piano. Born in New Brunswick, New Jersey, Johnson's family was from the South, and as a youth he was exposed to African American folk songs, ring shouts, and dances that would later impact his music. After moving to Jersey City in 1902, where he was inspired to play ragtime, his family settled in New York first in San Juan Hill (on the city's West Side) then in Harlem. By 1912, Johnson began to play all around the city, providing entertainment at bars, cabarets, and cafés, backing singers, and playing for films. He joined a vibrant piano scene with Luckey Roberts, Richard "Abba Labba" McLean, a student of Roberts and a major influence on Johnson; Paul Seminole, known for his deft left-hand work; Sam Gordon, a classically trained pianist with impressive technique who played in

Harlem; and Fred Bryant from Brooklyn, also known as the "Harmony King," who popularized the backward tenth, among many others.

In the spring of 1913, he became a regular pianist at Jim Allen's Jungles Cellar. It was located on a particularly bawdy street known as the "jungles" in the San Juan Hill neighborhood, an area that was later "removed" to make way for the present-day Lincoln Center complex as part of urban renewal. However, before World War I, it had the largest population of African Americans, and besides Johnson begot jazz pianists Thelonious Monk and Herbie Nichols. During this era, many of the best piano players played in the various cabarets and bars in that neighborhood.

Johnson landed another job in the area accompanying dancers at the Jungles Casino. He played the usual repertory of two-steps, waltzes, and schottisches, but many of the dancers were recent transplants from the South and their dances reminded him of the music and dance he was exposed to as a child. At the Jungles, he describes their dancing as "wild and comical" and adapted his music accordingly to their dance rhythms: "Breakdown music was the best for such sets, the more solid and groovy the better. They'd dance, hollering and screaming until they are cooked."[1] Another popular dance was the Charleston step, and Johnson made use of the dance's rhythm in his own songs including perhaps his most famous composition, "Charleston." "Mule Walk" and "Gut Stomp" were also based on dances he accompanied and thus the beginnings of stride are rooted in dance.

It was around this time that Johnson played his first rent party. Rent parties were a semiformal way to collect the rent by turning one's household into a performance space. Offering refreshments, pianists were brought in to provide entertainment, and cutting contests developed becoming part of the show. While experienced "ticklers" fought to maintain their status, new pianists in town could establish themselves by winning such a battle. Johnson would play several rent parties in one night, engaging others including Willie Smith (before he gained his nickname "the Lion"), Raymond Boyette, and a young Fats Waller whom Johnson took under his wing. Critical to the performance was one's presentation and dress: pianists displayed their elegant and custom suits, shoes, and accoutrements such as silver-knobbed canes and silk handkerchiefs. Everything was shown off prior to performance as suits were carefully laid out to reveal an inner lining of equal extravagance.

Despite his mild, easy-going manner, Johnson was a fierce competitor as he began immersing himself in classical lessons. He developed strong technique, using orchestral effects enhanced by a long reach in his hands, eventually playing double glissandos and double tremolos on the breaks to blow away his competitors. He also developed arrangements, one of which ended with "Dixie" played in the right hand as "The Star-Spangled Banner" was played in the other hand. He also developed rag versions of the classics including Rossini's *William Tell Overture*, Grieg's *Peer Gynt Suite*, and Rachmaninoff's *Prelude in C Sharp Minor*, but his specialty was his own, "Carolina Shout."[2]

"Carolina Shout" (Okeh)

Johnson recorded "Carolina Shout" for Okeh on October 18, 1921, and it is one of his best-known compositions. He had already made two piano rolls of "Carolina Shout," but the Okeh version is remarkably looser and helped establish stride piano. Fats Waller and Duke Ellington were among those who were inspired enough to slow the roll down to learn the music.

Perhaps the most remarkable aspect of the piece is its rhythmic vitality punctuated with syncopations, accents, and anticipations. Based off the ring shout, Johnson manages to produce a musical interpretation of the dances he heard at the Jungles Casino as he builds the intensity through the different sections of the piece. His extensive use of repetition, riffs, and call and response are highly characteristic of traditional folk and blues songs (see chapter 1).

Johnson establishes the orchestral approach of stride away from ragtime as the right hand plays single-note melodies, sometimes in thirds, chords, and octaves. Freed from strictly providing accompaniment, the left hand has a more prominent role, playing bass notes, chords, melodies, countermelodies, and walking bass lines. On the repeat of the first A (0:25), the left hand breaks away from the oom-pah pattern (alternating bass note and chord) and introduces new patterns such as "oom-oom-pah" that enabled a higher degree of rhythmic complexity and unpredictability in the accompaniment. Eubie Blake had said that a hallmark of a pianist's style was the creative use of the left hand, and with this ingenious variation on a normally rigid pattern Johnson sets a high bar.[3]

Johnson also combines his hands for effect, another advancement in stride from ragtime. After the introduction, he plays his low bass notes as anticipations to the chords in his right hand, giving the music a slight bounce. The figure also occurs more pointedly at E (2:19) as Johnson divides the left-hand part across the hands with the left hand playing the bass note and the right hand playing the chord. It is an astonishing effect that promotes swing and a percussive approach to playing piano.

Listening Guide: "Carolina Shout" by James P. Johnson
James P. Johnson: piano. Okeh 4495. Recorded October 18, 1921, in
New York.

Time	Section	Comments
0:00	Introduction	
0:05	A	Bass notes anticipate the beat.
0:15	A'	
0:25	A	Oom-pah of the left hand is varied considerably, often with oom-oom-pah.
0:35	A'	
0:44	Transitional	Repetitive figure in both hands that swings.
0:54		
1:04	B	Plays "riffs" with call and response between the hands: The call is a descending phrase in the right hand, while the response is an ascending one in the left hand.
1:13	B'	
1:22	B	Same as above.
1:31	B'	
1:40	C	Syncopated riff in the right hand.
1:51	C'	
2:00	D	Longer call in the right with a short response in the left.
2:09	D'	
2:18	E	Call and response begin with an off-beat syncopated figure played by both hands.
2:27	E'	
2:36	Coda	Announces the ending with a chromatic gesture.

Like his contemporaries in stride and his forbearers in ragtime, Johnson began to focus on composition starting with theater, composing the music for *Runnin' Wild* (1923) and *Keep Shufflin'* with Fats Waller (1928). He was also increasingly recording in small groups, including a handful of recordings with Waller where they played two pianos ("Chicago Blues") or with Johnson on piano and Waller on organ ("Willow Tree").

However, Johnson continued writing and releasing new stride material. "You've Got to Be Modernistic" is an exhilarating performance with the final C section repeated six times as Johnson spins out idea after idea. On each succeeding chorus he develops a single idea with each one distinguished by changes in register or texture. Johnson's 1930 version of Cole Porter's "What Is This Thing Called Love" is his first venture away from Harlem into the world of Tin Pan Alley. His genius is evident as he constantly changes the texture, using two-handed stomps, motifs, tenths, boogie woogie lines, and plenty of rhythmic variation.

In addition to his incredible solo work, Johnson was an expert accompanist for singers. He recorded fourteen sides with the great Bessie Smith, and their duet on "Backwater Blues" from 1927 is a classic performance. He is a sensitive accompanist who never intrudes over Smith's vocal and instead gives her plenty of space as he accompanies her with a loping boogie bass line, filling in the gaps with short riff-like ideas. The concept is simple, and the emphasis on the text becomes clear when Smith sings about thunder in the fourth chorus and Johnson brings out thunder sounds from the bass.

Amid all this activity, Johnson was also delving into classical composition, composing a concert work entitled "Yamekraw" in 1927. In 1930, it was part of a nine-minute film with an all-black cast. Johnson continued to compose, notably "Victory Stride," "Harlem Symphony," and "American Symphonic Suite," but he was frustrated by the business, segregation, and racism as the white establishment refused to acknowledge his music. Ill health was beginning to slow him down, but he continued to record mostly in small groups. Like Scott Joplin, Johnson arose from humble beginnings and desired to be taken seriously as a composer. Although Johnson was acknowledged by some for his work, like Joplin sadly, he died on November 17, 1955, mostly forgotten.

Willie "the Lion" Smith

Compared to his contemporaries or his predecessors, Willie "the Lion" Smith (1897–1973) forged his own path. For one, he did not work in theater and was not a major composer like Johnson or a songwriter like Fats Waller; instead he focused his talents on playing the piano though he did also sing in his later years. He was a key figure in the development of stride piano and a terrifying presence at cutting contests, known for his boastful swagger, his sharp appearance—with his red vest, derby hat, and an ever-present cigar—and, of course, his masterful playing. During the early jazz era, he was hardly known outside of Harlem and was largely an underground figure primarily because he did not publish his first song until 1925 (and none more until 1934) and did not make first solo piano recordings until 1934, although he recorded sporadically through the 1920s.

Born William Henry Joseph Bonaparte Bertholf in upstate New York in 1897, his family was immersed in music and entertainment as his grandmother played in a minstrel show, his uncle performed as a dancer in vaudeville, and his mother was a church organist who taught her son to play hymns and pop songs. Swept by the ragtime craze, Smith turned his attention to the piano, frequenting and eventually gaining work at dancehalls and saloons where he met James P. Johnson. He joined the army during World War I, and his bravery on the field led to his nickname as his commander called him "a lion with a gun."

Upon his discharge, Smith returned to New York and became a regular at rent party piano battles. He was the pianist on Mamie Smith's "Crazy Blues" from 1920, but otherwise only appeared on a handful of recordings. He did not record any solo pieces until 1934 with "Fingerbuster." Written to win cutting contests, it is all speed and flash, however the middle section transitions rather suddenly into a lovely waltz including a harmonic progression with a descending bass line that Smith would revisit in other compositions. Although brief, it is an indication of his interests. Already a strong pianist, he began taking classical piano lessons at age thirty-three, continuing his studies in piano, theory, harmony, and counterpoint into the 1940s.[4]

A landmark recording session came on January 10, 1939, when Smith recorded fourteen pieces, including eight originals. They represent his mature stride style, his classical studies evident in his compositions and his elegant touch. Smith had always had a flair for rich harmonies, a distinctive trait that set him apart from Johnson and Waller, a trait that was not lost on Duke Ellington whose "Portrait of the Lion" includes similarly rich harmonies. By this time Smith's reputation was spreading far beyond Harlem, and by the end of the 1940s, he was touring worldwide. Lauded by the jazz world, he continued his travels, headlining jazz festivals around the world until his death in 1973.

Fats Waller

If Fats Waller (1904–1943) was merely a stride pianist, his place in jazz history would be secured. Yet his was a monstrous talent as he was also a songwriter, performer, singer, entertainer, and comedian. His songs, "Squeeze Me," "Ain't Misbehavin'," and "Honeysuckle Rose" are time honored jazz standards and a mere sampling of his four hundred compositions. In addition, his hundreds of recordings showed that Waller's productivity matched his talent. He was also a pioneer in adapting the pipe organ and the Hammond organ to jazz performance, recording solo, behind a vocalist, and with a band. In the 1930s, his group, Fats Waller and His Rhythm, made Waller one of the most popular African American entertainers, mostly because of his singing, his showmanship, and his comedic talents. His successes and larger-than-life personality have obscured his contributions as a key proponent of stride piano along with James P. Johnson and Willie "the Lion" Smith.

Born Thomas Wright Waller in New York's Greenwich Village, his father was a preacher while his mother sang and played organ for church services. Waller started on the harmonium before becoming infatuated with the piano. His tastes ran to the secular, commercial world, rather than the church, and an early job playing piano and organ for silent movies was met with disapproval from his parents. He eventually left home to stay with another family through which he met James P. Johnson, who helped Waller establish himself, showing the young man pointers on how to play and taking him out to rent parties.

Thus, Waller's career as a stride pianist began, accompanying singers and shows, traveling with vaudeville acts, making his first piano rolls, and recording his first solo stride pieces on October 22, 1922. Only eighteen years old, he was already married with a child and had started writing his own songs. By the mid-1920s he had established himself working alongside Louis Armstrong in Erskine Tate's Vendome Orchestra in Chicago in 1925 and then recording with Fletcher Henderson's Orchestra in 1926.

Beginning in 1926, Waller made a landmark series of solo recordings on pipe organ. It was his favorite instrument as it offered a range of orchestral possibilities from the manual, stops, as well as the bass pedals. "St. Louis Blues" from November 17, 1926, demonstrates his ability to make the organ swing, particularly towards the end of the performance after he had built up the tension. He achieved this with a light staccato touch on the keyboard and short, accurate notes on the pedals.[5] "Beale Street Blues," another W. C. Handy composition, is even earthier. Recorded on May 20, 1927, with vocalist Alberta Hunter, at her request Waller is featured through most of the performance, playing solo through two blues choruses and two strains of the bridge before Hunter sings the final two blues choruses. It is a most elegant rendition as Waller highlights the organ's rich tones and range of colors, even bringing out the pedals with a walking bass line at the bridge.

Waller's pipe organ recordings represent a unique body of work in the jazz canon. In 1938 he began recording on the new Hammond organ, an instrument that would be adopted by a generation of jazz musicians in the 1950s and 1960s. However, few followed Waller to perform on the pipe organ, save Count Basie, who heard Waller perform when the future Kansas City pianist was still based in New York; Basie recorded sporadically on the instrument.

Waller began writing songs early in his recording career and soon established a partnership with lyricist Andy Razaf (1895–1973). Together, they began a fruitful collaboration that resulted in hundreds of songs, including a good deal more that was not credited to them as Waller was notorious for selling his songs at a pittance whenever he was desperate for money.

They also wrote for numerous shows including some music for *Keep Shufflin'* in 1928. Johnson also contributed music and played two pianos with Waller in the pit band, entertaining audiences with duets on the break. Their crowning achievement, though, was a revue called *Hot Chocolates* from 1929 that featured Louis Armstrong. It was a smash hit running for 219 performances featuring the standards "Ain't Misbehavin'" and "Black and Blue," an early commentary on race and prejudice.

Waller recorded his definitive stride pieces in 1929. His technique, as always, is flawless and the hallmark characteristics of stride are all present with three-against-two syncopations, dazzling speeds, and virtuosic passages, yet he has his own distinctive style. For one, he has a distinctive touch, likely the influence of the organ, as his bass notes ring out more than Johnson's. Also, being a noted songwriter, Waller is inherently more melodic than Johnson. There is also more variety. "Viper's Drag" starts in a medium tempo with a brooding minor theme, before going into a peppy double time feel in major. Along the way he mixes walking lines, shuffle rhythms, and stride accompaniment. Other highlights include "Numb Fumblin'." Waller's favorite piece was "Handful of Keys," an up-tempo number in the manner of Smith's "Fingerbuster" or even novelty pianist Zez Confrey's "Dizzy Fingers." It is based on a scale but he spins out numerous variations on the theme. The middle section which recalls "Them There Eyes" is merely a break in the action as he builds the momentum over the course of the performance. He really lets loose in the last two choruses, his creativity and his wit apparent as he bounces the motif around the piano, breaking the momentum with a sudden change in tempo that foreshadows the ending.

With all this activity, Waller was just getting started as he was about to become a huge star. But he led a turbulent life and was chased by personal demons that led him to indulge in food and drink. Combined with a rigorous schedule of composing, performing, recording, and touring. It led to his early death at the age of thirty-nine on December 15, 1943.

Chapter 7

The New York Dance Band Sound

From James Reese Europe to Duke Ellington

While stride piano was developing in Harlem, dance bands were quickly becoming popular in New York. The phenomenon is largely due to the vast popularity of ragtime and its dances, so that by the 1920s, dance bands, riding on the popular new sound of Paul Whiteman, were in demand as large dance ballrooms opened all over the country. The early development of the modern big band has its roots in New York, most explicitly through the dance bands of Fletcher Henderson and the work of arranger Don Redman and Duke Ellington whose artistic intents in composition were rooted in dance bands.

But the story of popular music and dance in New York began a decade earlier with the popular syncopated orchestras of the 1910s. Some of the most popular bandleaders originated from Washington, D.C., including Will Marion Cook (1869–1944), Ford Dabney (1883–1958), and James Reese Europe (1880–1919), one of the most important African American bandleaders of the era.

James Reese Europe

By 1913, ragtime dancing in the U.S. was an enormous phenomenon. The demand was such that public dance halls were erected everywhere from cabarets to amusements parks to the finest hotels.[1] Social reformers accustomed to the waltz, quadrille, or polka were alarmed by the dancing craze and found ragtime, its syncopated rhythms, and especially its dances, immoral.[2] Ragtime dances like the Turkey Trot or the Grizzly Bear required the dancers to be close, to touch, or to embrace, and this went against the prudish ideals of the Victorian Era that many still followed. However, the appearance of Vernon and Irene Castle changed the entire public perception of the dances with their stylish looks, clean-cut image, and elegant manner. Being a married couple, they brought a new sense of respectability to the dances, popularizing social dancing among the upper class. However, to perform their ragtime steps, they needed the right orchestra to play syncopated music, and they found their man in James Reese Europe who became the Castles' personal musical director.

Born in Mobile, Alabama, and raised in Washington, D.C., James Reese Europe (1880–1919) is an important figure in the evolution of jazz from ragtime. In 1903, he moved to New York and established himself in the burgeoning African American musical theater world as a composer, conductor, and musical director. By 1910, he formed the Clef Club, an African American–centered organization that functioned as a musician's union and booking agency, as well as an orchestra. Europe's groups were large, with over hundred musicians, and often played private functions for New York's elite.

Europe's crowning achievement was a performance at New York's Carnegie Hall on May 2, 1912. He broke a color line by presenting a historic first "Concert of Negro Music" by African American singers and instrumentalists.[3] Its success also changed public perceptions of African Americans and opened new doors of employment for African American musicians in New York. Demand for Clef Club musicians was high as they held a virtual monopoly on the band business at dance halls and private parties in New York.

His work with Vernon and Irene Castle led to Europe's first recordings, from December 29, 1913. The highlights are "Down Home Rag" and "Too Much Mustard," whose fast tempos are particularly riveting. Despite the prevalent stiff ragtime rhythms of the early 1910s, the music still retains the rhythmic vitality and forward momentum that "must have been electrifying to dance to."[4] "Castle House Rag," written by Europe and Dabney and recorded in February 1914, is a powerful performance that features Buddy Gilmore's show-stopping drumming. The dancer-musician relationship of the Castles and Europe is merely one example of jazz's ongoing connections with dance.[5] This trend that would continue during the early jazz era and onwards through the Swing Era as the development of new dances like the Charleston, the Black Bottom, and the Lindy Hop would have a significant impact on the direction of the music.

With the ongoing war, Europe enlisted with the Fifteenth Regiment before being asked to put together a band. As bandmaster of the 369th U.S. Infantry Regiment's "Hellfighters Band," he traveled to France to perform. Their version of the French national anthem, "La Marseilles," stunned audiences. Recordings made two weeks after returning from Paris in 1919 reveal that the syncopated orchestra had expanded their ragtime-based sound to include muted brass, unusual rhythmic or dynamic shifts, and "breaks," some of which are quite daring with moments of surprising improvisation. Europe was fatally shot weeks after this last recording session, on May 9, 1919, after a disagreement with a disgruntled musician. His death left a void as the monopoly on high society jobs held by African American musicians ended.[6]

Paul Whiteman

Despite the success of African Americans in New York in the 1910s, the mood quickly changed amid a turbulent time in race relations between black and whites. The influx of African Americans in cities in the north and west due to the Great Migration led to overcrowded cities as rents were raised to accommodate surging populations. Jobs became scarce and competitive as the situation worsened with the demobilization of thousands of soldiers at the end of World War I. Tensions exploded during the "Red Summer" of 1919 with violent attacks on African Americans and race riots in three dozen U.S. cities.[7] In Chicago on July 27, the murder of a black teenager who accidentally swam across an unmarked barrier separating the races in Lake Michigan sparked six days of race riots. A reign of terror in the South began with the reemergence of the Ku Klux Klan in the late teens (prompted by the 1915 film *Birth of a Nation*), the untold Tulsa Race Massacre of 1921, and increased cases of lynching. Though African Americans began to record from 1920, segregation was upheld by the recording industry with the new "race" record label, targeted to African Americans.

In this setting, the white bandleader Paul Whiteman (1890–1967) emerged as a hugely successful and influential dance band leader. His music was hugely popular in the 1920s, and his polite brand of jazz largely defined the genre to white audiences. He became known as the "King of Jazz," thus beginning the public dominance of white musicians as the face of jazz at the cost of African Americans. Whiteman is controversial for his jazz content was often minimal, though to his credit, he never claimed to play jazz. Still, his influence was widespread, and African American bandleaders followed his lead including Sam Wooding, Fletcher Henderson, and Don Redman.[8]

Whiteman was born in Denver, Colorado, and was a trained symphonic violist. Despite his early misgivings about playing the instrument, he won positions with the Denver Symphony Orchestra and the San Francisco Symphony. Before long, the young Whiteman was swayed by the sound of dance orchestras, and after playing in a band in the Navy during World War I he formed his own in San Francisco.

At the time, Art Hickman (1886–1930) was the leading bandleader in town. After a successful residency at the St. Francis Hotel, Hickman and his orchestra came to New York in 1919 for an engagement at Ziegfeld's restaurant and soon recorded. "Rose Room," later made popular by Benny Goodman and Charlie Christian, features the melody played by the brass augmented with a light saxophone countermelody. The arrangement by Ferdinand Grofe (1892–1972) was based on the African American music they heard in the Barbary Coast section of San Francisco, and the resulting counterpoint was unique, especially compared to the pervasive all-unison sound of syncopated orchestras.

Hickman was poised to become a breakout star; instead, he merely set the stage for Whiteman who based his sound on Hickman's and even hired Grofe as his arranger. Following regional success on the West Coast, Whiteman and his band eventually made their way to New York. Headlining at the Palais Royal in September 1920, the band became quickly popular as their quick ascent led to a recording contract with Victor Records.

Released in November, 1920, "Whisperin'" and "Japanese Sandman" were Whiteman's breakout songs that established him as a national star. They are good examples of Grofe's arranging style that would be copied by bands both black and white: shifting the instrumentation for every chorus and including more timbral contrast. The slide whistle on the second chorus of "Whisperin'" is an example of the eccentric or novel sounds that would continue to prevail in early jazz. "Wang Wang Blues," also recorded in 1920, had carefully arranged passages with breaks, comic trombone slides, growling trumpet, and Larry Shields–like clarinet playing that resembles a cleaned-up version of the Original Dixieland Jazz Band. It was enormously popular as Whiteman's brand of polite jazz resonated with the general public, especially affluent whites, who considered the wild, raucous sounds introduced by the ODJB as too edgy.

Whiteman's success led to a glut of white society bands specializing in "sweet" music, including his rival Vincent Lopez at the Pennsylvania Hotel, that quickly spread throughout the country with Isham Jones and the Benson Orchestra in Chicago and the Coon-Sanders Nighthawks Orchestra in Kansas City, among many, many others. These bands were the dominant forces in popular music at the time, and jazz content was often minimal. By 1922, Whiteman dominated New York and popular music with nineteen orchestras working out of his office that extended internationally with tours of Europe in 1923 and 1926. For all of his success, Whiteman longed to present jazz in the concert hall, and he finally did so on February 12, 1924, at Aeolian Hall in New York.

Entitled "An Experiment in Modern Music," it was Whiteman's answer to the overwhelmingly negative critical reception of jazz. Critics felt that it was an assault on respectable music and tastes and was a threat to national culture. They blamed America's loosening morals on the spread of the music.[9] The racial overtones of the critics were clear with many observers wary of accepting African American cultural forms into white American society. Whiteman's programming reflected how jazz evolved from its "crude" beginnings to become a "respectable" art form. It began with the Original Dixieland Jazz Band's "Livery Stable Blues" and concluded with Grofe's orchestration of George Gershwin's "Rhapsody in Blue," an example of "symphonic jazz," a merger of classical and jazz that was Whiteman's refined version of what jazz should be. The concert was a wild success, and critically reviewed, and led to a repeat of the concert's program at the more prestigious Carnegie Hall on April 21.

However, by the end of the year, the novelty of symphonic jazz had worn off, and Whiteman focused on being a dance orchestra playing popular songs, novelties, and some "hot" music. Remnants of the symphonic jazz concept, however, would still be audible in Whiteman's ambitious recordings of pop songs, the best of which would feature his new band from 1927 to 1929 featuring trumpeter Bix Beiderbecke (1903–1931).[10] Though no longer known as symphonic jazz, the classical-jazz merger would be a continually revisited theme throughout jazz history.

Fletcher Henderson

Arranger and pianist Fletcher Henderson (1897–1952) was the top African American bandleader during the 1920s. Based in New York, he started as a Whiteman imitator before developing a sound that gave birth to the big band style during the 1920s. Yet he has suffered the fate of being overshadowed by others. Later in the early 1930s, his own arrangements would help usher in the Swing Era, yet as an African American man he was denied fame and fortune while his own work instead helped make Benny Goodman famous. A retiring figure, Henderson was at that point not an effective business manager and a reluctant bandleader. However, the high quality of his band's music assured a roster of solid musicians including Louis Armstrong, Coleman Hawkins, Rex Stewart, Jimmy Harrison, Tommy Ladnier, Buster Bailey, Benny Carter, Cootie Williams, John Kirby, Russell Procope, J. C. Higginbotham, Henry "Red" Allen, Roy Eldridge, Chu Berry, Sid Catlett, Israel Crosby, and Ben Webster.

Born to a middle-class family in Cuthbert, Georgia, Henderson took piano lessons as a child. He went on to earn a bachelor's degree in chemistry at Atlanta University and then moved to New York to continue his graduate studies at Columbia, but was quickly made aware of the limited opportunities for aspiring African American chemists and instead opted for a career in music that would be more favorable to him. Fortunately, he began his career when the blues craze started, and Henderson found plenty of work as a pianist accompanying singers, eventually becoming the house pianist for Black Swan Records, the first record label owned and operated by an African American, Harry Pace, W. C. Handy's partner in his publishing company. Formed to give Africans American classical artists opportunities to record, Black Swan decided to capitalize on the blues craze, although many African Americans felt that the jazz and blues that it was recording was degrading.[11]

By 1923, Henderson was the most widely recorded accompanist in New York and playing regularly with what would become the nucleus of his orchestra: Elmer Chambers and Joe Smith on cornets, Coleman Hawkins and Don Redman on various reeds, Charlie Dixon on banjo, and Kaiser Marshall on drums. Henderson was elected leader of the band because of his distinguished appearance and college education. The Fletcher Henderson Orchestra made its debut at the Club Alabam in January 1924, but it rapidly moved up to the Roseland Ballroom in July, playing opposite Sam Lanin, as the club's policy was to have two bands, one white and one black, playing alternating sets. Roseland broadcast their shows on radio, a rare opportunity for an African American band at the time, and furthered Henderson's popularity and influence.[12]

Playing at such exclusive venues required the band to play a variety of music, including sweet music; however, Henderson's recorded legacy rests on his jazz performances, due to recording companies' segregated policy regarding race music.[13] His band was categorized and sold as a "stomp" band to African American communities, while its repertory of sweet music was left unrecorded, including their "rose" medley that combined "Roses of Picardy," "Broadway Rose," and other popular waltz songs with the word "rose" in their titles.[14] Nonetheless, it was well received at the Roseland Ballroom, demonstrating the band's talent in playing such material alongside "hot jazz" or fast dance numbers. That the band could play such a range of styles is a testament to the high level of musicianship of its individual members, whose collective experience included studio work, dance bands, and theater pit orchestras.

The addition of Louis Armstrong in October 1924 to Henderson's group propelled this already strong band even further. Henderson had heard the young cornetist as far back as 1922 while on tour with vocalist Ethel Waters and had tried to convince him to move to New York. Loyal to King Oliver, Armstrong refused, but on at the urging of his wife, Lil Hardin Armstrong, he finally relented. Initially ridiculed by the band for his country dress and demeanor, Armstrong's playing silenced any further comment as he brought with him authentic blues playing and phrasing along with a strong sense of rhythm and swing that astonished the other musicians.

Arranger and multi-reeds player Don Redman (1900–1964) was another critical member of the band. Born in West Virginia, Redman was a child prodigy, learning piano and all the wind instruments before going on to earn a degree in music composition. He came to New York with Billy Paige's Broadway Syncopators before immersing himself in the city's vibrant recording scene, meeting Henderson on his first record date and becoming his arranger. A highlight of his work is his arrangement of King Oliver's "Dipper Mouth Blues," recorded as "Sugar Foot Stomp."

"Sugar Foot Stomp"

"Sugar Foot Stomp" is a New York dance band arrangement of a New Orleans song with Louis Armstrong playing Oliver's famous three-chorus solo note-for-note. The tempo is considerably brighter as Redman's arranging skills are on display with melody paraphrases, solos, backgrounds, and a clarinet soli that would become his trademark. Most ingenuous are his two-bar breaks, which are different just about every time.

Redman repeatedly mixes sweet and hot approaches. The sweet approach is best heard in the whole-note backgrounds that are heard throughout the performance and featured explicitly before the grand finale–type chorus. During Armstrong's solo, Redman introduces rhythmic figures that are riff-like in their simplicity and that look ahead to developments in Kansas City jazz. Other harbingers of the future include the grand finale–style typical of the Swing Era ending in blues choruses eight and ten with saxophones and brass pitted against each other. More telling is the 4/4 time played by the tuba for these sections. Until this point of the performance, the rhythm section had maintained the 2/4 feel common to the era. But with tuba joining the banjo on all four beats, the feel intensifies. Of course, the tuba could not maintain such a momentum throughout an entire song, but the 4/4 time that King Oliver's music brought, through Louis Armstrong, is vividly demonstrated.

Then there is Armstrong's recreation of Oliver's solo which swings from start to finish, along with the exclaimed "Oh play that thing!" from the original recording. His rhythmic conception is advanced as the rest of the band easily follows his lead, especially drummer Kaiser Marshall. His cymbal hits match Armstrong's swing, particularly in the way he emphasizes beats two and four. Swing was largely a foreign concept at the time, let alone bringing out the off-beats, also evident in Redman's syncopated riffs behind the solo. The rhythms behind the solo are quite sophisticated, but the band plays through it flawlessly. On "Sugar Foot Stomp," the elements of swing come together with the 4/4 feel, the emphasis on beats two and four, and riff-like figures.

"Sugar Foot Stomp" ranked among the top-selling records of 1925 and made Fletcher Henderson nationally known.[15] It would become a Swing Era standard with recordings by Benny Goodman, Artie Shaw, Glenn Miller, and Chick Webb. The arrangement was so successful that even Oliver himself recorded his own version of "Sugar Foot Stomp" in 1927.

Armstrong left the band in November 1925, but Henderson's band remained strong. The arrangement of "Stampede," from 1926, with an excellent solo by tenor saxophonist Coleman Hawkins, is quite sophisticated as the blues form is augmented with four strains, three modulations, and constant changes in orchestration. "Whiteman Stomp" from 1927 was

Listening Guide: "Sugar Foot Stomp" by Fletcher Henderson and His
Orchestra
Fletcher Henderson: piano; Louis Armstrong, Elmer Chambers, Joe
Smith: trumpets; Charlie Green: trombone; Buster Bailey and Don
Redman: clarinet and alto saxophone; Coleman Hawkins: tenor
saxophone and clarinet; Charlie Dixon: banjo and exclamation; Ralph
Escudero: tuba; Kaiser Marshall: drums. Columbia 395-D. Recorded
May 29, 1925, in New York.

Time	Chorus	Comments
0:00	Introduction	Same introduction from Oliver's "Dipper Mouth Blues."
0:04	Blues form Chorus 1	Melody played by alto saxophone with "sweet"-backgrounds (whole notes) that land on the beat. The last two bars are a break for saxophones and brass.
0:18	Blues Chorus 2	Paraphrase of the melody played by the brass. Band initiates the break with a sudden "hit" on beat two of the last bar of the form to set up the next section.
0:32	Interlude	Sixteen-bar clarinet soli with a short interjection from the band on the last bar of both eight-bar sections.
0:41		Soli continues with a slow blues-like slide.
0:50	Blues Chorus 3	Trombone solo by Charlie Green backed only by banjo and tuba. The last two bars feature a break for the saxophones.
1:04	Blues Chorus 4	Recreation of King Oliver's classic solo from "Dipper Mouth Blues" by Louis Armstrong on cornet without the wah-wah effect. The saxophone plays backgrounds that are riff-like in nature, and the rhythm section accompaniment now includes Kaiser Marshall on cymbals. The last two bars are again a break for the saxophones.
1:18	Blues Chorus 5	Cornet solo resumes with syncopated rhythmic figures from the entire band during the first four bars before resuming the time on the fifth measure. The saxophones also revert back to the sweet backgrounds from the first chorus. The last two bars are a break for the band.
1:33	Blues Chorus 6	Cornet solo resumes (with repetitive rhythmic figures from the saxophones), and this time the syncopated rhythmic figures occur from the fifth bar and conclude not with a break but with banjoist Charlie Dixon exclaiming: "Oh play that thing!"

continued on next page

Time	Chorus	Comments
1:47	Blues Chorus 7	A hymn-like section with the whole band minus the banjo playing whole notes that recalls the sweet backgrounds from the first chorus. Meanwhile the banjo plays quarter notes throughout. The last four bars build in anticipation with rhythmic figures and the punctuated trumpet note on beat two of the last bar of the form.
2:01	Blues Chorus 8	A grand finale of sorts with brass and saxophones (playing a paraphrase of the melody) pitted against each other, while the tuba begins playing in 4/4, a harbinger of the Swing Era.
2:15	Blues Chorus 9	Repeat of chorus 7.
2:29	Blues Chorus 10	The final statement of the melody with backgrounds with the last few bars replaced by the coda.
2:41	Coda	

commissioned by Paul Whiteman and features one of Redman's more complex charts, featuring instrumental interludes, complex harmonies, stop-time passages, as well as a focus on contrasts and timbres: solo piano and hi-hat both punctuated with full ensemble gestures. Henderson also looked to the past with material from ragtime, the New Orleans era, and four numbers associated with the Original Dixieland Jazz Band. The updated versions, especially the ODJB songs, are practically reinvented and modernized for the big band with solos. However, Redman's departure for McKinney's Cotton Pickers in July 1927 signaled the end of an era for Henderson's band.

Without Redman, Henderson turned to "head arrangements," on the spot arrangements determined by the band; "King Porter Stomp" is one example from 1928, a reworking of an old composition by Jelly Roll Morton. By the time Henderson rerecorded it in 1932 as "New King Porter Stomp," it had morphed into a template for big bands in the Swing Era.

McKinney's Cotton Pickers

Don Redman's new band McKinney's Cotton Pickers (MKCP) was one of the great African American bands of the late early jazz era that rivaled Duke Ellington and Cab Calloway as the most popular band. Based out of Detroit, their music was also transitional to the Swing Era, particularly in the brilliant arranging of Redman, trumpeter John Nesbitt, and later alto saxophonist Benny Carter. Still, the band grew out of practices from the early jazz era as their recorded output reflected their diverse repertoire, hot songs alongside sweet ones, various vocal songs, and even light comedy.

MKCP was started in 1921 by drummer William McKinney as Synco's Trio in Springfield, Ohio. About 1922 or 1923, they became a large dance band that included Dave Wilborn on banjo, Claude Jones on trombone, and Wesley Stewart on violin (who became a reeds player). McKinney became the manager and replaced himself on drums with Cuba Austin, a talented drummer, tap dancer, and entertainer. Later, McKinney further strengthened the group adding George "Fathead" Thomas on saxophone, June Cole on sousaphone, and John Nesbitt on trumpet. The band put on a terrific show dancing, singing, playing, and doing comedy. In 1926, McKinney signed on with Jean Goldkette's organization, playing in the Arcadia Ballroom in Detroit before gaining a permanent engagement at the more prestigious Graystone Ballroom.

With these changes, the band became McKinney's Cotton Pickers and lured arranger Don Redman away from Fletcher Henderson to play saxophone and to lead the band. Redman brought with him the precise, arranged style of Harlem bands to the Midwest as the band grew to include Prince Robinson on woodwinds and Ralph Escudero, also from the Fletcher Henderson Orchestra, on tuba. The band quickly became a success playing for mostly white audiences who were thrilled by the band's musicianship and showmanship flair. Their weekly schedule included playing special events, contests, and holiday shows as well as backing singers. The Graystone Ballroom also broadcast the band's shows live on the radio and was an important aspect of their success. Because MKCP was an excellent sounding band, playing precisely and with good intonation—traits associated with white dance orchestras by critics, musicians, and listeners[16]—renaming the band McKinney's Cotton Pickers was a strategic move that positioned the band as black, southern, and rural for radio listeners.[17]

For this reason, MKCP was not bound by record company executives enforcing stomps or hot jazz; instead, they were marketed as both a race band and as a mainstream one. As a result, the group's recorded output is diverse, recording sweet songs, "To Whom It May Concern," hot songs, "Crying and Sighing," blues/hokum numbers, "It's Tight Like

That," and Duke Ellington jungle-style numbers, "Blues Sure Have Got Me." The sweet material is punctuated by arrangements with pervasive use of the glockenspiel and crooning vocals. Vocals was an important part of the band's music with instrumentalists doubling as singers and employing a variety of singing styles including scatting, quartets, and crooning. Surprisingly, Redman sang as well and is mostly known for his singing-speaking style as heard on "Wherever There's a Will There's a Way," but he could be comedic as he is on his scat solo on "Beedle Um Bum." The quartet singing was limited to backup singing, most notably on "Four or Five Times," but perhaps established a precedence followed by the Jimmie Lunceford Orchestra.

Redman's contributions are strong and diverse. His arrangement of Jelly Roll Morton's "Milenberg Joys" is excellent with his trademark clarinet trios that recall Henderson's music, especially the slow slide in the low register during the break. However other aspects are different including the stunning backgrounds that are now riff-oriented and the call-and-response finale with brass. The individual solos are energetic with Claude Jones on trombone being especially strong as Austin's dancing accents on the hi-hat are a powerful rhythmic counterpoint. On the more commercial material, Redman is equally strong. On the introduction of "Come a Little Closer," he introduces a wide timbral variety pairing two clarinets with trombone and juxtaposing that unusual combination of instruments with glockenspiel and later hot trumpet. Other highlights include "Cherry," with Redman taking advantage of four multi-reed players to write a saxophone soli, and the introduction of his standard "Gee, Ain't I Good to You."

Overshadowed by Don Redman, trumpeter John Nesbitt (1900–1935) was also responsible for MKCP's material, having several important arrangements. "Crying and Sighing" from the first recording session features plenty of variety: a merry theme played by the brass, punctuated with saxophone responses, is contrasted with a glockenspiel solo with light saxophone backgrounds. The subsequent full ensemble section is notable for its syncopation, surprise interludes, and a terrific solo by tenor saxophonist Prince Robinson.

Because Goldkette would not allow the band to record in New York,[18] MKCP's catalog is augmented with a few recording sessions that feature numerous guests including Sidney DeParis on trumpet, Benny Carter on alto saxophone, Coleman Hawkins on tenor saxophone, Fats Waller on piano, and Kaiser Marshall on drums. Don Redman's "Plain Dirt" and Nesbitt's "Peggy" both from November 1929 are exciting performances that certainly predate the Swing Era. "Plain Dirt" features short solos by DeParis, Jones, and Hawkins, but the focus is on the ensemble works that are increasingly riff-oriented, the insistent quarter-note punctuations played by the saxophones being particularly strong, and the excellent call-and-response passages between brass and woodwinds. The walking tuba behind Carter's full chorus solo on "Peggy" is also indicative of the Swing Era, but the ensemble passages, which build from start to finish are again the focus. Nesbitt's writing is strong, with syncopated sections that break up the pulse, astonishing passages for brass and woodwinds, and an exciting finale. All of it is extremely well played, likely better than "Plain Dirt" simply due to the tempo.

The onset of the Depression altered the dance band business considerably. MKCP managed to record into 1931, but the band was also no longer working with Goldkette and shifted its focus as a touring band. Redman left in 1931 as high personnel turnover and mismanagement led to the band's demise in 1933. The band got rid of McKinney and toured under the banner "The Original Cotton Pickers" led by Cuba Austin, while McKinney reformed the MKCP with local Detroit musicians.

Duke Ellington

Edward Kennedy "Duke" Ellington (1899–1974) is among jazz's greatest composers. During the early jazz era, he shaped his identity as a pianist, composer, and bandleader, leading to his residency at the Cotton Club in 1927, which gave him national attention and success. Using his orchestra as his instrument, Ellington wrote music that catered to his sidemen's strengths.

Ellington was born in Washington, D.C., on April 29, 1899, to a middle-class family and grew up around music. The young Ellington was also exposed to African American music at church and took his first piano lessons when he was around seven or eight. Ellington showed an early interest and talent in painting and drawing, but by his teen years he was more interested in music, going out to hear and watch pianists playing in the then-popular ragtime style, taking lessons, and eventually forming his first group, Duke's Serenaders, and writing his first composition, "Soda Fountain Rag." Even in high school, Ellington carried himself with aplomb with elegant clothes and a noble demeanor that earned him his nickname "Duke."

By the early 1920s, Duke managed to earn a good living as a dance band leader, playing for black and white audiences while honing his business skills. It was during this period that he developed a coterie of musicians to play with him including childhood friends Otto Hardwick (1904–1970) on saxophone and Arthur Whetsol (1905–1940) on trumpet, along with William "Sonny" Greer (1895–1982) on drums. Ellington was growing as a musician, taking lessons in harmony with a local teacher and studying the new stride techniques of James P. Johnson by slowing down a piano roll of "Carolina Shout." In February 1923, New York–based vaudeville clarinetist Wilbur Sweatman hired Greer to play drums, who agreed on the condition that he also hire Ellington and Hardwick. Leaving the comfortable life of Washington, Ellington soon set his heights for bolder challenges in New York.

HARLEM RENAISSANCE

In 1913, James Reese Europe and other musicians left the Clef Club and founded another African American booking agency, the Tempo Club in Harlem. The move paralleled the influx of African Americans moving uptown, from midtown west where the Clef Club was located, and was central to the birth of Harlem entertainment proper as the city's top all-black and mixed-race nightclubs moved up to Harlem.[19] By the 1920s, Harlem was the cultural capital for African Americans, attracting aspiring artists, musicians, thinkers, poets, and intellectuals who became part of what was known as the Harlem Renaissance. The literary movement was particularly strong, producing a plethora of writers in all mediums including Zora Neale Hurston, Langston Hughes, Rose McClendon, and James Weldon Johnson. It was a time of deep racial pride as important civil rights groups formed including the National Association for the Advancement of Colored People (NAACP), headed by W. E. B. DuBois, and the National Urban League. The success of Mamie Smith's "Crazy Blues" in 1920 and the all–African American production and cast of *Shuffle Along* in 1921 sparked a demand for black entertainment and art. Many whites-only clubs opened in Harlem, and it became fashionable for rich whites to go to Harlem and spend an evening at the Cotton Club, Connie's Inn, Small's Paradise, or the Savoy Ballroom.

Ellington arrived amid all this activity in March 1923. A proud African American, Ellington soaked in Harlem's creative energy and in the process became a key figure of the era. He immersed himself in the cutting sessions and rent house parties of Harlem, developing his stride technique while furthering his connections. He met and befriended Fats Waller and Willie "the Lion" Smith, who took Ellington under his wing. Fellow Washingtonians Will Marion Cook and Will Vodery, veteran composers of the heyday of African American musical theater, became his mentors, providing professional advice and informal lessons in harmony, counterpoint, and orchestration. However, work became scarce when the musicians quit Sweatman's band, and they soon decamped back to Washington. In June the band returned under Elmer Snowden's name, and a turning point was landing a gig at the Hollywood Club in September 1923. By February 1924, Snowden was expunged from the group, and Ellington assumed its leadership. The group would spend most of the next four years at this club, which eventually was renamed the Kentucky Club, developing their sound and taking the new name of the Washingtonians.

A musical turning point came in the fall of 1923 when trumpeter James "Bubber" Miley (1903–1932) replaced Whetsol, who returned to Washington to finish high school. Miley was from South Carolina but raised in New York and was deeply influenced by King Oliver and New York trumpeter Johnny Dunn. He was inspired to create his own wah-wah timbres and developed an innovative sound with a "plunger," the rubber suction cup, that enhanced his gutbucket blues playing. His presence greatly changed the conception of the group as they previously had been playing polite, sweet music to appeal to their audiences. Miley's raspy tone and percussive attack created a unique voice, and Ellington used it as the basis for the group's sound that was further enhanced with the addition of trombonist Charlie Irvis, a blues specialist, who joined in January 1924.

It was late 1926 when Ellington met Irving Mills (1894–1985), who would become his manager. Born to a Jewish family in the Lower East Side of Manhattan, Mills began as a singer and song plugger promoting popular songs to performers before founding his own publishing firm in 1919. Aimed at signing young unknowns, his roster of composers and songwriters eventually included Ellington, Hoagy Carmichael, Dorothy Fields, Jimmy McHugh, Harold Arlen, and others. Upon meeting Ellington, Mills signed him to a major record label. Like many other Jews who entered the U.S. in the late nineteenth-century, Mills encountered a lot of racism and discrimination; and like African Americans, he turned to the growing entertainment industry for better opportunities, as did performers (Al Jolson, Sophie Tucker, and Fanny Brice), songwriters (Irving Berlin, George Gershwin), and other entrepreneurs and business managers within the nascent music industry such as Mills, Florenz Ziegfeld, and Joe Glaser (who later managed Louis Armstrong among others). Mills built Ellington's reputation by marketing him as a bandleader and composer. But Ellington was unhappy with Mills's cut, which was approximately half of what Ellington himself made. Armstrong had a similar deal with Joe Glaser, and such financial arrangements were common between African Americans performers and white managers. Despite the practice, Ellington and Armstrong both knew that they needed a white manager to succeed in the music business.

"BLACK AND TAN FANTASY"

Ellington's signature sound finally comes through on "East St. Louis Toodle-Oo" from November 29, 1926, but is further perfected on "Black and Tan Fantasy." First recorded in October 1927, the song is a blues, a central theme in Ellington's music as he would revisit the form repeatedly throughout his career. The title is a reference to "black and tan" nightclubs who catered to a mixed-race clientele. The dualities are presented in a series of musical contrasts: major versus minor blues forms; muted brass versus sweet alto saxophone; plunger technique on trumpet and trombone; a relentless quarter-note beat versus two-beat feel; and solo versus ensemble sections.

Miley's wah-wah trumpet is the central figure, but he is joined by his counterpart on trombone, Joe "Tricky Sam" Nanton (1904–1946). Nanton, who replaced Irvis in June, achieved his sound by placing a trumpet mute in the trombone. He also altered his tone with careful use of a rubber plunger, evoking vocal-like sounds that sound closer to "yah-yah" than "wah-wah." The pair's loose phrasing and decorative gestures signal a vocal-like approach that strongly evokes blues and novelty sounds.

The orchestral approach of stride piano undoubtedly influenced Ellington's writing and his conception of the orchestra. His stride solo here is excellent and acts as an interlude between brass solos. It is rich in harmonic substitutions, foreshadowing the captivating harmonies that would permeate his later works. Such details indicate the depth of Ellington's compositions that would only grow in the years and decades to come.

Listening Guide: "Black and Tan Fantasy" (1927) by Duke Ellington and His Orchestra
Duke Ellington: piano; Bubber Miley, Louis Metcalf: trumpets; Otto Hardwick: alto saxophone; unknown: tenor saxophone; Fred Guy: banjo; Mack Shaw: tuba; Sonny Greer: drums. Brunswick 3526-B. Recorded April 7, 1927, in New York. Originally credited to "The Washingtonians."

Time	Section	Comments
0:00	A (minor blues)	Melody by muted brass.
0:25	B	Sudden shift in mood to major with alto saxophone melody played very sweetly by Otto Hardwick. Section ends with a gesture from the saxophones.
0:41	B	Same as above with a break for the saxophones at the end with a choked cymbal hit.
0:57	A (major blues)	Wah-wah trumpet solo by Bubber Miley.
1:22	A (major blues)	Same as above.
1:45	A (major blues)	Solo stride piano by Duke Ellington with colorful harmonic substitutions on the form.
2:09	A (major blues)	Muted trombone with plunger by "Tricky Sam" Nanton and a horse whinny sound at 2:25.
2:34	A (major blues)	Wah-wah trumpet solo by Miles with aggressive choked cymbal hits.
2:54	Coda	Return to minor tonality and a quote from Chopin's "Funeral March."

COTTON CLUB

On December 4, 1927, Ellington began a four-year residency at New York's Cotton Club, an engagement that continued his artistic and commercial growth. Winning the job over King Oliver and Sam Wooding, the orchestra played two shows a night, six to seven nights a week, giving Ellington an opportunity to fine-tune his work as he learned how to write for his sidemen. In addition to playing the show's revue, accompanying chorus girls, a floor show, and skits, the band entertained during intermission.

The Cotton Club along was a whites-only venue, and like other New York establishments with African American entertainment such as the Log Cabin, Club Alabam, Kentucky Club, or Plantation Café, all conjured up the Old South from the name of the venue to the décor to the club itself with plantation scenes and images of southern mansions.[20] Even Ellington's music was referred to as "jungle music," and the moniker stayed. Ellington was partially responsible, embracing the term and writing "Jungle Blues," "Jungle Nights in Harlem," and "Echoes of the Jungle." Despite the minstrel-implications of his surroundings at the Cotton Club and the derogatory description of his music, with its primitivist overtones, the residency made Ellington a star and a national success through the orchestra's regular performances that were nationally broadcast live on the radio from February 1929.

By 1927, radio had become an important form of entertainment and transformed American life. In the same way that the internet changed life in the 1990s, radio connected people across the nation to a network of shared experiences. It also contributed towards a decline in sales of sheet music and records. For example, in 1921, record sales peaked at over 105 million units, before dropping down four years later to fewer than 60 million per year.[21] For Ellington, performing at the Cotton Club meant that his music reached an audience beyond the club and New York. Combined with a busy recording schedule, including recording for several record companies that was standard practice of the day, Ellington reached a higher level of fame than his contemporaries.

OTHER HARLEM BANDS

Ellington faced stiff competition with other popular Harlem bands during the late 1920s including Leroy Smith, Lloyd Scott, the Savoy Bearcats, Charlie Johnson and his Paradise Ten, and Fess Williams and His Royal Flush Orchestra. Smith's group was the most symphonic sounding, but otherwise the other bands were mostly in the mold of Fletcher Henderson with musicians equally adept at playing "hot" jazz as they were reading in pit bands.

One of the stronger bands was led by pianist and bandleader Charlie Johnson (1891–1959). In residence at Small's Paradise since 1925, his band is remarkable, featuring Jabbo Smith and Sidney De Paris on trumpets, Jimmy Harrison on trombone, and Edgar Sampson, Benny Waters, and

Benny Carter on reeds. "You Ain't the One" and "Charleston Is the Best Dance After All" features Carter's first recorded arrangements, but otherwise most of the arrangements were done by Waters. "The Boy in the Boat," an amalgamation of Fletcher Henderson's and Duke Ellington's styles, is one of his best and features intricate hi-hat work from George Stafford and excellent solos by Harrison on trombone and De Paris on muted trumpet with clarinet responses by Ben Whitted.

ELLINGTONIANS

Beginning with Miley and Nanton's wah-wah sounds, Ellington crafted his band's sound around the skills of his valuable sidemen. Many remained loyal to Ellington for decades. Baritone saxophonist Harry Carney (1910–1974) joined in 1927 and stayed in the band even after Ellington himself died. He developed a distinctive sound that would support the saxophone section and was an excellent clarinetist as well. "Cotton Club Stomp" is a thrilling performance from 1929 and features Carney playing intricate counterpoint on baritone sax during the statement of the theme.

Alto saxophonist Johnny Hodges (1907–1969) arrived in 1928 and would remain with the group, save for a few years in the 1950s, until his death in 1970. One of Ellington's most distinctive voices, he was perhaps the orchestra's greatest soloist, renowned for his exquisite ballad playing. At this stage in his career, however, Hodges had not yet developed the rich tone and powerful phrasing that he would be lauded for. Instead, he was known for his up-tempo playing. "Tishimongo Blues" from 1928 begins with short trading between Nanton and clarinetist Barney Bigard followed by solos from Hodges and Miley. Along with Bigard, Hodges's sound, clear and warm, contrasted to the bluesy, rough timbres played by Miley and Nanton. Moreover, their lines are far more fluid, and Bigard is particularly flashy in comparison to the riff-like playing of the brassmen. Hodges shines throughout, contributing an outstanding solo, leading a dynamic saxophone section, and filling in the ensemble passages with his impassioned playing. His soprano saxophone solo on "The Blues with a Feelin'" from November 1928 is excellent and recalls his mentor, the great New Orleans clarinetist and saxophonist Sidney Bechet. With Hodges's Bechet-inflected sound and Miley taking his cues from King Oliver, Ellington found his voice by incorporating the sound of New Orleans in his New York–style band. A fact he further exploited by always having a Louis Armstrong–influenced trumpeter and by bringing New Orleans musicians into his band, including clarinetist Barney Bigard and bassist Wellman Braud.

Bechet himself had a brief tenure with the group in 1923 as did vocalist Adelaide Hall (1901–1993). Before becoming one of the most popular African American singers of the late 1920s and a major star in England during the 1930s, Hall sang briefly with the Duke Ellington Orchestra in 1927 and left a strong impression with her wordless singing on "Creole Love Call," a reworking of Oliver's "Camp Meeting Blues." Like Louis Armstrong, she treated her voice like an instrument, albeit in a very different manner as her singing is as much informed by opera as it is by the blues, while her growling scat is reminiscent of Miley's playing. It was a memorable performance that remained in the Ellington's repertoire for decades to come.

Other important Ellingtonians to join include Juan Tizol on valve trombone and Cootie Williams who replaced the increasingly unreliable Miley in early 1929. Together with Carney, Hodges, Bigard, and Braud they would form a powerful nucleus that would carry the Ellington orchestra into the Swing Era.

Chapter 8

Louis Armstrong

The greatest soloist to emerge during the early jazz era was trumpeter Louis Armstrong (1901–1971). Over the course of his Hot Five and Hot Seven recordings from 1925 through 1928, Armstrong set a standard of improvisation that has resounded throughout jazz history with a definitive sound, strong command of the blues, a keen melodic sense, and an impeccable sense of rhythm and swing. But instead of following through with his innovations, he infuriated critics by becoming a popular entertainer and emerged as one of the greatest vocalists in jazz and popular music history. With a gravelly and rough-sounding voice, he was an unlikely candidate to attain this status, but he did so with his charisma, his outstanding musicianship, and his sharp entertainment skills. Armstrong is a towering figure in jazz history and one of the few to attain an iconic status in American culture.

Early Life

As one of the most celebrated entertainers and figures of the twentieth-century, Armstrong's life in jazz and music has often been wrapped in myth. Even his birthdate was unclear; he was said to have been born on July 4, 1900, a seemingly appropriate date for such an American icon, and a fact that Armstrong perpetuated throughout his lifetime. He was, in fact, born on August 4, 1901, in New Orleans, the illegitimate son of William Armstrong and Mary Albert, an unwed teenager. His father abandoned the family, and Armstrong was left in the care of his grandmother before living with his mother from age five. Growing up in an area of uptown

New Orleans known as "the Battlefield," he was raised in abject poverty, amid the violence, crime, and prostitution that dominated the area. He was sent to work at the age of seven, delivering coal to prostitutes in the red light district, but he was already exposed to music through the Baptist and Sanctified churches, early street musicians with a repertoire of work songs and nascent forms of the blues, and barbershop quartets, where Armstrong first made his reputation among musicians, becoming known as "Little Louis."

A turning point in his life was when Armstrong was arrested for shooting blanks in the air on New Year's Day 1913. Sent to the Colored Waif's Home for Boys, he thrived in such a stable environment with strict disciplinary rules. He played in the school band, moving from tambourine to alto horn to bugle, before finally being placed on cornet. Steeped in African American vernacular traditions, he was introduced to a Eurocentric musical pedagogy, taking "legitimate" private lessons and learning about different standards of musical technique that would provide the basis of his later acclaimed work.[1]

When his time at the Waif's home was finished, he was reluctant to leave as he had to return to hard labor. However, the experience on cornet allowed Armstrong to immerse himself deeper in the music scene, playing in honky-tonks and on advertising wagons, and listening to a lot of music. Being in New Orleans, he admired many of the city's cornetists, including Bunk Johnson, Buddy Petit, and especially Joe Oliver, who took young Armstrong under his wing (who addressed him as "Papa" or "Papa Joe"). When Oliver left for Chicago in 1918, he recommended Armstrong for trombonist Kid Ory's band. However, Armstrong too left New Orleans the following year when he joined Fate Marable's band on the Mississippi riverboats.

Riverboats and Chicago

Fate Marable (1890–1947) led entertainment bands on the Streckfus Riverboats that traveled through the Mississippi and Ohio rivers. His bands of ten to twelve musicians typically played a mixed repertoire of music and often relied on commercial arrangements. Many of the musicians played by ear, but Marable taught them to be professionals, placing an emphasis on reading music and learning how to behave on a job. A famous photograph from 1918 features one of Marable's best bands with Armstrong joined by Pops Foster, Johnny St. Cyr, and

Johnny and Baby Dodds. Armstrong not only improved his reading but also his ability to play songs and styles beyond New Orleans. Marable is renowned as a great talent scout employing scores of musicians who would achieve greater success including Zutty Singleton, Henry "Red" Allen, Tommy Ladnier, and Jimmy Blanton. Armstrong stayed on until 1921 and finally broke through to some of the better full-time work in New Orleans playing at Tom Anderson's outside of Storyville and in the Tuxedo Brass Band. A year later, Oliver sent for him to join his band in Chicago; Armstrong had already turned down an offer to join Fletcher Henderson's band, but the chance to play with his mentor was too good to turn down and he went north.

The addition of Armstrong as second cornetist furthered the band's popularity as he brought strength to the dual cornet lines, particularly because Oliver was no longer at his peak. On the Creole Jazz Band's 1923 recordings, Armstrong's assertive tone and strong lines, even at this stage, are already evident on "Chimes Blues," his first recorded solo with Oliver, and "Tears," where he is featured on nine breaks. Interestingly, both solos feature heavy use of arpeggios and their various permutations as favored by New Orleans clarinetists. By the late 1910s, Armstrong had memorized clarinet war-horses like "High Society" and "Clarinet Marmalade," which he likely learned to help him stand out; playing "clarinet style" on the cornet informed his first solos. By June 1924, at the urging of his second wife, pianist Lil Hardin Armstrong, he left the band and finally accepted an offer to join Fletcher Henderson and moved to New York.

New York

At the time of Armstrong's arrival in New York, the most highly regarded trumpeter there was Memphis-born Johnny Dunn (1897–1937). Singled out by Garvin Bushell for his drive, use of dynamics, and his use of double-time, he was a proficient blues player also noted for his wah-wah plunger mute technique, a rare sound in New York during this period.[2] His playing on Edith Wilson's "Dunn's Cornet Blues" from April 11, 1924, is excellent where his strong tone is on display playing short, syncopated phrases and a long bend as a highlight. Still, Dunn was stuck in ragtime and march rhythms, and his feel was stiff. Armstrong's appearance in New York changed everything.

Armstrong's stay with Fletcher Henderson only lasted about a year, but his impact on the band was tremendous.[3] His solo on "Shanghai

Shuffle" is indicative of Armstrong's creative agenda. Basing his solo around one note, his focus on rhythm and groove creates a swinging solo that clearly inspires the rhythm section to dig into the rhythm. Working with Fletcher Henderson also meant that Armstrong was privy to his connections in the New York jazz scene, freelancing on various recording sessions organized by pianist and industry man Clarence Williams (1893–1965). Originally from New Orleans, Williams worked for Okeh Records from 1923 to 1930, running a large number of studio groups backing blues singers and hiring many musicians from Henderson's band. Armstrong played on a number of Williams's led sessions including a series of recordings with the great Sidney Bechet on soprano saxophone, who at the time was the only person who could play at or beyond Armstrong's level. The two men had known each since childhood and have been rivals ever since.

Sidney Bechet (1897–1959) was born to a musical Creole family in New Orleans and started out as a clarinetist at an early age and then studied under the great early clarinetists in New Orleans including George Baquet, Big Eye Louis Nelson, and Lorenzo Tio Jr. He spent his formative years in the 1910s working in New Orleans before touring with various shows, including a traveling carnival, and ended up in Chicago in 1917 where he played with Freddie Keppard, one of his idols. In 1919, Bechet joined Will Marion Cook's large concert band, the Southern Syncopated Orchestra, for a tour of Europe as featured soloist. Bechet's playing impressed audiences and critics everywhere, including Swiss conductor Ernest Ansermet who raved about Bechet in a review of their performance, the first serious review of a jazz concert. For the next ten years, Bechet would travel far and wide, returning to Europe often and even visiting Russia in 1926, in the process helping disseminate jazz around the world. He also picked up the soprano saxophone, which became his primary instrument. He freelanced often, including a three-month stint with Duke Ellington in 1923, but never stayed in any band for too long because of his volatile temperament. During his heyday, he recorded infrequently, and as a result his most famous recordings were recorded well after New Orleans jazz was established.

However, Bechet's performances with Armstrong from late 1924 and early 1925 are some of the most important recordings of the early jazz era. While "Texas Moaner Blues" from October 1924 showcases their masterful solos and mutual affinity for the blues, two versions of "Cake Walking Babies (from Home)" contain their most famous "duels" on record. Recording as the Red Onion Jazz Babies, the first version from

December 1924 for Gennett Records, with Alberta Hunter and Clarence Todd on vocals, is the most famous version. Bechet commands attention with sheer raw power, loud volume, dramatic entrances with wide leaps, and aggressive staccato articulation. Armstrong, on the other hand, is more sophisticated, utilizing melodic motifs and gestures to generate excitement. He is more controlled, but ultimately both are highly skilled improvisers. On the version recorded as Clarence Williams' Blue Five (with Eva Taylor on vocals) in January 1925 for Okeh, Armstrong comes through as the winner. However the two men's dominant performances can be explained by an engineering imbalance; Bechet is louder on the former, while Armstrong is louder on the latter.[4] Regardless, it features some of the most dynamic playing of the early jazz era.

Armstrong also accompanied in the studio many blues singers, some of whom would not be remembered if not for his presence. However, recording with Bessie Smith and "Ma" Rainey, he is again matched with a musical personality comparable to his own. Overall, his playing is simpler as he emphasizes his blues vocabulary of slow bends and slides. Sometimes he plays in the style of his mentor "King" Oliver, as he does on Smith's "Cold in Hand Blues" where he even gets a chorus for himself. However, while he was not Smith's favorite accompanist as his playing often took the spotlight away, the results still reveal the possibilities of interaction and improvisation.

A summer tour with the Fletcher Henderson Orchestra introduced Armstrong's music all over the country. Performing in band battles and jam sessions, Armstrong grew stronger as a musician while broadening his appeal to audiences everywhere. His wife, who felt that Armstrong should receive first billing, secured a job for him at the Dreamland Café in Chicago. An offer to record for Okeh further prompted Armstrong to leave Henderson's band in 1925 and relocate.

Lil Hardin Armstrong

Of the early jazz female pianists, Lil Hardin Armstrong (1898–1971) was one of the most visible and the best known, having played on landmark recordings by King Oliver and Louis Armstrong. Her skills as a pianist and arranger have been overshadowed by her marriage to the famous trumpeter and her subsequent influence on his career. In fact, she was a fine all-around pianist and arranger who later became a bandleader. She was also instrumental as a composer, but her songs were often credited to "L. Armstrong." This was often done to capitalize on her husband's name but unfortunately diminished her contributions.[5]

Armstrong was from Tennessee and was born in Memphis. Classically trained on piano and organ, she took courses at Fisk University and later moved with her family to Chicago. She had played in church but was always attracted to popular music. A job at a music store as a music demonstrator led to an opportunity to work with trombonist Lawrence Duhé's band which morphed into King Oliver's Creole Jazz Band. She traveled to San Francisco in 1921 with the band and then again back to Chicago for the group's famed appearance at Lincoln Gardens in late 1922. Her big sound and exuberant energy can be heard on the group's 1923 recordings, but her work has been unfairly dismissed. She establishes her solo style on "I'm Going to Wear You Off My Mind" from April 6, 1923, with octave work and syncopations.

On her work with Louis Armstrong's Hot Five, her rhythmic approach to solos had matured quite a bit with a stronger feel and a greater grasp of the hot jazz language. On "Put 'Em Down Blues" from 1925, she comes out of her husband's vocal with ringing octaves before ending with another octave flourish down to the lower register of the piano, while "Come Back, Sweet Papa" features syncopated figures between the hands as well as an ending hemiola figure.

As a leader, Armstrong secured gigs for her and her husband at the Dreamland, persuading management to hang up a sign: "The World's Great Cornetist, Louis Armstrong." She eventually secured a recording contract to record her own material which she composed or arranged. Recording as either the New Orleans Wanderers or the New Orleans Bootblacks in July 1926, it was a similar group to the Hot Five with George Mitchell on cornet and the addition of Joe Clark on saxophone. Although Armstrong does not solo, her rhythmic drive adds to the joyous performances that are excellent examples of New Orleans jazz.

Hot Five: 1925–1926

Louis Armstrong's first Hot Five recording sessions from late 1925 and early 1926 featured veteran New Orleans musicians including ex-King Oliver bandmates Johnny Dodds on clarinet and his wife on piano, as well as Johnny St. Cyr on banjo and the great trombonist Kid Ory (1890–1973). Right from the start, Armstrong is the focal point; even during the collective improvisation passages he is the clear lead voice.

It is not just his sound but the execution of his lines that demands attention.

Armstrong recorded strong solos on "Oriental Strut" and "Muskrat Ramble," but "Cornet Chop Suey" from February 26, 1926, is a particularly astounding performance. His "clarinet style" playing is on full display, as he is featured from start to finish, save a short piano solo, during a series of brilliant breaks and stop-time figures. Unable to play with the mute in the tradition of his mentor, Armstrong instead uses speed and agility on the cornet as a gimmick. Conceived as a novelty, "Cornet Chop Suey" is a showcase piece designed to impress his audience.

While the Hot Five records contain outstanding examples of Armstrong's playing, they also contain his first recorded vocals. He always loved to sing but was not allowed to during his tenures with Oliver and Henderson. On "Heebie Jeebies," also from the February 26 session, he scat-sings for the first time on record. Legend states that Armstrong dropped the music during the recording session and began to scat, thus inventing a unique art form off the cuff. But scat had been part of the recorded musical lexicon for at least a decade and had been attributed to older minstrel comedians. Jelly Roll Morton, Tony Jackson, and others claimed to have learned scat from comedian Joe Sims. Armstrong, who never claimed to have invented the technique, had been scatting since his early vocal quartet days.[6] On the Hot Five and Hot Seven records, scat was a natural extension of his trumpet playing and though Armstrong may have thought of scat as a gimmick, the results were purely art.

Armstrong was also not above recording comic, novelty, or minstrel-style songs with mini-skits such as "Big Fat Pa and Skinny Ma," "Don't Forget to Mess Around," or "Big Butter and Egg Man." But even on such hokum material, his artistry was undeniable. "Big Butter and Egg Man," the title being a reference to a big spender, represents a breakthrough for Armstrong as he frees himself from repetitive rhythmic phrases. By instead relying on smaller musical motives and varying them rhythmically and melodically, Armstrong is able to construct lines that develop from the preceding one. Thus, his solo is a cohesive statement and has been universally praised by critics.

Armstrong played this song while accompanying tap dancers Herbert Brown and Naomi McGraw at the Sunset Café. In the mid-1920s, it was not unheard of for trumpeters to accompany dancers, and in Armstrong's case it was an imitative act as he played back the dancers' steps on the trumpet.[7] The sudden change in Armstrong's rhythmic conception suggests that he was informed and influenced by the dancers' intricate tap work and would be a remarkable example of the synergy between music and dance in early jazz history.

Chicago Dance Bands

The Hot Five were only a studio band, and at night Armstrong was busy leading a larger band at the Dreamland Café, accompanying singers and dancers. He also began to work with Erskine Tate's Orchestra at the nearby Vendome Theater. They were part of an important network of Chicago dance bands that are overshadowed by its great small jazz groups. Playing in the theater meant accompanying films, but also meant playing for sing-alongs, overtures, accompanying singers, etc. A wide repertoire was required including classics, jazz, popular dance numbers, and novelty songs; the orchestra's members were expected to have formal experience, some classical training, and the ability to read music. These musical values were also cultivated by bandleaders, many of whom were violinists and college-educated, such as Tate, Charles Elgar, Charles "Doc" Cooke, and Clarence M. Jones, who were also continuing the New Orleans tradition of violin-playing bandleaders. As a result, the Chicago dance band sound was generally polite with the occasional "hot" solo and was closer in spirit to Paul Whiteman's brand of jazz. Many jazz musicians gained import-ant professional experience in these bands including clarinetists Jimmie Noone, Buster Bailey, Omer Simeon, Barney Bigard, tubists Hayes Alvis and Quinn Wilson, trumpeters George Mitchell and Shirley Clay, pianists Earl Hines and Teddy Weatherford, and drummers Jimmy Bertrand and Zutty Singleton.

Tate (1895–1978) was from Memphis and studied at the American Conservatory of Music in Chicago. He held a residency at the Vendome Theater from 1919 to 1928, accompanying vaudeville acts and supplying mood music for films. Tate had already recorded in 1923, but "Stomp Off, Let's Go" and "Static Strut" with Louis Armstrong, recorded on May 28, 1926, might be the finest examples of a Chicago band, rivaling even Fletcher Henderson's best work. With strong ensemble passages featuring Dodds on clarinet, Teddy Weatherford on piano, and Jimmy Bertrand on drums, the band plays with precision and gusto, seemingly invigorated by the presence of Armstrong who had switched from cornet to trumpet.

Armstrong was the star soloist, prioritizing showmanship in his nightly gigs as he entertained audiences with his high-register playing and flair for the dramatic. On Tate's recordings, he played some of his

most exciting material to date with scintillating breaks on "Stomp Off,
Let's Go" and flashy solos on "Static Strut." Of course, he is part of the
band's entertainment formula that includes slap tongue solos on baritone
sax and novelty washboard breaks; however, it's Armstrong's musicianship and virtuosity that grabs the spotlight.[8] The work of pianist Teddy
Weatherford (1903–1945) is noteworthy, not only for his inspired solos
but for his exciting accompaniments with octave figures, foreshadowing
Earl Hines.

Undocumented on record, until the Hot Five, though was Armstrong's vocals and entertainment skills. For the first time, Armstrong
was in a situation where his boss allowed him to sing, and he thrived
in this setting. But he did not stop there, taking part in comedy skits
including a cross-dressing act, an "instrument argument" with saxophonist Stump Evans, and a preaching act.[9] The most significant stunt was
his high-note playing which extended his reputation even more and
resulted in the blistering recordings with Tate. From the perspective of
the 1920s, Armstrong's ability to play high notes astounded audiences
and critics alike and was perceived as novelty and sometimes referred to
as "freakish."[10] His various stunts, one of the most famous being when
he reportedly playing 350 high Cs in a row, are based in difficulty rather
than humor and recall similar vaudeville or stage performers such as the
highest high-wire act or the strongest strong man; Armstrong's abilities
lay far beyond ordinary trumpet players.

By April 1926, Armstrong broke up with Lil and went to work
with Carroll Dickerson at the Sunset Café. Besides the music, there was
an elaborate stage show with tap dancers, chorus girls, comedians, and
other acts; Armstrong relished the spotlight, playing for the audiences
and even getting involved with the floor show. Eventually, thanks to the
club's manager, Joe Glaser, Dickerson was ousted, and Armstrong became
the headliner; later, Glaser would oversee the trumpeter's career. Like
so many ballrooms and clubs across the nation, the Sunset was run by
gangsters. Armstrong's celebrity as a soloist was strong enough that two
books about his playing were published, *Louis Armstrong's 125 Jazz Breaks
for Cornet* and *Louis Armstrong's 50 Hot Choruses for Cornet*.

Hot Five and Hot Seven: 1927–1928

Armstrong reentered the studio in May 1927 and expanded his Hot
Five lineup with a tubist and drummer, making them the Hot Seven.

All of his solos from the recording sessions reflect his obsession with the upper register, stemming from his work at the Vendome. Perhaps his most impressive performance is his solo on "S.O.L. Blues" from May 12, 1927, and "Gully Low" recorded the next day and featuring virtually the same solo, with five high Cs. Today that note can be played by high school students, but at the time, it was considered the peak of the instrument's written range and would have sounded very impressive. Each of Armstrong's high Cs are emphasized with his characteristic "rip," an aggressive ragged, ascending glissando that leads up to the note, followed by his characteristic "shake," an exaggerated vibrato.

Trumpet pedagogues of the era thought that proper embouchure for high-note playing was best achieved by placing the lips in a "smile" position. By the late 1930s, a "puckering" position was deemed to be more effective. In the late 1920s, Armstrong had already stumbled upon this technique by accident and amazed listeners with the mass and weight behind his notes.[11] By expanding the instrument's range, he set an example that would be imitated by countless jazz trumpeters after him as no trumpeter could match him for sheer range until the 1940s.

The Hot Seven recordings from May 1927 also begin to move away from New Orleans practices towards an emphasis on solo improvisation. Armstrong was increasingly basing his improvisations on the harmonies of the song rather than the melody. "Potato Head Blues," from May 10, was a breakthrough in this regard. Besides containing his highest note from this era, a high D that he plays at the climax of his solo, Armstrong outlines the harmony by playing arpeggios, a hallmark of his earlier solos, that are now fully integrated into the body of his solo instead of during breaks. Combined with his advanced rhythm conception, that first surfaced on "Big Butter and Egg Man," Armstrong's solo is a milestone of jazz improvisation.

He manages to sustain the drama of his solo through an entire chorus of stop-time by masterfully balancing the relationship between melody and rhythm. The notion in jazz that all musicians are drummers and that everyone plays their instrument like a drum is evident on "Potato Head Blues," where Armstrong displays a sophisticated sense of rhythm that would resonate in jazz solos for decades. He creates a powerful sense of forward momentum with his strong sense of swing. Weak beats are accented in a way that displace the pulse but are resolved with figures that fall on the beat. Introducing tension and release as a device to propel a solo, Armstrong creates a solo full of beauty that resolves beautifully with the re-entrance of the band. It is a truly captivating performance that announces the art of the jazz solo.

Afterward, Armstrong returned to his Hot Five for recording sessions in September and December of 1927. Highlights from this period include "Struttin' with Some Barbecue" and "Hotter Than That," featuring one of his best scat solos from the era with an early hemiola (two against three) phrase. He also scats with guest guitarist Lonnie Johnson on a remarkable out-of-time call-and-response duet. A fellow native of New Orleans, Johnson was one of the few musicians who played at Armstrong's level with an intimate knowledge of the blues language.

"Savoy Blues," a reference to the Savoy Ballroom in Chicago not Harlem, also features an eloquent solo from Johnson, but the character of Armstrong's own solo represents a new direction for him. No longer strictly in the domain of "hot" jazz with swinging rhythms, Armstrong imbues his solo with a variety of rhythms including swing, straight, or even eighth notes, triplets, and a rubato-like (meaning free rhythm) fluidity.[12] Harmonically, he enriches the chords with the "color" tones, particularly sixths and ninths. Such devices are hallmarks of "sweet" bands of the era known for creating such soft and dreamy moods and a far cry from Armstrong's performances that tended to be either upbeat and celebratory or simply bluesy. He now has a diverse palette of emotions as his playing expresses tenderness and intimacy in a manner that allows for sadness and sentimentality.

After a failed nightclub enterprise with friends drummer Zutty Singleton (1898–1975) and pianist Earl Hines (1903–1983) in late 1927, Armstrong was unemployed. Moreover, his status as the "Greatest Trumpet Player" was temporarily challenged by a newcomer, classically trained African American trumpeter Reuben Reeves (1905–1975).[13] Championed by the conservative music critic and pianist Dave Peyton, the battle was brief and ended when Armstrong outplayed Reeves sometime in early 1928. The impact was evident on the next set of Hot Five recordings which featured a revived Armstrong, whose playing was stronger than ever.

Back in the studio in June 1928 for the final Hot Five sessions, Armstrong chose new musicians, selecting his bandmates from his gig with Carroll Dickerson at the Savoy Ballroom. The showband influence is evident with a polished ensemble sound and an increasing emphasis on arrangements. Furthermore, with the exception of Singleton, the musicians were all northerners: Hines on piano, Jimmy Strong on clarinet and tenor saxophone, Fred Robinson on trombone, and Mancy Carr on banjo. The "sweet" style, introduced on "Savoy Blues," now informs newer material like "A Monday Date" or "Two Deuces," but is also evident on Armstrong's most celebrated performance, "West End Blues."

"West End Blues"

"West End Blues," recorded on June 27, 1928, is a pinnacle of Armstrong's performances from this era. His opening cadenza is one of the most fabled moments in jazz history and, despite being only twelve short seconds, is a summary of achievements learned thus far including a wide range of rhythms, a triumphantly held high note, and logical phrase structure that evoke a range of styles and moods, including hot, sweet, classical, blues, and clarinet. Despite the hybridity of styles, Armstrong's strength of character unifies all of the elements as he seamlessly flows from one idiom to the next.

Listening Guide: "West End Blues" by Louis Armstrong and His Hot Five
Louis Armstrong: trumpet; Jimmy Strong: clarinet; Fred Robinson: trombone; Earl Hines: piano; Mandy Carr: banjo; Zutty Singleton: drums. Okeh 8597. Recorded June 28, 1928, in Chicago.

Time	Section	Comments
0:00	Introduction	Perhaps the most famous twelve seconds in jazz history. Trumpet cadenza by Armstrong bursts with energy as he unleashes a cascade of notes and rhythms that seem to call forth the art of jazz improvisation.
0:16	Chorus 1	Preceding the entrance of the band, Armstrong leads the statement of the melody with support from clarinet and trombone (sometimes playing independent phrases) as the piano plays strict staccato time.
0:50	Chorus 2	Distinct change of texture with trombone stating the melody, tremolo chords from the piano, and Singleton's novelty "clip-clop" accompaniment that resembles horse's hooves.
1:24	Chorus 3	Another change in texture with the clarinet playing in the low register with "sweet" responses from Armstrong on vocals.

Time	Section	Comments
1:59	Chorus 4	Piano solo by Earl Hines, who alternates between sweet and hot styles, continually changing his right-hand texture, alternating between fast, florid lines with octaves and tremolos.
2:33	Chorus 5	Armstrong returns on a triumphantly held high note, before unleashing a cascade of notes that stems from the opening cadenza.
2:56	Coda	Hines's cascading chords full of lush harmonies signal the end of the performance.
3:05		Armstrong returns for a final phrase before the performance ends with the closing of Singleton's finger cymbal.

The variety of styles in the opening cadenza is echoed throughout the entire performance. After the introduction and the statement of the melody by the full band comes Robinson's bluesy, poignant trombone solo accompanied by Hines's tremolo chords and Singleton's clip-clop accompaniment that recalls the sound of horse's hooves, thus combining blues, novelty, and classical elements. The third chorus begins with a low-register clarinet solo sounding particularly reedy that is offset with Armstrong's sweet vocalization responses. Described variously as gorgeous and heartwarming, his tone is gentle, his phrasing rubato-like, and his choice of notes colorful, often bringing out the sixth, the major seventh, and at one point the eleventh. Hines then plays the next chorus on his own, alternating between sweet and hot. The final statement by the full band has a triumphant character highlighted by a long held high note by Armstrong before releasing a cascade of descending blues phrases. Hines's own cascading chords at the end of the performance is enchanting and changes the mood back to wistful. Despite a hybrid of styles and textures, the changes are logical and natural, and "West End Blues" ranks among the most cohesive performance of the Hot Five and Hot Seven recordings.

Armstrong's singing style on "West End Blues" is representative of a new vocal style that was in vogue, "crooning," the art of singing softly while relying on the microphone for volume. Until this time, his vocal style, such as on "Heebie Jeebies" or "Hotter Than That" was exclamatory and loud, based on the mindset of filling large spaces. By 1927, microphones were in widespread use, and Armstrong learned to sing into one at the Savoy Ballroom. He is now more nuanced, tender, and able to display a wider emotional range. Armstrong's incorporation of this new technique would eventually transform his career.

Earl Hines

Pianist Earl Hines (1903–1983) is a key figure in the development of modern jazz piano. Known for playing "trumpet-style piano," which was essentially code for "Louis Armstrong"-style, Hines was always adamant that he developed independently of Armstrong. Originally from Pittsburgh, he made his first recordings in 1923, accompanying vocalist Lois Deppe, and his solo from "Congaine" reveals a restless pianist already experimenting with displacing the beat and playing single-note lines in his right hand. His light touch and his speed and agility are also in place, suggesting that he indeed developed on his own.

Hines made a name for himself in Chicago in the mid-1920s before establishing himself with New Orleans clarinetist Jimmie Noone at the Apex Club in Chicago in 1928. The group deviated from the traditional New Orleans style with a two-person front line consisting of clarinet and alto saxophone and Hines's idiosyncratic playing. Based in stride piano, Hines developed a clear, light touch that enabled a linear approach in his right hand, ensuring that he was a more than capable third voice in the ensemble. He was so strong he sometimes stole the show. On Noone's "Sweet Sue (Just You)" from May 1928, the sweet rendition of the melody is offset on the second chorus by Hines's exciting solo. Swinging and full of ideas, he plays startling double-time lines, octaves, and long phrases. However, his most celebrated performance is his stunning duet with Armstrong on "Weather Bird," recorded on December 7, 1928.

"Weather Bird"

"Weather Bird" is a classic performance from Hines and Armstrong. First, there are the remarkable exchange of phrases as both musicians are highly attuned to what the other is playing, often echoing the other's phrases in attempt to outplay the other. Although Hines is technically the accompanist, he does not limit himself to this role, acting as a matching lead voice alongside Armstrong. This blurring of the lines between soloist and accompanist, a form of call and response, would resonate tremendously in jazz history. In addition, by playing syncopations, cross-accents, and phrasing on and off the beat, it is abundantly clear that they are challenging each other's sense of rhythm and pulse in attempt to throw the other off. When Hines steps away from the steady pulse of stride piano, Armstrong continues to play undaunted, coming up with his own unique phrasing. In the process of such daring playing, mistakes and weakly articulated notes are evident, but this is beside the point as the focus is on the musical battle. Hines occasionally uses harmonic devices to throw Armstrong off, including his break at 2:07, but such methods seem to only empower Armstrong who comes back forcefully with his own line.

The possibilities of improvisation as a spontaneous journey is most evident in the ending coda when the musicians trade short one-bar phrases. There is a sense that neither musician knows how to end the performance until Armstrong finally plays an ascending phrase that points to its end. Freed of rhythm section backing and away from the demands of the audience, the possibilities of jazz as a music to listen to rather than dance to is also evident.

Listening Guide: "Weather Bird" by Louis Armstrong
Louis Armstrong: trumpet; Earl Hines: piano. Okeh 41454. Recorded on December 7, 1928, in Chicago.

Time	Section	Comments
0:00	Introduction	
0:04	A	Trumpet by Louis Armstrong states the melody with piano accompaniment by Earl Hines who anticipates Armstrong's pauses with quickly articulated responses.
0:23	B	Hines's lines develop from responses to countermelody before sounding more like collective improvisation with the two musicians echoing the other's phrases.
0:41	B	Piano solo: beginning with octaves, Hines takes advantage of the break at 0:48 to move into a syncopated section (0:50–0:55) before ending off as he did in the beginning of his solo.
1:00	A	Armstrong returns with the melody as Hines's accompaniment becomes less on the beat and more syncopated.
1:19	Interlude	Armstrong returns Hines's rhythmic jabs by playing behind the beat, creating polyrhythm and momentary rhythmic tension as the pulse almost disappears!

continued on next page

Time	Section	Comments
1:24	C	Piano solo begins by reestablishing the pulse.
1:42	C	Armstrong returns on the break. Hines continues to challenge Armstrong rhythmically with an altogether syncopated accompaniment. However, Armstrong continues undaunted, responding with his own phrasing of the beat.
2:01	C	Hines brings out his upper register. Note his break at 2:07!
2:19	Coda	Beginning with Armstrong, the two trade short phrases that become increasingly shorter. Hines's first answer falters slightly, but Armstrong responds in kind. The drama of determining an ending continues until 2:29 when Armstrong begins a phrase that slows down signaling the end. His high note is responded to with Hines adding ending harmonies.

"Weather Bird" is the only duet from the December recording session which was otherwise firmly in the New York tradition with the addition of a sixth member, Don Redman as the second reeds player. His presence further bolsters the small dance band style that characterizes the music from this session. The expanded instrumentation allowed for sophisticated arrangements with intricate parts. "Beau Koo Jack," written and arranged by the underrated Alex Hill, boasts a variety of textures that results in an unpredictable performance. Armstrong's solo, of course, is outstanding with complex chromatic phrases and well-articulated phrases as he displays remarkable control jumping through three octaves in one measure. "Muggles," slang for marijuana, is another highlight featuring Singleton's exquisite brushwork and two extraordinary choruses from Armstrong, one at a double-time tempo and the other in a slow blues vein.

Response to the Hot Five and Hot Seven

Armstrong's Hot Five and Hot Seven records sold well leading to other record companies to feature similar virtuoso trumpeter-singers such as Brunswick's Jabbo Smith and Victor's Henry "Red" Allen. Although neither musician had Armstrong's personality or charisma, their playing completes the picture of jazz trumpet during the early jazz era, beyond

Armstrong, Bubber Miley, and Bix Beiderbecke, while providing new approaches that would lead to the instrument's further development.

Jabbo Smith (1908–1991) was respected for his technical and creative abilities. Born in Georgia, he was raised in the Jenkins Orphanage in Charleston, South Carolina, which boasted a strong music program. He subsequently developed rapidly as a musician in the school's famed band. Smith played in the group from the time he was ten, but left as a teenager to become a professional musician. He freelanced in New York during 1927 and 1928, recording sessions with Charlie Johnson and Duke Ellington, before relocating to Chicago where he made his first recordings as a leader in 1929. Despite being marketed as an alternative to Armstrong, Smith still had his own distinctive sound, and there is not a bad solo among his twenty sides. He is perhaps at his most technically fluent on "Jazz Battle," while his muted phrases behind clarinetist Omer Simeon on "Sweet and Low Blues" have been praised for their creativity and unpredictability. Yet he is equally capable of simpler blues phrasing as exhibited on "Sleepy Time Blues." Conveniently, Smith was also an adept scat singer. "Sleepy Time Blues" and "Got Butter on It" features some of his best scat solos while "Decatur Street Tutti" features an equally exuberant performance by Smith on both trumpet and voice. Perhaps due to the timing of the recordings, they did not generate any sales, and Smith left music, languishing in obscurity for decades. Still, Smith's driving, energetic attack was influential on Roy Eldridge, displaying a harder edged sound that would become prominent with Dizzy Gillespie.

Victor's singing-trumpet answer to Louis Armstrong was Henry "Red" Allen, Jr. (1908–1967), the last of the great New Orleans trumpeters. Born into a family of musicians, he started on violin and alto horn before settling on trumpet, soon becoming a member of his father's band, the Henry Allen Brass Band. He also played with King Oliver in New York in 1927 and was with Fate Marable on the riverboats when he was discovered by a Victor talent scout in 1929. Recording under his own name and with the Luis Russell Orchestra, he soon became the most celebrated trumpeter in New York. His solo on "Louisiana Swing" gained Allen the immediate respect of his peers. He even recorded with Armstrong on "I Ain't Got Nobody" from December 1929, and the pair sounded indistinguishable from each other. Allen would develop a more personal manner of playing marked by a legato style. Translating the Armstrong language into swing, he became an important transitional player, although he would later focus on his New Orleans legacy.

Dolly Jones (1906–1975) is the first female jazz trumpet player on record, recording "That Creole Band" and "When" with trombonist Al Wynn in 1926. Jones's sound is powerful as she soars above her bandmates who sound frantic by comparison. With modern phrasing and strong command of the instrument, she sadly never got any proper respect or encouragement from the male-dominated jazz world. Such discrimination continued to plague her as discographers doubted that the trumpet playing on the Wynn tracks was Jones and instead crediting Armstrong although it is clearly not him.[14] Jones spent most of her life in Chicago, later playing with Lil Hardin Armstrong, freelancing under other surnames, and making a cameo appearance in the film *Swing!* from 1938 playing excellent versions of "China Boy" and "I May Be Wrong."

Her mother, Dyer Jones (1890–?), was known as one of the great trumpeters of her day. Oral testimony reveals the respect that her fellow musicians had for her musical talents. Drummer Tommy Benford exclaimed that:

> Dyer had a big name in those days, yes she did. A lot of people knew her and a lot of people wanted her. She was one of the great ladies of the trumpet . . . oh my God she was wonderful. That lady, she used to hit so many high notes, a lot of the guys in the band wanted to know where she got 'em from. Man, she was something else . . . and Dolly was right behind her.[15]

When the elder Jones was in New York in 1929, she played with Sammy Stewart's band at the Arcadia, and Benford added, "anytime you take a band like Sammy Stewart's and feature her in New York, she's got to be outstanding, because we didn't have nothing but good musicians in our band—-people like Sid Catlett, 'Big' Charlie Green, Johnny Dunn."[16]

Dyer taught trumpet to Valaida Snow (1900–1956) who was also a vocalist and became a star during the Swing Era. During the 1920s, Snow was active in vaudeville and toured Shanghai in 1926. She never rid herself of the comparisons to Louis Armstrong, a common criticism of women jazz musicians and an unfair assessment, considering the number of male players who also sounded like other musicians early in their careers (like Red Allen). The primary difference was that they were subsequently encouraged by their peers to develop their own voice whereas women were not.

Armstrong in New York

The final Hot Five sessions from 1928 reveal Armstrong's interest in dance bands, and he pursued this direction, finding himself back in New York in early 1929. By this time, broadcasts from Chicago's Savoy Ballroom had made him a star, and his evening performance at Harlem's Savoy on March 4 with Luis Russell's band was followed by a banquet welcoming Armstrong to New York. The best musicians came out including banjo-ist Eddie Condon, who organized an impromptu recording session for the next morning. It was an integrated all-star session with trombonist Jack Teagarden, tenor saxophonist Happy Caldwell, pianist Joe Sullivan, guitarist Eddie Lang, and drummer Kaiser Marshall. Two songs were recorded, but only "Knockin' a Jug," a slow blues, was released. Named after a jug of whiskey that was consumed prior to the session, it is a classic performance with outstanding solos by all.

The next day Armstrong recorded two songs, but they signaled a change in musical direction. Besides "Mahogany Hall Stomp," he recorded a sweet rendition of the ballad "I Can't Give You Anything but Love," his first recording of a Tin Pan Alley song. His trumpet solo is outstanding, building from the song's melody to include double-time phrases before ending with a false climax. In addition, his vocal performance is definitive with impassioned singing, a speechlike approach, and the liberties he takes with the melodic and rhythmic phrasing while filling in the spaces with scat.[17] It was the first of many Tin Pan Alley songs that Armstrong would turn into jazz standards. Ethel Waters paid tribute to Armstrong's vocal performance by copying it note for note, while imitating his voice, on a 1932 recording with the Duke Ellington Orchestra.

"I Can't Give You Anything but Love" became the template for Armstrong's subsequent work: performing current Tin Pan Alley, or pop, songs, recording with a big band, and emphasizing his singing. The backing arrangement was sweet with lush chords, strong vibrato, and a two-feel as the band would become increasingly anonymous. Armstrong still played trumpet, but the emphasis on his vocals was part of a larger plan to make him a star. The commercial direction was a stark contrast to his Hot Five and Hot Seven records and disappointed many critics, many of whom felt that he was selling out in contrast to Duke Ellington or Coleman Hawkins who still maintained a commitment to the art of jazz. However, such criticism is unfair, because Armstrong musicality *was* jazz. He simply transferred his artistry to his singing with breathtaking performances on "Ain't Misbehavin'," "Black and Blue," "All of Me," "Stardust," and many others that are not only gems of vocal jazz but also for male popular singing. Moreover, Armstrong did not share the views of his critics and never thought much of his Hot Five and Hot Seven recordings, considering them mere stepping stones towards his greater goal.[18] After all, he was an entertainer at heart. He became a major star and a household name and, in the process, broke down racial barriers for African Americans in radio and film. He was a larger than life figure who ultimately delivered his music to a broader audience beyond jazz.

Chapter 9

The Chicagoans and Bix Beiderbecke

Chicago jazz in the 1920s refers to a wide range of musicians, black and white, and groups, large and small. This chapter profiles a group of white Chicago musicians active in the mid-1920s known as the "Chicagoans" as well as the great cornetist Bix Beiderbecke who spent time in Chicago. The Chicagoan label is confusing and even more misleading since many of its musicians hailed from other parts of the Midwest including Frank Teschemacher (Kansas City), Pee Wee Russell (St. Louis), George Wettling (Topeka, Kansas), and Eddie Condon (Goodland, Indiana). But as a group, they came together in Chicago and devised an updated form of New Orleans jazz that became known as "Chicago style."

A core group of the Chicagoans met while they were attending Austin High School, and consisted of Teschemacher on clarinet, Bud Freeman on tenor saxophone, bassist Jim Lannigan, and the brothers Jimmy and Richard McPartland on trumpet and guitar. Together, they congregated at a nearby soda parlor to listen to and discuss the latest jazz records. They gained the nickname the "Austin High Gang," but that is not accurate as well because this initial group of friends grew to include musicians from other high schools such as drummer Dave Tough.

Inspired to play jazz from listening to the Original Dixieland Jazz Band (ODJB) and other early jazz groups, they are among the first generation of jazz musicians to learn from recordings. They were also fortunate to hear live performances by King Oliver at the Lincoln Gardens and the New Orleans Rhythm Kings (NORK) at the Friar's Inn, which furthered their dedication to jazz. Soon the circle of musicians grew to include trumpeter Muggsy Spanier, clarinetist Mezz Mezzrow, as well as drummers George Wettling and Gene Krupa.

However, the leading and central figure of the Chicagoans was banjoist Eddie Condon (1905–1973). Although he primarily played rhythm and rarely soloed, his importance lay in his fierce commitment to the Chicago style of jazz. He also promoted the music any way he could by organizing concerts, later leading an early jazz program on television in 1942 and hosting a series of jazz radio broadcasts in 1944. He is best remembered for running jam sessions, often at his club, Eddie Condon's in New York, from 1945 through 1967. A colorful character with a quick wit, he preferred the informal jam session insisting that "jazz can't be scored."[1]

Though not formally a Chicagoan, bassist Thelma Terry (1901–1966) was on the scene at the same time. She holds the distinction of also being one of the few significant female bandleaders in an otherwise all-male band. Born in Michigan, at eighteen she was first chair in the Chicago Women's Symphony Orchestra before switching over to jazz.[2] She was active in the music scene playing with Eddie Condon and leading a theater pit band that included Chicagoans Dave Tough and Bud Freeman, before branching out on her own with six recordings from 1928. "Mama's Gone, Goodbye" and "Lady of Havana" are the best tracks and feature her strong playing as well as her slap technique.

In January 1927, Spanier on cornet and Teschemacher on clarinet were among the first Chicagoans to appear on record, playing for amateur saxophonist and local butcher, Charles Pierce. Spanier had made his first recordings back in 1924 in the years prior to the Chicago style being solidified. By 1927, the Chicagoans' jam sessions at the Three Deuces attracted many musicians, including Benny Goodman, Bix Beiderbecke, and singer and comb player Red McKenzie from the Mound City Blue Blowers who helped Condon secure the first all-Chicagoan recording session.

Chicago Style

In December 1927, four songs were recorded, "Sugar," "China Boy," "Nobody's Sweetheart," and "Liza," which garnered a lot of attention and introduced the new Chicago style, a modification of New Orleans jazz practices. The next all-Chicagoan recording session was in April and showcased the musicians playing with more authority and confidence. "Friar's Point Shuffle" is a brilliant blues with a vocal by Red McKenzie, but "There'll Be Some Changes Made" and "I've Found a New Baby" from

April 6–8, 1928, have been hailed by some as the greatest jazz records ever made. With Spanier on cornet, Teschemacher on clarinet, Mezzrow on tenor saxophone, Joe Sullivan on piano, Lannigan on bass or tuba, and Krupa on drums, they are also sublime examples of Chicago style jazz.

Listening Guide: "I've Found a New Baby" by the Chicago Rhythm Kings
Muggsy Spanier: cornet; Frank Teschemacher: clarinet; Mezz Mezzrow: tenor saxophone; Joe Sullivan: piano; Eddie Condon: banjo; Jim Lannigan: tuba; Gene Krupa: drums. Brunswick 03413-A. Recorded April 6, 1928, in Chicago.

Time	Section	Comments
0:00	AA	Collective improvisation with the main melody played by cornet and clarinet with added fills by the clarinet and the tenor sax.
0:20	B	The front line plays the melody together.
0:30	A	Collective improvisation by the front line resumes.
0:39	AABA	Clarinet solo by Frankie Teschemacher.
1:05		At the end of the B section is an example of an explosion with a held note by Teschemacher and a drum response from Krupa.
1:15		Flare up led by Muggsy Spanier on cornet.
1:17	AABA	Piano solo by Joe Sullivan.
1:44		At the end of the B section: quiet explosion from Krupa who accents beat four with Sullivan.
1:52		Flare up led by Spanier with Teschemacher punctuating a held note.
1:54	AABA	Tenor saxophone solo by Mezz Mezzrow.
2:13		Shuffle rhythm played by Mezzrow and Krupa on the rims of his snare drum at the B section.
2:30		Flare up by the front line.
2:32	AABA	Collective improvisation by the front line.
2:40		Mezzrow on tenor saxophone plays a flare up figure before the second A.
2:51		Spanier plays the melody as Teschemacher plays the shuffle rhythm at the B section.
2:58		Flare up before the last A.
3:10	Ending	Break for the tenor sax followed by the "Charleston" rhythm on the hi-hat.

"I've Found a New Baby" reflects the Chicagoans preference for current popular songs with shorter forms, in this case AABA, discarding the older ragtime and march forms that were favored by New Orleans jazz ensembles. The impact of Louis Armstrong's Hot Five recordings and his appearances at the Sunset is particularly noticeable with Armstrong-like figures played throughout and the emphasis on individual solos over collective improvisation. The front line has been rearranged with tenor saxophone as a competing third voice replacing trombone and its accompaniment-type figures. Furthermore, the clarinet favors simpler melodic lines and riffs over the decorative, arpeggiated figures that were common.

The drums underwent the biggest change. Drums were often absent during early jazz recordings for fear of overwhelming the other instruments, but advances in recording technology allowed the entire drum set to be recorded with the use of multiple microphones to record the instruments and headphones used by the engineers. Therefore, Krupa is heard clearly throughout, playing his bass drum on all four beats throughout the performance. This was a remarkable step forward that predates the Swing Era. The elimination of the woodblocks and other novelty percussion sounds allowed Krupa to focus on timekeeping and to be more interactive in the music, including an enthusiastic backbeat with the snare drum on beats two and four that sometimes concluded a performance.

On these early recordings, the Chicagoans retained breaks, but introduced new devices to create tension and release: the "flare up" is particularly prominent: a short and loud figure that announces a new section, most often a polyphonic outburst of collective improvisation, but at other times a punctuated held chord with a drum response. It is often used as a dynamic tool and to signal a new soloist or section. An "explosion" is a syncopated figure played by the drums that anticipates a new section. Finally, there is the "shuffle rhythm," a staccato, heavily accented eighth-note pattern typically applied to the bridge of a song.

The individual solos are simply excellent. Best known for influencing Benny Goodman, Teschemacher (1906–1932) on clarinet has been criticized for his technique and his faulty intonation, but others consider him a genius. His solo on "I've Found a New Baby" led the French critic Hugues Pannasié to compare Teschemacher with the work of Bach.[3] A former violinist, he had been playing clarinet for barely three years when he recorded with the Chicagoans. Aggressive and full of nervous energy, his solos are sometimes spastic, with their jabbing rhythms, but are always played with intention and are boundless in ideas. His work is exemplary of the Chicago style.

Sullivan on piano is next, and he was far and away the best white jazz pianist of the era. Accompanied only by Krupa on drums, his driving two-handed style is exciting with a strong focus on rhythm. Normally a clarinetist, Mezzrow is on tenor saxophone here, and his solo language is steeped in the blues. Spanier, also making his Chicagoan debut, plays simply and directly, sticking close to the melody as the Armstrong influence is quite evident in his flare ups and his ensemble work.

The Chicagoans made two more significant recordings: "Jazz Me Blues" from April 28, 1928, but not issued until 1939, features more great playing from Sullivan and especially Teschemacher, who wrote the arrangement and solos brilliantly on clarinet, alto saxophone, and then returning on clarinet for a rousing finale. "Baby, Won't You Please Come Home," from May 2, is perhaps the most cohesive rhythmically as the band swings particularly hard. Teschemacher again dominates as his declamatory style could not contrast more with Spanier's straightforward approach. His solo is short but memorable for its intensity as he continues his jabbing rhythms during the ending collective improvisation.

Coming to New York

The Chicagoans' recordings had made a tremendous impression on easterners, and egged on by McKenzie, they began to dream of coming to New York. In mid-1928, with the promise of work, Condon, Krupa, Teschemacher, and Sullivan made their move. The trip was rocky as the musicians spent a period without work, but they did attract the attention of trumpeter Red Nichols who, like other New Yorkers, admired the Chicagoans' music. Their influence was practically immediate as the New York scene would adopt many of the devices pioneered by the Chicagoans.[4]

Bix Beiderbecke

Leon "Bix" Beiderbecke (1903–1931) was one of the great soloists of the early jazz era. Noted for his distinctive sound on cornet, he was extremely well-respected and admired during his lifetime and was among the first white jazz musicians to gain respect from African Americans. Yet he lived a tragically short life and died largely unknown to the public. Rumors about his life filtered out and he came to symbolize the "Roaring Twenties," romanticized as a troubled genius who had to make commercial sacrifices for his art, while drowning his sorrows with alcohol. The legend exploded with the release of Dorothy Baker's best-selling 1938 novel, *Young Man with a Horn*, that was based on his reported life. Later made into a movie, the myths surrounding Beiderbecke continued unabated in articles, memoirs, and biographies. Ultimately, alcohol problems did catch up with Beiderbecke, but otherwise he was content with his music. Playing with Jean Goldkette and Paul Whiteman, Beiderbecke was allowed the musical freedom to be himself and contributed breathtaking solos. Moreover, while he did experiment with classical music, his compositions and his playing clearly reflect his interests in popular music.

Born March 10, 1903, in Davenport, Iowa, to an upper-middle class family, Beiderbecke demonstrated a talent for music at a young age with his keen ears, learning to play piano a little. A turning point came in 1918 when his older brother Charles came back from the service and brought a new phonograph and some records, including one by the ODJB, and the younger Beiderbecke was intrigued by this new music. He taught himself cornet, learning the songs from the 78 and developing unique fingerings that contributed to his famous sound.

In 1921, Beiderbecke was sent to the Lake Forest Academy in Illinois. By this time, jazz became the focus of his life, and he took every opportunity to play, neglecting his studies. His obsession with jazz worried his parents who strongly disapproved of his interest, hoping that the academy would improve Beiderbecke's academic performance. But the school brought Beiderbecke closer to Chicago where he often went to hear live jazz: either at the Friar's Inn to hear the NORK, or to the Sunset Cafe on the city's South Side where he heard African American groups like King Oliver's Creole Jazz Band. Around this time, Beiderbecke heard Emmett Hardy (1903–1925), a white cornetist who played in the two-cornet edition of the NORK and is said to have had a great influence on Beiderbecke's sound. As word spread of his talent, Beiderbecke began to meet musicians with whom he would later collaborate, including a young pianist and composer, Hoagy Carmichael (1899–1981), the future composer of such jazz standards as "Georgia," "Stardust," "The Nearness of You," and "Heart And Soul." The late nights he spent at jazz clubs had an impact on his schoolwork, and he was continually late for the school's curfew. It was during this time as well that Beiderbecke developed a taste for alcohol that would be his downfall. After a year, he was expelled from the school.

THE WOLVERINES

At the end of 1923, Beiderbecke joined two old friends from the academy for a gig at the Stockton Club in Ohio. Soon they became known as the Wolverines, basing their sound on the New Orleans Rhythm Kings. A New Year's brawl brought an end to the engagement, and the group began working in Cincinnati at Doyle's Dancing Academy. Their popularity attracted the attention of Gennett Records, and in February 1924, the group recorded, starting with songs associated with the ODJB, "Fidgety Feet" and "Jazz Me Blues," featuring Beiderbecke's first playing on record. Even on the primitive recording equipment, he is clearly heard through the ensemble sections, and his sound is already striking. His first solo on "Jazz Me Blues" already highlights his tendency towards harmonic color. It has been suggested that this aspect of his playing stems not only from his background in piano but from the influence of clarinetists such as Larry Shields from the ODJB and Leon Roppolo from the NORK. Reportedly one of the few white musicians to be allowed to sit in with King Oliver's band, Beiderbecke's musical conception also owes much to Oliver and other African American musicians.

The Wolverines also played for dances at Indiana University, and in May and June, the group recorded seven more selections. The ODJB and NORK standards "Tiger Rag" and "Royal Garden Blues" highlight the band's energy, while "Riverboat Shuffle," the first song penned by Carmichael to appear on record, features a spectacular Beiderbecke solo. In the fall of 1924, the group went to play in New York, and recordings from this time indicate how much Beiderbecke had improved in his playing, even while the rest of the band sounded the same. He plays confidently with a crisper sound and stronger phrases on "I Need Some Pettin'" and "Big Boy," which is also notable for featuring his first recorded piano solo. However, despite being the Wolverine's star soloist, he resigned from the band in October 1924 and prepared to join Jean Goldkette's group.

On October 10, Beiderbecke participated in a recording session where he met C-melody saxophonist Frankie Trumbauer (1901–1956). Trumbauer, whose nickname was "Tram," was born and raised in St. Louis and was a great musical counterpart to Beiderbecke, possessing a whimsical melodic sense that complements Beiderbecke's light, airy sound. He was one of the first saxophonists to dispense with the popular slap-tongue technique in favor of a smooth, legato one. He already displayed this style on his first recordings from 1923 with the Benson Orchestra. On "I Miss the

Sunshine," from June 14, his unique sound is easily discernible during the ensemble sections, and his solo was widely copied by saxophonists both black and white.[5] In spite of his choppy rhythms, Trumbauer is otherwise understated, playing with a light vibrato and taking his time while leaving a lot of space, all uncharacteristic of jazz musicians in 1923.

Still, Trumbauer had a wide musical conception and was prone to novelty sounds as well. "Trumbology" from 1927 is his answer to Rudy Wiedoft, a popular novelty saxophonist of the era who specialized in double-tonguing resulting in absurdly fast, staccato passages. Trumbauer even experimented with the bassoon, taking a few forgettable solos on record. However, his work with Beiderbecke rubbed off on him considerably as he began to play in a more legato style, emphasizing his airy sound. Although he was overshadowed by Beiderbecke, he was ultimately a pioneer on his instrument who would have a profound effect on Lester Young who adapted Trumbauer's style to the tenor saxophone.

Unfortunately, Beiderbecke's inability to read music adequately led to a failed audition with Goldkette, who, nevertheless, kept him close, providing him with work as he freelanced in New York—where he met Red Nichols—and Michigan, and played in St. Louis with Trumbauer's group at the Arcadia into 1926. By May, Beiderbecke was back as a permanent member of the Goldkette orchestra.

Jean Goldkette

By the 1920s, Detroit established itself as an important training ground for dance bands largely due to the successful enterprise established by pianist, bandleader, and entrepreneur Jean Goldkette (1892/99–1962). A Frenchman born in Greece and raised in Moscow, Goldkette came to the United States in 1911 and found himself in the dance band business in Chicago, He ended up in Detroit and by the mid-1920s had stopped playing piano and focused on management, expanding his business from contracting dance bands to part- or full-ownership of the top ballrooms in Detroit as well as others located as far away as Chicago, Kansas City, and Toronto.[6] Through a partial monopoly on the band business in Detroit, he fostered a number of groups, many of whom would become the most popular dance bands of the era including his own group, McKinney's Cotton Pickers, and Glen Gray's Orange Blossoms later known as the Casa Loma Orchestra.

Goldkette's early recordings from 1924 already boasted a strong group, but the addition of Beiderbecke and Trumbauer provided the basis for his best group, which also featured Danny Polo on clarinet, Eddie Lang on guitar, and Steve Brown on bass. The group entered the studio in October 1926, and while Beiderbecke rarely solos at length, his presence in the band was still strong. This was largely due to the work of arranger Bill Challis (1904–1994) who crafted his charts around Beiderbecke, allowing him to improvise freely around the arrangements, in the process elevating such performances as "I'm Looking over a Four-Leaf Clover," "I'm Gonna Meet My Sweetie Now," and "Clementine." Born in Wilkes-Barre, Pennsylvania, Challis learned violin before becoming a C-melody saxophonist in his childhood. He began his arranging career writing arrangements for his campus band at Bucknell University. In 1926, he submitted arrangements to Goldkette and was hired as staff arranger. "Sunday," "Hoosier Sweetheart," and "Proud of a Baby Like You" are some of his finest arrangements as he deftly combines sweet and hot passages.

Listening Guide: "Clementine" by the Jean Goldkette Orchestra
Bix Beiderbecke: cornet; Fred Farrar and Ray Lodwig: trumpets; Don Murray, Doc Ryker, and Frankie Trumbauer: reeds; Bill Rank and Lloyd Turner: trombones; Joe Venuti: violin; Irving Riskin: piano; Eddie Lang: guitar; Howdy Quicksell: banjo; Steve Brown: bass; Chauncey Morehouse: drums. Victor 20994-B. Recorded September 15, 1927, in New York.

Time	Section	Comments
0:00	Introduction	Melody played by clarinets and trombone.
0:11	Chorus 1 (AABA)	AA: Brass theme with responses from hi-hat and/or cornet.
0:33		B: Trombone solo by Bill Rank.
0:44		A: Brass theme resumes and ends with saxophone soli.
0:55	Interlude (sixteen bars)	New theme by the full ensemble with solo breaks for guitar (at 0:58 and 1:03).
1:17	Chorus 2 (AABA)	Melody played by the saxophone section led by Frankie Trumbauer with hi-hat fills.
2:00	Chorus 3 (AABA)	AA: Cornet solo by Bix Beiderbecke (with brass backgrounds).
2:22		B: Violin solo by Joe Venuti ending with a two-bar break.
2:32		A: Beiderbecke's solo resumes and ends with a guitar break.
2:43	Final theme (A)	A: Full ensemble.
2:51	Coda	

"Clementine" is one of the two "hot" jazz songs recorded by Gold-kette with solos from Rank, Venuti, Lang, and Beiderbecke, his longest recorded solo with the band. His playing is superb as his infectious swing feel permeates the entire performance. During ensemble sections, he is let loose, freely playing fills during the opening statement and dominating overall with his distinctive sound. Trumbauer is unmistakable as well during the reeds feature, an early saxophone solo by Challis, a sound he helped pioneer.

That "Clementine" swings is also due to one of the strongest and cohesive rhythm section teams of the era with Chauncey Morehouse on drums (formerly of the OM5), Steve Brown on bass, and Eddie Lang on guitar. The support is strong with Brown's full, round sound and Eddie Lang's acoustic guitar playing quarter notes. Morehouse's parts are not audible, but his featured hi-hat fills swing and are indicative of his time feel. Their collective sound anticipates upcoming changes in the jazz rhythm section.

"Singin' the Blues"

1927 was a busy year for Beiderbecke, and he recorded some of his best work, often under Trumbauer's name, churning out brilliant solos that include his most revered performances that cemented his legacy. "Singin' the Blues," recorded on February 4, 1927, is a landmark recording in the history of jazz with superb solos by Trumbauer and Beiderbecke. Overall, the performance is tidy with the band in the background during the solos except for guitarist Eddie Lang's wonderous fills. Beiderbecke's solo is simply astounding, demonstrating how eloquent a musician he was. Despite being only twenty-three years old at the time of the recording, it features his "mature" style relying on note choice, phrase development, and his sound to carry his solo, while establishing a lyrical approach to jazz improvisation that allowed for introspection and thoughtfulness. His characteristic rip, heard twice, is also discernible and was mimicked by his admirers. Trumbauer's solo is excellent, and although his approach to the chords is overall more traditional, his whimsical phrasing and light tone complement Beiderbecke's own solo.

"Singin' the Blues" also established the popularity of the jazz ballad in a "hot" jazz context. During this era, slow songs were not often played and, if played, would have been almost always a blues, Louis Armstrong's

"West End Blues" being one example. Additionally, "Singin' the Blues" is a popular, sweet song, and such songs were often played to dramatic effect, with their sentimental moods augmented with strings and "sweet" orchestrations. Here, the group's performance maintains the sweet, sentimental nature of the song without sacrificing any authentic jazz feeling, particularly during the solos.

Listening Guide: "Singin' the Blues" by Frankie Trumbauer and His Orchestra
Bix Beiderbecke: cornet; Frankie Trumbauer: C-melody saxophone; Jimmy Dorsey: clarinet, alto saxophone; Bill Rank: trombone; Paul Mertz: piano; Eddie Lang: guitar; Chauncey Morehouse: drums. Okeh 40772. Recorded February 4, 1927, in New York.

Time	Section	Comments
0:00	Introduction	
0:07	AB	C-melody saxophone solo by Frankie Trumbauer with accompaniment by Eddie Lang.
0:35	AC	Trumbauer's solo continues, preceded by a short break at the end of the previous section.
1:03	AB	Cornet solo by Bix Beiderbecke.
1:31	AC	Beiderbecke's solo continues, preceded by a short break at the end of the previous section.
2:00	A	Collective improvisation.
2:15	B	Clarinet solo by Jimmy Dorsey.
2:29	AC	Collective improvisation led by Beiderbecke.

Originally recorded by the ODJB in 1920, Beiderbecke's version of "Singin' the Blues" is considered definitive and was extremely well received. Benny Carter's arrangement for Fletcher Henderson was recorded twice in 1931. Carter orchestrated the entire performance including Trumbauer's solo scored for three reeds with trumpeter Rex Stewart interpreting Beiderbecke's solo. It was a cover version, an anomaly in jazz, with all the details of the original recording accounted for including Lang's guitar fills and a rare instance of African American musicians openly acknowledging the influence of white musicians. Another stunning tribute is vaudeville singer Marion Harris's 1934 cover, wherein she anticipates vocalese by adding lyrics to Trumbauer's and Beiderbecke's solos. She reverses the order of solos and loosely interprets them, but the performance is unprecedented.

The next Trumbauer session on May 13, with largely the same musicians, produced more classics. "I'm Coming Virginia" is a superior ballad performance that is easily the equal to "Singin' the Blues" with Lang's fills and Beiderbecke producing one of his most moving solos. "Way Down Yonder in New Orleans," reminiscent of the Goldkette sound, features one of Trumbauer's loveliest solos. Improvising off the melody, his playing is calm, dreamy, and light, with his sound predating alto saxophonist Paul Desmond. Beiderbecke comes next, and while he too bases his solo off the melody, he is far more assertive rhythmically, swinging harder and inspiring the rhythm section to "dig" into the rhythm. "Riverboat Shuffle" is a significant improvement from the Wolverine's version with Beiderbecke leading the way in a stunning performance. His solo is remarkable with an entirely unique conception of phrase structure, melodic sense, and breaks that grabs the listener with impressive feats of musicality and not virtuosity.

In early September, Beiderbecke entered the studio to record his own composition on piano, "In a Mist." Beiderbecke's piano work is an important aspect of his recorded legacy. Strong enough to record with the Wolverines and on a trio number with Trumbauer and Lang called "No Reason at All in C," he was Lang and Venuti's choice of pianist in October 1926, a session that was never released.[7] "In a Mist" caused a sensation as few musicians of the era could double on another instrument at that level. His interest in harmony and admiration for French Impressionist composers is quite evident based on his voicings: fourth structures, parallel seventh and ninth chords, and whole tone scales that also hint as his influences on cornet. It was one of four published solo piano compositions that include "Candlelights," "Flashes," and "In the Dark," all notated and transcribed by Challis.

In the fall of 1927, Beiderbecke began to rehearse with bass saxophonist Adrian Rollini's band at the Club New Yorker. Consisting of his bandmates from Goldkette including Beiderbecke, Trumbauer, Rank, Venuti, Lang, and Morehouse, it was a musician's band, and the group recorded under Trumbauer's name. Two of the three songs recorded on September 28 are among the best examples of progressive late 1920s jazz. "Krazy Kat," by Trumbauer and Morehouse, is meticulously arranged with sudden textural changes, unusual themes, and unexpected harmonies, but "Humpty Dumpty," written and arranged by reeds player Fud Livingston, is even more daring, bordering on experimental. His work with Red Nichols, notably "Imagination," had already established him as an adventurous writer, and he is harmonically driven with chords that are sometimes dissonant, chromatic, and often unexpected. Unusual for the era, it is a serious piece of music with an unusual form and a carefully crafted arrangement with short piano interludes, played by Frank Signorelli, and solos by Trumbauer, Venuti, and Beiderbecke. Unfortunately, Livingston never continued the path he started, but his work certainly predates other jazz movements by decades. Rollini's engagement at the Club New Yorker was short lived, however, and Beiderbecke and Trumbauer soon accepted an offer to join Paul Whiteman's Orchestra.

PAUL WHITEMAN

Since Whiteman's successful 1924 Aeolian concert, his orchestra had toured cross-country nonstop and had grown larger with more strings, brass, and vocalists, but Whiteman wanted to augment his jazz content. Unable to hire African American musicians in his band, he instead resorted to hiring the best white musicians, and he turned his attention towards Jean Goldkette's Orchestra, whose recent win in a "battle of the bands" against Fletcher Henderson at the Roseland Ballroom had spread quickly. When Goldkette disbanded in the summer of 1927, Whiteman slowly hired his musicians, and the impact was immediate, especially when Beiderbecke and Trumbauer joined. The band also included former Goldkette musicians Jimmy and Tommy Dorsey as well as Challis, who was given the freedom to write music based on the new instrumentalists' strength. The old guard of the Whiteman orchestra, led by longtime trumpeter Henry Busse, did not take kindly to the new "hot" jazz musicians, and though there was tension, Beiderbecke's impact on Whiteman's material is remarkable.

Beiderbecke dominates Challis's chart for "San" from January 12, 1928. Scored for only ten musicians, it is an atypical Whiteman jazz chart and is a considerable improvement from the orchestra's 1924 recording with a wide variety in textures, solo and collective improvisation, and two ensemble passages. The written sections are highly syncopated but well played and, most importantly, swing. Challis's writing is ahead of its time, but would not have worked without Beiderbecke's feel and sound.

Other Beiderbecke highlights from the Whiteman oeuvre include his solo on "Dardanella," where, accompanied by Brown's slap-bass playing, he abruptly changes the mood and relaxes the band's feel. Beider-becke takes charge on Malneck's arrangement of "From Monday On." Following an introduction from the vocal trio, he lets out a sudden rip, or Chicagoan explosion-type idea, into his solo, later leading the closing full ensemble statement. Challis's arrangement of "Sweet Sue (Just You)" from 1929 begins with three minutes of light symphonic gestures and a horrifyingly out-of-date "sweet" vocal, sung falsetto, before the listener is treated to a gem of a solo by Beiderbecke accompanied by the rhythm section. Coming out of nowhere and transforming the performance, he swings hard playing into a mute and paraphrases the melody. The solo is a perfect example of how modern he really was.

However, for all his artistry, Beiderbecke's alcoholism was catching up to him, and he left Whiteman's band in late 1929 after a series of breakdowns. Despite spending time with his family in Iowa and undergoing treatment, he continued to drink as his health deteriorated. Beiderbecke shuttled back and forth between Davenport, Iowa, and New York, where he died on August 6, 1931.

Chapter 10

Other Pioneering Soloists

The full story of the early jazz era would not be complete without an overview of important musicians by instrument. Influential cornetists and trumpeters are outlined in the King Oliver, Louis Armstrong, and Bix Beiderbecke chapters (chapters 4, 8, and 9) while pianists are discussed in context of stride piano (chapter 6), the work of Earl Hines (chapter 8), and Mary Lou Williams (chapter 11).

Clarinetists

The clarinet was a dominant instrument in the early jazz era, and its greatest practitioners have had a lasting influence, beginning with the great Tio family of clarinetists, Lorenzo Tio Sr. (1867–1922), his brother, Louis "Papa" Tio (1862–1922), and his son Lorenzo Tio Jr. (1893–1933). They preferred the thirteen-keyed Albert system, a simpler mechanism than the seventeen-keyed Boehm system that has since become standard, while producing musicians with a solid foundation in music theory and solfege. Tio Jr. played in the Excelsior and Olympia Brass Bands, and his warm and exquisite clarinet work can be heard on "Louisiana Swing" and "Bright Star," recorded with Armand J. Piron from 1923. Collectively, the Tio family's pupils include Sidney Bechet, George and Achille Baquet, Charles Elgar, Alphonse Picou, Omer Simeon, Barney Bigard, Louis Cottrell Jr., Albert Nichols, Jimmie Noone, and Darnell Howard.

Perhaps the greatest New Orleans clarinetist during the early jazz era was Johnny Dodds (1892–1940). Born and raised in New Orleans, he was largely self-taught and learned to play by watching others including his idol, Sidney Bechet. Early work included time on the Streckfus riverboats with one of Fate Marable's legendary bands with his younger brother, Baby, on drums; Pops Foster; and Louis Armstrong, before moving to Chicago in 1920, when he replaced Jimmie Noone in King Oliver's band. He developed into a fundamentally blues player with a growling tone and a distinctive vibrato. After leaving Oliver in early 1924, Dodds freelanced, heavily recording with Freddie Keppard, Tiny Parnham, Lil Hardin Armstrong, Jelly Roll Morton, and most famously with Louis Armstrong's Hot Five and Hot Seven. He was also flexible enough to record with down-home blues musicians, including guitarist Blind Blake and the Dixieland Jug Blowers. The latter's "House Rent Rag" mixes city and country aesthetics with an unusual instrumentation of violin, clarinet, alto saxophone, banjo, and jugs that predates the work of the Harlem Hamfats.

Dodds also had a long run at the mob-run Burt Kelly's Stables and led his own record dates, including a number of washboard bands, popularized by Jasper Taylor in 1925. "The Blues Stampede" is a particular highlight that also features washboard player Jimmy Bertrand, the barrel-house Chicago pianist Jimmy Blythe, and Armstrong on cornet. Dodds's session from July 6, 1928, features four songs—"Bucktown Town Stomp," "Weary City," "Bull Fiddle Blues," and "Blue Washboard Stomp"—whose cohesiveness in form and feeling have led many to consider the pieces as part of a four-movement suite.[1] The tracks also feature excellent playing by Natty Dominique on cornet, Honoré Dutrey on trombone, and Bill Johnson on bass.

Compared to Dodds, Jimmie Noone (1895–1944) was a far more refined clarinetist, with strong technique, advanced command of his instrument, and a cleaner sound. He too was a descendant of the Tio school, but his style evolved due to his later formal studies with Frank Schoepp, who also taught Benny Goodman and Buster Bailey. Having played with King Oliver's Creole Jazz Band, appearing on four recordings from 1923, Noone's greatest work was with his own band during his engagement at the Apex Club.

The group's front line featured only clarinet and alto saxophone with the great Earl Hines on piano allowing him to be the third voice, but Noone's dazzling playing negated any need for another horn. "Apex Blues," from the group's famed 1928 recordings, showcases his smooth tone as he moves with ease around his instrument. He is more aggressive on faster numbers like "My Monday Date" or "I Know That You Know," which showcase his fluid technique. Yet, despite his dexterity, Noone maintains an affinity for the blues and the New Orleans tradition. Unfortunately, his work has been overshadowed by others as his playing looks ahead to the future, foreshadowing Benny Goodman and even Artie Shaw. With the presence of Hines, another modernist in the group, Noone's music ultimately defines a transitional period in jazz falling somewhere between New Orleans and the Swing Era.

Omer Simeon (1902–1959) was a journeyman clarinetist who was a good improviser and a solid section man. He played on a number of important early jazz recordings with Jelly Roll Morton's Red Hot Peppers in 1926 and King Oliver's Dixie Syncopators in 1927. He was a strong improviser as well, recorded in a trio setting on his own and with Morton on "Shreveport Stomp" from 1928, showcasing his high and low registers on two solos. Later during the Swing Era, he was flexible enough to adopt the alto saxophone in the big bands of Earl Hines, Horace Henderson, and Jimmie Lunceford.

"Gaspipe" Clarinet

Novelty, or hokum, sounds were extremely popular and prevailed among white and African American musicians during the early jazz era. Examples included muted brass with plungers, novelty instruments such as the slide whistle, the comb, or the washboard, and clarinetists who specialized in playing squeaks, honks, growls, and other unusual sounds. They were known as "gaspipe" clarinetists, due to the resemblance to the squeal of a leaking gas pipe.[2] Some of the more extreme techniques include slap-tongue (a "popping" sound caused by pulling the reed away from the mouthpiece), exaggerated growls on the low notes, laughing sounds, and playing only with the mouthpiece; some were also good improvisers. Gaspipe clarinetists were popular in traveling shows and vaudeville, and there was a wide variety within this specialized genre including George McClennon, Wilton Crawley, Ted Lewis, Fess Williams, and Wilbur Sweatman, although Johnny Dodds, Jimmy O'Bryant, and Larry Shields also used the technique.

George McClennon (1890/91–1937), the adoptive son of Bert Williams, specialized in laughing sounds and danced while he played. Wilton Crawley (1900–1967), who doubled as a contortionist, might be among the best known having recorded two songs with Henry "Red" Allen, Jelly

Roll Morton, Teddy Bunn, and "Pops" Foster. On "New Crawley Blues," Crawley takes two solos. The first shows off his blues skill in a more traditional manner, while his second solo, played without a mouthpiece, features abrupt laughing-like sounds.

However, the most famous gaspipe clarinetist was Ted Lewis (1890–1971) who was a major star in the 1920s. Born in Ohio, Lewis, who was Jewish, was a star attraction in circuses and vaudeville before coming to prominence with Earl Fuller's Jazz Band in the late 1910s. Known for playing repeated trills, he was signed to Columbia Records as a solo act in 1918 and emerged as a star. Donning a black suit, top hat, and cane, and emphasizing his comic-like vocals, he gradually deemphasized his clarinet playing in favor of singing and became a superstar known as "Mr. Entertainment" singing his most famous song "Is Everyone Happy?"

His music was stiff, but he typically employed hot jazz soloists. Highlights include "Shim-me-sha-wabble" from 1928, with excellent solos by George Brunies on trombone and Don Murray on clarinet, and "Farewell Blues," which begins with train effects before featuring Muggsy Spanier on trumpet and Frankie Teschemacher on clarinet. "San" from 1930 begins as an excellent example of "hot" jazz with excellent solos by Spanier before ending up in slapstick territory with Lewis's gaspipe clarinet solo, his duet with a comb player, and the "doo-wacka-doo" ending.

Stanley "Fess" Williams (1894–1975) was probably the most interesting gaspipe clarinetist. "Here 'Tis" and "Friction" demonstrate how creative he could be in getting a wide range of timbres on his clarinet, playing only the mouthpiece, staying in the low or high register of his instrument, or using slap-tongue; Williams also applied such tactics to the saxophone. His saxophone solos on "Playing My Saxophone" are especially wild and climax with circular breathing before ending in the altissimo register. In addition to such advanced techniques, his thrusting rhythms and asymmetrical phrasing borders on outright free jazz and foreshadows Ornette Coleman, Eric Dolphy, and other free jazz saxophonists of the 1960s. Known as the black Ted Lewis, even wearing a top hat, Williams was quite the showman; a publicity photo shows him playing the clarinet like a guitar, and he was for a time a draw in Chicago and New York.

Clarinetist Wilbur Sweatman (1882–1961) was an important transitional figure between ragtime and jazz. However, his music does not fit neatly into either category and is shaped by his experiences in tent shows, minstrel shows, and vaudeville where he was a star attraction during the 1910s and 1920s, specializing in playing three clarinets at the same time.

He was also a composer, and "Down Home Rag" from 1911 is one of his best-known compositions. However, his 1916 recording marks Sweatman as the first African American to record jazz.

Born in Brunswick, Missouri, in 1882 to a middle-class family, he worked under some of the most important African American bandleaders of his day including Major Nathaniel Clark Smith in a youth band, Perry G. Lowery in the circus, and W. C. Handy in the most popular African American minstrel show, Mahara's Minstrels. Afterwards, Sweatman lived in Minnesota for a few years leading his own groups and where he reportedly made a cylinder wax recording of "Maple Leaf Rag" in 1903 that has been lost. He then moved to Chicago in 1908 where he gained attention for his "moaning" clarinet playing.[3] In 1911, Sweatman started publishing his own rags, but he left Chicago to tour on the vaudeville circuit, where he became known for his solo three-clarinet performances. His arrangement of "The Rosary," a lovely, popular song from the turn of the century would be echoed in Roland Rahsaan Kirk's tender three-saxophone rendition of his own composition "The Inflated Tear" from the 1960s.

In December 1916, Sweatman made his first recordings. "Down Home Rag" was one of two songs recorded and is perhaps the best example of a secondary rag, a repeated three note figure against a duple meter. He decorates the melody liberally with blues gestures and accents, and though he may be improvising, the group playing behind him is not. On record, Sweatman's gaspipe playing seems toned down, and while his sound is rather shrill at times, often awash with a thick vibrato, his playing is more animated than anything else. New currents in music revolving around Art Hickman and Paul Whiteman led to his release from Columbia, but he remained active on the vaudeville circuit until the 1930s, recording sporadically.

Novel sounds and instruments were initially played by musicians to help them stand out. But, with the notable exception of muted brass with plungers, the practice has been long extinguished from jazz performance. But the notion of an identifiable sound remained and continued through the swing era, bebop, and hard bop.

Saxophone

The saxophone was a staple instrument in vaudeville, circuses, and ragtime and was later adopted by dance bands, starting with Art Hickman.

Although the clarinet held forth during the early jazz years, the saxophone became increasingly prominent; the era's notable saxophonists already discussed include Sidney Bechet on soprano (chapter 8), Frankie Trumbauer on C-melody (chapter 9), Johnny Hodges (chapter 7) and Jimmy Dorsey (chapter 5) on alto, Harry Carney on baritone (chapter 7), and Adrian Rollini on bass saxophone (chapter 5).

Alto saxophonist Loren McMurray (1897–1922) was an early innovator on the instrument. Born in Kansas, he learned the saxophone playing in his father's saxophone band. After establishing himself in Kansas City with the Kuhn-Chaquette Orchestra, he moved to New York where he worked with bandleader and contractor Sam Lanin. McMurray appears on several recordings by Kuhn, Lanin, and the Original Memphis Five, but his best recording is his own "Haunting Blues" from June 1922. He is featured on two choruses, the first is a bluesy rendition of the melody, but the second is a solo beginning with stop-time breaks. His sound is full and light, and his phrasing is smooth with a sophisticated sense of rhythm and melody with hemiola figures and chromatic gestures. The cornet and trombone return at the bridge, but McMurray keeps going, playing through the break at the end. His solo conception is advanced for 1922, but unfortunately he passed away suddenly that October of blood poisoning.

Coleman Hawkins (1904–1969) was a dominant voice on the tenor saxophone during the 1920s. As the Fletcher Henderson Orchestra's star soloist, he helped establish the tenor saxophone in the big band and its dominance in jazz for decades to come. Hawkins was born in Missouri to a middle-class family and attended high school in Chicago and in Topeka, Kansas. He was gigging by the time he was twelve years old, having already learned piano, cello, and the clarinet before settling on the tenor saxophone. Playing in school bands he attended college in Topeka for two years studying composition and harmony and went out on the road in 1922 with Mamie Smith and Her Jazz Hounds. In June 1923, Hawkins ended up in New York where he recorded with Henderson. His solo on "Dicty Blues" demonstrates what an enormous sound he already possessed although his phrasing was unsure and he still relied on the then-popular "slap-tongue" technique.

Louis Armstrong's brief tenure with Henderson left a tremendous impact on the band, and Hawkins's playing changed as he began to develop a smoother sound. In 1926, he heard sixteen-year-old Art Tatum in Toledo, Ohio, whose harmonic approach also had a lasting effect on

Hawkins. "Stampede," from 1926, shows how far he had come with a tough, deep, muscular sound on the tenor saxophone that would become standard for the instrument. His technique had improved, allowing him to outline harmonies, a device he would later elaborate on. As the star tenor saxophone player in Henderson's band, many bands followed suit and made sure they too had a star tenor saxophone player who played like Hawkins.

"One Hour" from a 1929 recording session with Red McKenzie's Mound City Blue Blowers features a landmark solo by Hawkins. Despite the novel sounds of McKenzie's comb, Hawkins sounds like the future having mastered a legato or smooth sound that allowed for an expressive and mature performance. His vocal-like approach is punctuated by wide articulations, a perfected vibrato, and articulations that fed his sophisticated sense of phrasing. It was the first entry in Hawkins's ballad trilogy that would continue with another brilliant solo on 1933's "It's the Talk of the Town" by Fletcher Henderson and that would culminate with his classic performance on "Body and Soul" from 1939, a solo that displays his utter mastery of the instrument and an advanced harmonic approach that foreshadowed bebop.

Trombone

The slide trombone has been a part of early jazz bands since the turn of the century brass bands in New Orleans. Playing "tailgate" trombone, the best early trombonists include Vic Gaspard, Buddy Johnson, Frankie Duson, and Alvin "Zue" Robertson (1891–1943). A member of the Excelsior and Onward brass bands, Robertson spent most of his career in circuses and tent shows. He later recorded with Jelly Roll Morton in 1923, but the best known New Orleans trombonist was Edward "Kid" Ory (1886–1973).[4] He led the top New Orleans band in the 1910s, whose members included Johnny Dodds, King Oliver, and Louis Armstrong. Ory relocated to Los Angeles in 1919 where he made the first jazz recording by an African American in 1922. In the mid-1920s, Ory moved to Chicago joining King Oliver's Dixie Syncopators and later recording with Louis Armstrong's Hot Five and Jelly Roll Morton's Red Hot Peppers. Although not the most technically proficient, Ory was perhaps the most expressive of the tailgate trombonists with a rhythmic style and extensive use of slides.

A step forward in jazz trombone can be heard in the work of Miff Mole (1898–1961) and Jimmy Harrison (1900–1931), who represent opposite sides of the development of the instrument. Originally from New York, Irving Milfred Mole (1898–1961) was known for his technical contributions to the trombone. He was active in New York in the early 1920s playing and recording with the Original Memphis Five before working with Red Nichols, with whom he is most associated. His advanced technique allowed him to construct lines on trombone, and he played them well with good intonation, range, and sound. Harrison, on the other hand, was the first to adapt the language of Louis Armstrong on the trombone. His concept, "to swing it like a trumpet" is heard on his solo and break from Fletcher Henderson's "Hop Off" from November 4, 1927.[5] His solo on Charlie Johnson's "Walk That Thing" from 1928 is aggressive and even more impressive with off-beat syncopations and a wide range.

While Harrison was considered the "Father of Swing Trombone," his playing developed even further after meeting trombonist, Jack Teagarden (1905–1964), the most accomplished of the early jazz trombonists. Teagarden was also a fantastic singer and bandleader who became a star later in his career. His arrival in New York in 1927 shocked trombonists as he usurped Mole's dominance of the instrument with his blues-based sound and his smooth, legato delivery aided by his use of the lip to execute fast passages while still sounding relaxed.[6] Teagarden was born in Vernon, Texas, just south of the Oklahoma border where he was in contact with African Americans and a culture of folk songs and the blues. Taking up trombone, he played throughout the Southwest, making frequent trips to Mississippi and Louisiana, where he learned New Orleans music. Along the way he heard Armstrong, who heavily impacted Teagarden's approach.

When Teagarden finally made it to New York in 1928, his playing impressed everyone, and he went to work right away playing in the large dance bands of Ben Pollack and Roger Wolfe Kahn. His solo on Kahn's "She's a Great, Great Girl," one of his earliest, is on the technical skill level of Mole but is far more expressive with a broad blues vocabulary. By 1929, he was in demand, appearing in over one hundred recordings, many with Red Nichols, swinging hard on "Indiana" and playing chromatic lines on "Rose of Washington Square." "After You've Gone" also features his singing and his "natural tendency to transform popular songs into the blues."[7] His voice is deep, rich, and expressive, and he already sounds world-weary though he is only in his early twenties. Blues also punctuates his trombone solo on Louis Armstrong's "Knockin' a Jug" from March 5, 1929, with natural behind-the-beat phrasing and calculated use of space.

Banjo, Guitar, and Eddie Lang

During the early jazz era, the banjo was the dominant stringed chordal instrument in popular jazz and dance orchestras before being usurped by the guitar. However, though it played a primarily accompaniment role, the banjo was at the time among the most popular of instruments. An instrument of African origin, it was largely introduced to a broader audience in minstrel shows from the 1840s with the banjoist accompanying singers. By the end of the nineteenth century, the banjo enjoyed a renaissance with banjo orchestras, banjo clubs at top universities, and transcriptions of the latest marches and rags adapted for banjo. Moreover, the instrument was especially popular among the elite, thanks to the marketing scheme of banjo maker Samuel Swain Stewart who wished to elevate the instrument's status by deemphasizing the instrument's origins with enslaved people.

The first ragtime songs were recorded with banjo accompaniment, often played by Vess Ossman (1868–1923). Later on, Fred Van Eps (1878–1960) recorded ragtime songs on banjo. At the time, the five-string banjo was the standard instrument and usually fingerpicked. But the new four-string variant, known as the tenor banjo, became the favored instrument in emerging popular jazz and dance orchestras of the day. There were virtuoso banjoists, like Harry Reser, but otherwise, banjo was strictly a rhythm instrument, playing chords on the beat. Typically played with a plectrum (or flatpick), it was louder and better suited for the new dances which required faster tempos. Amongst the best-known banjoists were Chicagoan Eddie Condon, Fred Guy with Duke Ellington, and Johnny St. Cyr, known to play a six-string banjo, who played on recordings by Armstrong's Hot Five and Jelly Roll Morton.

During the mid- to late 1920s, the acoustic guitar began to assert itself into the jazz ensemble largely through the pioneering efforts of Eddie Lang (1902–1933). While he played strong solos and had fluid technique, Lang preferred the background and was a great accompanist with excellent time, a deep understanding of harmony, and superb knowledge of his instrument. He brought the acoustic guitar to the forefront with his excellent musicianship and technique, but also by taking advantage of the microphone to amplify his sound. An extremely versatile musician, he was well suited to studio work, playing and recording with jazz groups, dance orchestras, radio commercial bands, hillbilly singers, crooners, and novelty acts during a remarkably prolific and short career.

Lang had a precedent with other pioneering acoustic guitarists especially Nick Lucas (1897–1982) and his astonishing 1922 record "Picking the Guitar" and "Teasing the Frets." The titles indicate novelties, but Lucas's single note dexterity is remarkable as is his knowledge of harmony on the guitar. The seeds of Lang's style can be heard as Lucas plays bass notes, chords, and melodies. "Picking the Guitar" even features arpeggiated chords that would be a staple of Lang's work. Lucas continued his work as a session guitarist but, on record, he never played anything again like his solo work from 1922, and instead he became a pop singer in the late 1920s. In his place, Lang applied Lucas's work in a jazz context.

Born in Philadelphia as Salvatore Massaro, Lang studied violin for eleven years before adopting first the mandolin, the banjo, and then the guitar, his father having been a fretted instrument maker in Italy. He became friends with violinist Joe Venuti in school, and they began a long-lasting musical partnership. At some point, he became "Eddie Lang," and he made his first recordings on banjo with Charlie Kerr's Orchestra in March 1923. The following year he was on the road with the Scranton Sirens, a band that at different times included the Dorsey brothers, Bill Challis, and Russ Morgan, before joining Red McKenzie and his Mound City Blue Blowers, a novelty band, in late 1924.

Formed in St. Louis by vocalist and entrepreneur McKenzie on comb, Dick Selvin on kazoo, and Jack Bland on banjo, the group scored a major hit in 1924 with "Arkansas Blues" and were a draw in vaudeville and nightclubs. Despite the novel sounds, McKenzie and Selvin were in fact competent. "Deep Second Street Blues" from December 1924 revealed that McKenzie could play slow blues with surprising feeling and authenticity. Lang is also outstanding, showing off his command of the blues. "Morning After Blues," recorded after a two-month long tour of England in 1925, features his most impressive outing on guitar with chord and melody-type accompaniment and a solo introduction that is stunning in its harmonic movement. Later editions of the band featured integrated sessions with Coleman Hawkins, Jimmy Dorsey, Pee Wee Russell, Red Nichols, Adrian Rollini, and others.

In 1926, a job at the Silver Slipper with Venuti in Atlantic City led to the pair's first recordings in September of that year. Soon afterwards, the pair moved to New York and Lang became an in-demand guitarist, playing with popular bands including Jean Goldkette, Roger Wolfe Kahn, and the Ross Gorman Orchestra, who, in addition to Lang, also employed guitarists Tony Coluccio and Dick McDonough. It was through this group that Lang met Red Nichols, and his visibility spread throughout the industry as he became a ubiquitous figure on the studio scene, backing singers, novelty acts of all kinds, and various bands. Lang was a strong presence on Bix Beiderbecke's famous 1927 recordings with the Frankie Trumbauer Orchestra, providing valuable contributions on ballads with his smooth chordal accompaniment and fills on "Singin' the Blues" and "I'm Coming Virginia."

1927 continued to be a busy year for Lang with solo, duo, and trio recordings with Venuti that further showcase his style. Evidence of his classical training and technique abound with his solo adaption of Rach-maninoff's "Prelude (Op. 3, no. 2)," "A Little Love, a Little Kiss," and also on "April Kisses" where Lang revives the "bel canto" sound of Italian classical guitar in the tradition of Giuliani, Carulli, and Carcassi. Duets with Venuti on "Stringing the Blues," "Wild Cat," and "Sunshine" highlight Lang's accompaniment skills as he plays substitute and passing chords, countermelodies including numerous arpeggios, and fills, all of which is underpinned with a strong rhythmic pulse. By doing so, he demonstrates the possibilities of the guitar as a powerful rhythm instrument without the need of piano. Furthermore, as jazz was gravitating towards a 4/4 feel, the gentle sound of the acoustic guitar was preferable over the banjo.

Lang's versatility led to appearances on race records by African Americans Louis Armstrong, King Oliver, Wilton Crawley, Victoria Spivey, Eva Taylor, Bessie Smith, and others, albeit anonymously as white musicians were not supposed to "understand" an African American genre despite Lang's natural affinity for the blues. To improve marketability, Lang was sometimes billed as "Blind Willie Dunn," a reference to the numerous "blind" blues artists, such as Blind Lemon Jefferson or Blind Boy Fuller, implying that Lang was African American. Yet another example of deception by a record company.[8] This pseudonym was even used for his own solo recordings that featured his blues playing, includ-ing "Church Sobbing Blues" and his classic duet recordings with fellow pioneer guitarist Alonzo "Lonnie" Johnson (1894–1971), who also had been exploring the potential of the guitar.

A bluesman at heart, Johnson's accomplishments on guitar allowed the instrument to thrive in a jazz setting. Born in New Orleans and starting on violin before making guitar his primary instrument, Johnson was already not a typical blues artist of the era. His recordings from 1925 focus on his singing, but he was already a fluent guitarist, contributing single note solos and playing strong rhythm. "Away Down in the Alley Blues," a solo instrumental from 1928, is a captivating performance. Combining advanced knowledge of harmony with fluid single-note lines, his language is fundamentally the blues with solid rhythm and an earthy feel. It is perhaps his flexibility that allowed Johnson to work and record with jazz musicians such as Lang, Louis Armstrong, Duke Ellington, and the Chocolate Dandies.

The Lang-Johnson duets from 1929 are landmark recordings. Falling in the jazz-blues category, they are stylistically irrelevant as their influence stretches to all guitar players regardless of style. Johnson is often the featured soloist showing off his creativity and marvelous technique on up-tempo numbers like "Hot Fingers" and "Handful of Riffs," as Lang dazzles in his treasured accompaniment role. But on "Guitar Blues," Lang steps out of the spotlight as the two guitarists trade lines. In retrospect, being ex-violinists, both Lang and Johnson appear to be applying that instrument's techniques on the guitar, in the process contributing to the instrument's development in popular music by providing a performance practice and vocabulary for the instrument.

Sadly, despite high profile gigs with Paul Whiteman, appearing briefly in the 1932 film *The King of Jazz* with Bing Crosby, Lang died suddenly in 1933. Still, as few banjoists made the successful transition to the guitar, Lang dominated his instrument, largely overshadowing his contemporaries Dick McDonough (1904–1938) and Carl Kress (1907–1965) who were also part of the New York scene, playing and recording with many of the same artists. The left-handed McDonough was the more precise player as demonstrated by his playing on the Ross Gorman Orchestra's "I'd Rather be the Girl in Your Arms" and "No More Worryin'." Kress, on the other hand, retained the spirit of the banjo by adapting the perfect fifth tuning on banjo first to the four-string tenor guitar, then the guitar itself, normally tuned in fourths. The new tuning allowed for closer voicings of chords and bass lines with a buoyant chordal style. In addition to working with the Red Nichols and Frankie Trumbauer bands, he also recorded duets with Lang in 1932 and McDonough in 1934.

Other notable acoustic guitarists include African Americans Teddy Bunn (1910–1978) and Eddie Durham (1906–1978). Bunn had a long and distinguished career based in blues and swing. Born in Long Island, New York, he made a splash in 1929 with his work for Duke Ellington. His excellent playing is featured on "Oklahoma Stomp" by the Six Jolly Jesters, an Ellingtonian small group with Greer on washboard, and "Haunted Nights" where he also trades eloquent phrases with clarinetist Barney Bigard. Bunn also recorded with gaspipe clarinetist Wilton Crawley, playing an outstanding solo on "New Crawley Blues" with his blues inflections and back-phrasing, playing behind the beat. Texas-born Durham was a guitarist and trombonist who is best known for helping build the Kansas City sound with his arrangements for Bennie Moten from 1929 through 1932. Overlooked is his excellent guitar playing featuring a broad vocabulary with fluid lines and strong chordal work. He later pioneered the electric guitar by using homemade pickups to amplify his instrument.

Tuba and Double Bass

During the early jazz era, tuba was more visible than the string bass in recordings due to its loud volume allowing it to be heard over the other instruments and its ability to continuously play short quarter notes to establish a two-feel pulse. The string bass was also important as most tubists doubled on that instrument as well: Walter Page, Pops Foster, Steve Brown, Hayes Alvis, Moses Allen, Joe Tarto, and others have appeared on record playing both instruments. Ralph Escudero (1898–1970) with Fletcher Henderson's Orchestra and later McKinney's Cotton Pickers is among the few who only played tuba, providing a solid foundation for Don Redman's sometimes complex charts.

Cyrus St. Clair (1890–1955) was one of the best tubists of the era. A powerful presence in the rhythm section with a rich sound, he helped anchor the bands of Charlie Johnson and Clarence Williams, with whom he often worked. He dominates the groove on Williams's "Freeze Out" from 1929 and even plays a short feature on "Left All Alone with the Blues," beginning in the very low register of his instrument before moving upward. This was a rare moment as tubists were rarely asked to solo or even featured, solely playing a supportive role. Bert Cobb, with King

Oliver's Dixie Syncopators, takes a graceful half-chorus on "Someday Sweetheart" from September 17, 1926, accompanied only by Bud Scott on banjo. Joe Tarto (1902–1986) doubled on tuba and bass and was an in-demand sideman, flexible enough to play from written parts for large dance orchestras and improvise through jazz pieces in small groups. He took short solos occasionally, such as on Miff Mole and the Molers' "Hot Time in The Old Town" and "Darktown Strutters Ball," and Joe Venuti's "I Must Have That Man" that showcase his sound and wonderful sense of phrasing, but like most tubists he was primarily an ensemble player.

Despite limited recording opportunities prior to 1926, the string or double bass has always been present in early New Orleans ensembles as photographic evidence proves, including the only known photo of Buddy Bolden. Interestingly, most bassists during the early jazz era were from New Orleans, from Jimmy Johnson, Henry Kimball, Billy and his son Simon Marrero, Arnold Loycano, Chester Zardis, "Chink" Martin Abraham, and Ed Garland through the pioneering recorded efforts of Wellman Braud, Pops Foster, Bill Johnson, Steve Brown, John Lindsay, and Al Morgan. Notable exceptions were John Kirby from Baltimore, Walter Page from Oklahoma, Thelma Terry from Chicago, and Joe Tarto from New Jersey.[9]

Among the best of the first generation of New Orleans bassists was Henry Kimball (1878–1931). Primarily a bow player, he led his own band and also played with the Excelsior Band with John Robichaux on violin and Dee Dee Chandler on drums in 1893.[10] William "Mr. Billy" Marrero (c. 1873–1920), however, was regarded "as the greatest bass violinist" by musicians and bassists alike in New Orleans.[11] A respected bandleader, he led the Superior Orchestra and was a noted bass teacher, having taught Pops Foster, Wellman Braud, and Al Morgan. His son Simon Marrero (c. 1897–1935) is among the first bassists to be recorded, his bass lines faintly heard on three tracks by the Original Tuxedo Jazz Orchestra, recorded in New Orleans on January 23, 1925.

During the early jazz era, performance practice for string bassists varied considerably, as all bassists frequently alternated between pizzicato (plucked with the fingers) and arco (played with the bow), often on the same song. They also primarily stayed in a two-feel, but by the end of the 1920s, bassists would also play walking bass lines in a four-feel, but this was typically reserved for an exciting part of the performance, such as behind a solo. Slap bass is also associated with New Orleans bassists, an aggressive manner of playing wherein the plucked note by the bassist's right-hand fingers is accompanied by a percussive hit on the fingerboard.

Allowing the bass to be heard above the band in live performance as well as on recordings, it was typically used to contribute to the rhythmic intensity of the performance, but also accompanied walking bass lines.

Steve Brown (1890–1965) was one of the first significant jazz bassists to appear on record and had a prodigious slap technique. He first played tuba, adding the string bass later. He went to Chicago in the early 1920s and played with the New Orleans Rhythm Kings and Elmer Schoebel's Midway Dance Orchestra before joining Jean Goldkette's Orchestra in 1924. On "Dinah," from January 27, 1926, he drives the band when playing in two with the bow and then appears to lead Don Murray's clarinet solo with his slap playing. His best work is on "My Pretty Girl" recorded four days later, an up-tempo dance piece with a brilliant, Beiderbecke-led full ensemble passage that features Brown's dynamic and syncopated slap bass lines driving the band. Along with other members of Goldkette's band, Brown joined Paul Whiteman in 1927 and remained an important member during his brief time with the band. Although he did not play any solos on record, he was given a solo feature in live performance, perhaps one of the first jazz bassists to have one.

Among the premier New Orleans bassists was George Murphy "Pops" Foster (1892–1969). His recordings with Red Allen, Louis Armstrong, and Luis Russell from 1929 and 1930 show that he followed the lead provided by Brown and used his bass to drive the band with his powerful quarter-note pulse. He began on cello before switching to bass and was active in New Orleans from 1906 playing early gigs with just about everyone including the first generation of jazz musicians including Freddie Keppard, King Oliver, Buddy Petit, Manuel Perez, and Mutt Carey. Foster left New Orleans in 1917 to play on the Mississippi riverboats with Fate Marable's band before moving to Los Angeles to play first with Kid Ory and then Mutt Carey. By 1923, he was in St. Louis making his first recordings on tuba with Charlie Creath, later recording with Dewey Jackson's Peacock Orchestra in 1926.

Foster moved to New York in 1929 to play with pianist Luis Russell's band, immediately recording first with Red Allen then Louis Armstrong. "Mahogany Hall Stomp" from March 5, 1929, features an astonishing performance by Armstrong with *three* different solos. Building up from a two-feel, the energy from Armstrong's climactic third solo increases with Foster launching into a swinging walking bass line before Armstrong ends on a long, held triumphant note. It is an astounding performance that hints at the Swing Era. Incidentally, the band minus Armstrong would follow this path as a proto-swing band first backing Red Allen then as its own entity recording as the Luis Russell Orchestra in 1929 and 1930.

Bill Johnson (1872/1874–1974) is the oldest jazz string bassist to appear on record. Beginning as a guitarist, before settling on bass around 1900, he was among the first of the New Orleans musicians to leave, departing in 1904, eventually moving to the West Coast in 1908 and leading a band that became known as the Original Creole Orchestra. By the early 1920s, he settled in Chicago where he played with numerous groups including King Oliver, appearing on the Creole Jazz Band records as banjoist. His main body of work on bass is from various small-group recordings from the late 1920s, including short features on Johnny Dodds's "Blue Piano Stomp" and "Bull Fiddle Blues" from July 5–6, 1928. Other highlights from this era include his forceful attack and solo on the Dixie Four's "St. Louis Man" and his impressive up-tempo walking lines on Ikey Robinson's "My Four Reasons."

Sidney Brown (1894–1968) was born south of New Orleans in Deer Range and started on violin which was his primary instrument then moved to New Orleans in the early 1910s. He joined Sam Morgan's band before switching to bass, later adding tuba. Brown played more consistent walking lines on eight songs with Sam Morgan's Jazz Band from October 1927. On these recordings, the band is a commercial New Orleans band loosely mixing collective improvisation with written parts. Its repertoire was quite varied, playing multiple styles, mixing hokum vocals on "Short Dress Gal" as well as recording three spirituals, one of which is sung in vocal quartet style. The instrumental "Boogalusa Strut" is the group's "jazz" showcase with hot solos and breaks and best showcases Brown's powerful playing. In fact, on the eight songs, he spends most of his time playing walking bass lines, his quarter notes sometimes augmented with slap. His note choices are repetitive, but his playing is strong.

Drums

Jazz drums emerged during the early jazz era through a combination of styles including New Orleans parade and marching bands, vaudeville, and ragtime. The drum set was not yet established, and the early history of jazz drumming parallels its development. However, the drums suffered on record by being underrepresented due to engineers who refused to record full drum sets until the advent of the electric microphone in 1927. From the onset, though, the drummer was often the main improviser in the band. At its most fundamental, though, drumming during the early jazz era was not that different from today, to participate in the ensemble by keeping time and adding color.

Within the context of parade, marching, and brass bands in New Orleans, drummers learned formal drum techniques and how to read music. The drummer played an important role during funeral parades, signaling a change from a dirge or similarly somber piece to one that is more festive. In interviews, Baby Dodds explained that he was often hired to play such music "because I knew just when to cut in and start the real jazz home."[12] Among the early generation of drummers in New Orleans at the turn of the twentieth century were those playing under John Robichaux's leadership including Edward "Dee Dee" Chandler (c. 1866–1925), the first to use the bass drum pedal in a dance band, and Louis "Old Man" Cottrell Sr. (1878–1927), who is thought to have been one of the first to apply vaudeville "trap" drums to dance bands.[13]

The drummer in vaudeville held an important job that was highly informed by similar work in the theater pit, for traveling shows, at the circus, and later, at silent movie houses. Often playing in cramped spaces, it was more economical to have one drummer to play and to improvise different sound effects to accompany the show. The need for different colors and the imitation of various sounds (the clip-clop of the horse's hooves was accomplished by hitting the rim of the snare drum, a roll on the bass drum imitates thunder, etc.) were important aspects of the job thus requiring a wide range of instruments including Chinese tom-toms and cymbals, woodblocks, and temple blocks as well as nonmusical instruments like cowbells, washboards, sandpaper, and fly swatters, an early ancestor of the wire brush, and for comedic effect, slide whistles and fire gongs. This wide array of instruments led to vaudeville drummers being labeled as "trap-drummers."[14]

The early jazz rhythmic vocabulary of drumming, however, was derived from ragtime. African American Buddy Gilmore (1880–?) and his improvisatory style led early jazz historians to consider him to be the first jazz drummer, and undoubtedly his work is an important step from reading to interpreting the written page. Born in Raleigh, North Carolina, he was a star in James Reese Europe's Society Orchestra with his own drum features. His drumming so impressed dancer Vernon Castle that Castle learned drums from Gilmore, and a drum battle between the two became part of the act.[15] "Castle House Rag," recorded by James Reese

Europe in 1914, features Gilmore's drumming. Despite claims that the drums were too loud for recording at this time, the drums are easily heard and are being clearly played at a loud volume. In the final section, he plays a stop-time solo before the final coda where he never repeats himself, improvising a short solo and embellishing the final "shave-and-a-haircut" ending. Original Dixieland Jazz Band's Tony Sbarbaro (1897–1969) was originally from New Orleans, but his style falls more neatly into ragtime, with his tendency to change textures by switching instruments.

During the early jazz era, different styles of drumming developed in New Orleans, Chicago, and New York. The second generation of New Orleans drummers played their best work in Chicago and include Andrew Hilaire, Tubby Hall, and Paul Barbarin, but the most import-ant were Warren "Baby" Dodds and Zutty Singleton. Their beginnings were remarkably similar, learning their craft from teachers and informal settings, playing in dance and parade bands, and gaining valuable pro-fessional experience onboard Fate Marable's riverboat bands. However, their contributions were considerably different.

As a member of King Oliver's Creole Jazz Band, Dodds maintained a style informed by ragtime and was a pivotal figure in the evolution of drumming from ragtime to the Chicago style. More than other drummers before him, he was concerned with what to play behind the soloist that would better complement or support their rhythms.[16] He is well featured on "Wolverine Blues," a trio number with his brother Johnny and Jelly Roll Morton from June 10, 1927, where he plays in his usual ragtime style, changing instruments or sounds for each chorus, but playing con-temporary rhythms: Charleston, off-beat accents, and a ride cymbal beat.[17]

Singleton became well-known through his exquisite brush work with Louis Armstrong's Hot Seven from 1928 and trio recordings led by Jelly Roll Morton on piano with Barney Bigard on clarinet. A flexible musician, he assimilated the work of the Chicagoans and is an important link between New Orleans drumming with the Swing Era. His influence is noticeable on Morton's "My Little Dixie Home" as Singleton grooves hard behind Bigard while even playing a ride cymbal pattern for a short while at the end.

Drumming is an essential component of the Chicagoan style. Inspiration came from recordings and local drummers like Baby Dodds and the New Orleans Rhythm Kings' Ben Pollack, who for one chorus on "Sweet Lovin' Man" plays woodblock rhythms on the cymbal. The style was further developed by Bob Conselman, Paul Kettler, and Dave

Tough (1907–1948); however, the style became known to the world through the early work of Gene Krupa (1909–1973) on the landmark Chicagoan recordings from December 1927.[18] The new drumming techniques included bass drum on all four beats, off-beat syncopations and accents, and the use of rim shots while discarding the more novel sounds including the woodblocks and temple blocks. The drummer also initiated devices like the shuffle rhythm, continuous cighth notes on the rim of the snare during the bridge, as well as the explosion, a strong accent on beat four before a new section. Krupa's playing is compelling on the early Chicagoan records from December 1927 through spring 1928, and he made a strong impression on New Yorkers as the Chicago style and feel was quickly absorbed by other drummers.

New York–style drummers differed from their New Orleans and Chicago counterparts. These drummers had reading knowledge and the ability to play in larger formal dance bands while also being flexible enough to excel in small-group jazz. Among the best were Kaiser Marshall, George Stafford, and Chauncey Morehouse. Morehouse (1902–1980) took an early drum solo on brushes on the Georgians' "Land of Cotton Blues" from September 1923. He also played and recorded with Jean Goldkette, Bix Beiderbecke, Frankie Trumbauer, and Red Nichols.

Vic Berton (1896–1951), known for his work with Nichols, was an unusually versatile drummer. He experimented often with the role of the drummer, starting with his remarkable cymbal work. On "Poor Papa" by the Red Heads from February 1926, Berton's cymbals are clearly heard behind the clarinet solo as he improvises rhythms, complementing and even mimicking the clarinet's rhythms. He was also known for his "hot timpani" playing, playing short fills and accompanying soloists. Lastly, he was an early advocate for the hi-hat, then variously known as top hat, hi boys, lo boys (when the cymbals were foot-level), or snow shoes, and even patented his own version in 1925. Ultimately, he still maintained a ragtime approach to playing drums by switching instruments for different sections or soloists, a style that would vanish upon the arrival of the Chicagoans.

Violin

A less common instrument in modern times, the violin was more visible in the early jazz era. It was introduced to jazz through ragtime ensembles and especially early New Orleans dance ensembles, whose violinists played classical but also Cajun, fiddle music, and other folk styles that were popular in the American South. Often, the band's leader was a violinist, a tradition that goes back to John Robichaux at the end of the nineteenth century (and likely further) and continued into the 1920s with Armand J. Piron, Charles Elgar, and Carroll Dickerson. James Reese Europe and W. C. Handy's bands had strings, and Art Hickman's band out of San Francisco had one violinist which may have inspired Whiteman, himself a violist, to add strings to his ensemble.

The top jazz violinist of the early jazz era was Giuseppi "Joe" Venuti (1903–1978). A notorious prankster, Venuti was virtuoso musician steeped in classical music, and his strong tone and fluid technique enabled him to become a brilliant soloist with Jean Goldkette and Paul Whiteman, as well as his own recordings. He also overcame the volume limitations that accompanied his instrument, during pre-amplification times, that allowed him to be easily heard in both small and large ensembles.

Venuti's best work was with his own group with childhood friend Eddie Lang on guitar from the late 1920s. Most songs were jam session–type material to showcase Venuti's brilliant improvisations: "Stringing the Blues" was not a blues but based on the chord changes of "Tiger Rag"; "Wild Cat" was based off of "China Boy"; and "A Mug of Ale" is "Limehouse Blues." "Kicking the Cat," which also features Rollini on the goofus, is more involved with an introduction, interlude, and modulations. Regardless of the setting, Venuti is brilliant from start to finish, playing with fluid technique and a bag of tricks that were usually played during breaks and designed to impress his audience: fast lines, octave jumps via harmonics, and double- or triple-stops. Despite his obvious virtuosity, he is lighthearted about his music as he brings a certain elegance and charm to the music.

Stuff Smith (1909–1967) and Eddie South (1904–1962) began their careers in the early jazz era, but their best work was done later. Smith recorded with Alphonso Trent in 1928, and South's work steps outside the box of hot jazz and reflects his diverse interests. He grew up in Chicago where he studied with Charles Elgar and played with Erskine Tate. South made his first recording in 1923 with Jimmy Wade, but his 1927 recordings with his group the Alabamians are unusual in their instrumentation (violin, piano, guitar, and drums) and choice of material.[19] "By the Waters of Minnetonka" is programmatic featuring Native American rhythms, classical-like textures, unusual wordless, not scat, vocals, a hot jazz section, and an outstanding chordal guitar solo by little known "Little Mike" McKendrick (1903–1961).[20] "Two Guitars" from 1929 reveals the influence of gypsy music on South with a plaintive, minor theme. The arrangement with an out-of-time introduction and bass clarinet is a convincing merger of classical technique in a jazz setting that is strikingly modern.

Chapter 11

Territory and Other Bands

Away from the major music centers in New York and Chicago, dance bands sprouted across the country. Based in smaller cities such as Kansas City, St. Louis, Omaha, Dallas, and others, they typically operated within the vicinity of their home state and are known as territory bands. The best ones had strong local followings and received the best jobs. Band battles were common among local bands, but they also competed with bigger name bands that passed through town. Some musicians from territory bands were recruited by the bigger bands based in New York and Chicago, and in this sense, territory bands can be thought of as a training ground, or a minor league system, where musicianship and talent was fostered and developed. However, as recordings prove, the best musicians, for whatever reason, did not always leave, and many territory bands' performances were outstanding and rivaled those of Fletcher Henderson or Duke Ellington.

Life in a territory band was often difficult. Bands used two to three cars to travel great distances, driving hundreds of miles in one day often on dangerous roads and sometimes in unpleasant weather. Travel for African Americans was a real concern because segregation laws made it difficult for bands to find a place to eat, to get their vehicles serviced, or to find a place to stay. The threat of physical violence from locals was also a reality and prompted many musicians to carry guns. The publication of *The Negro Motorist Green Book* helped African Americans navigate the perils of travel, but it was not published until the 1930s. Moreover, many bands would travel hundreds of miles only to play to an empty hall and not get paid. Some ran out of money on the road, leaving musicians stranded and taking whatever jobs they could to work their way back home. Despite these experiences, a band was family and the most successful bands had loyal musicians who stayed together, bonding through thick and thin.

Individual territory bands' recorded output is meager, with some bands only recording two songs, but testimony from musicians reveals a deeper influence. Cincinnati bandleader Zach Whyte, for example, only has six recordings from 1929 to his name, but his best years were reportedly between 1931 and 1933 when trumpeter Sy Oliver—known for his later work with Jimmie Lunceford, Tommy Dorsey, Ella Fitzgerald, and others—was writing for the band. Alphonso Trent only recorded eight songs, yet they reveal a remarkable band with outstanding arrangements, excellent ensemble work, and top-rate soloists.

Cities across the country had excellent bands, and there are simply too many to mention, including Red Perkins and Lloyd Hunter's Serenaders in Omaha, Grant Moore and his New Orleans Black Devils in Milwaukee, the Black Birds of Paradise in Birmingham, Maynard Baird in Knoxville, and Troy Floyd in San Antonio. Memphis boasted many bands including Slim Lamar and his Southerners, the Memphis Stompers, and the Chickasaw Syncopators who would later become known as Jimmie Lunceford and his Orchestra.

Collectively, territory bands were important institutions, nurturing local talent and helping establish local jazz scenes that, in many cases, remain in place today. This chapter focuses on bands from the Southwest, particularly Kansas City which outgrew its territory status to become a major center for jazz on par with New Orleans, Chicago, and New York.

Kansas City

Based in New Orleans jazz and using the Northeast dance bands as a model, Kansas City developed its own unique brand of jazz. Key sources for the city's music was blues, originating from nearby Mississippi and the southwestern states of Oklahoma and Texas, as well as the ragtime influence with Sedalia, Missouri, located ninety-four miles away. That Kansas City could boast a thriving and fertile music scene was largely due to rampant corruption that can be traced to Thomas Pendergast. A powerful politician who largely controlled Kansas City and Jackson county, Missouri, from the mid-1920s through his downfall in 1939, Pendergast used intimidation and voter fraud to make sure his political friends were in power, allowing bootlegging and gambling to thrive through his control of the police force. With live music serving as a distraction for such illicit activities, opportunities for bands to play were plentiful as musicians gravitated to Kansas City for work.

Jam sessions, where musicians would come in and play or sit in, were common and became legendary. During an era before formal jazz education in schools, colleges, and universities, jam sessions served as an informal way of learning about jazz performance. They could act as cutting sessions, where young musicians could prove themselves, perhaps earning recognition or a place in a band while winning the acceptance of the older musicians. Musicians in traveling shows and bands were regular attendees at jam sessions, keen to learn about the local talent while maintaining their own reputation. Tenor saxophonist Coleman Hawkins was such a regular, who enjoyed delighting audiences as much as he enjoyed intimidating other musicians with his own abilities. In such a charged atmosphere, bar owners quickly realized that it was more economical paying a few musicians to host a jam session than hiring a large dance band.

Kansas City already boasted its own white dance bands, however, it was the vibrant African American scene centered around 18th Street and Vine where a distinctive Kansas City, or Southwest, sound emerged. Kansas City jazz rose to national prominence with the Count Basie Orchestra in 1938. However, the architect of that band was largely the work of pianist and bandleader Bennie Moten (1893–1935).

BENNIE MOTEN'S EARLY BANDS

Moten was born and bred in Kansas City in 1893. He learned piano from his mother before going on to study with Scott Joplin's students, Thomas "Scrap" Harris and Charles Watts. He played his first gigs at rent house parties and brothels before forming a trio, B. B. and D., in 1918, specializing in blues and popular songs. The group started out playing gambling rooms and parties before moving on to more respectable venues, dance halls, and social events for African Americans and whites.

By the time the group made its first recordings for Okeh Records in 1923, they had expanded to six pieces and were billed as Bennie Moten's Radio Orchestra. It was a young band with Lamar Wright on cornet, Thamon Hayes on trombone, and Woodie Walder on clarinet, but they would form a steady presence in Moten's band for the next few years. They were all recent graduates of Lincoln High School who studied under Major Nathaniel Clark Smith, a prominent music educator whose students include Harlan Leonard, Milt Hinton, Walter Page, Ernie Wilkins, and Ray Nance.

The band was still rooted in the sounds of ragtime, New Orleans, and vaudeville, but their playing would steadily improve over the next few years. King Oliver is a notable influence on the band, with Creole Jazz Band–like two-cornet breaks on 1924's "Goofy Dust" and "South," but more explicitly in trumpeter Wright's recreation of Oliver's "Dipper Mouth Blues" solo on "18th Street Strut" from 1925. By 1927, the band had developed a robust sound expanding to eleven pieces including Jack Washington on baritone saxophone to anchor the four-man saxophone section. They had become a strong band, sounding equally precise and at ease on fast tempo tunes as they were on slower material. The fast-paced "Moten Stomp" from June 12 is flawlessly played and exciting with breaks and strong, gutsy solos. The pulse is also noticeably stronger as is the groove. "New Tulsa Blues" swings with Moten's barrelhouse piano, the band's loose phrasing, and drummer Willie McWashington playing the "Western beat" with the drums accenting beats two and four. Other highlights include blues-informed solos by trumpeter Ed Lewis and Leonard on soprano sax, and the closing call-and-response sequence between the trombone and trumpets. It is far superior to the 1924 version which lumbers along by comparison.

JESSE STONE AND GEORGE E. LEE

For all of Moten's success, he had to battle many other local bands for continued popularity including Jesse Stone and his Blue Serenaders, George E. Lee's Novelty Orchestra, and Walter Page's Blue Devils. Jesse Stone (1901–1999) was born in St. Joseph, Missouri, and raised in show business beginning at the age of five singing and dancing in his uncle's minstrel show. He moved to Kansas City and studied music before starting his own band, the Blues Serenaders, in 1918. Playing a variety of gigs, including dances, concerts, and fairs, many band members doubled on other instruments as the band juggled a vaudeville-like stage show with Stone's tight arrangements in the style of his idol, Fletcher Henderson. At one point, Coleman Hawkins was a member before he joined Mamie Smith's Jazz Hounds.

Stone was a first-class entertainer, singing, dancing, acting, and playing piano, but the group's stage show did not translate in their recordings that instead focus on his brilliant arrangements. The group only recorded two songs in 1927. "Starvation Blues" is an outstanding performance that merges blues language with arranged sections. Stone brings out the ominous side of the blues with dissonance, emphasis of the blue note, and primal-like wails from his musicians.

Listening Guide: "Starvation Blues" by Jesse Stone and His Blues Serenaders
Jesse Stone: piano, arranger; Albert Hinton and Slick Jackson: trumpets; Glenn Hughes: alto saxophone; Elmer Burch: tenor saxophone; Jack Washington: alto and baritone saxophones; Druie Bess: trombone; Silas Cluke: banjo; Pete Hassel: tuba; Max Wilkinson: drums. Okeh 8471. Recorded April 27, 1927, in St. Louis.

Time	Section	Comments
0:00	A	Theme played on trumpet with responses played by muted trombone. The other instruments (second trumpet and tenor and alto saxophone) play light backgrounds.
0:19	A'	Same as above.
0:37	B	Muted trumpet solo with rhythm section (banjo, piano, tuba, and drums) answered by high shrill clarinets wailing on a single note. Tuba outlines a tritone interval in the accompaniment.
0:56	B'	Same as above.
1:14	B	Muted trombone solo accompanied by rhythm section only.
1:33	B'	Same as above.
1:51	B	Alto saxophone solo with a two-bar break leading to the next section.
2:10	B'	Same as above.
2:28	A	Theme is played as the beginning, but with the second trumpet adding a chilling countermelody in the upper register.
2:47	A'	Same as above.

The arrangement is sparse, with low backgrounds from the rhythm section (piano, banjo, tuba, and drums) and other instruments (trumpet and tenor and alto saxophones.) The opening theme is played on trumpet by Slick Jackson and answered by muted trombone played by Druie Bess. The first chord is the tonic, but the second chord is harmonically ambiguous. In essence a subdominant chord, Stone's arrangement, with the tuba staying on the tonic, suggests other possibilities (such as diminished). His painterly interpretation of that chord creates an unsettling atmosphere that seems to bring out a raw interpretation of the blues. This is further emphasized by Jackson who leans into the blue note, or flatted fifth of the scale, with slow slides.

Modulating to the relative minor for the B section, the ominous mood continues with the continued presence of that ambiguous second chord, now alternating with the new tonic minor chord and the tuba outlining a tritone interval. Meanwhile, there is a muted trumpet solo with wailing responses from the high clarinets, a chilling effect, followed by a muted trombone solo. The blues informs those solos, but is especially evident in the alto saxophone solo played by Glenn Hughes. Filled with bends and slides, his gliss to the root at B' is particularly poignant. Reportedly, Stone was known to write solos in his arrangements, though it is unknown whether he did so here or not.[1] An expressive countermelody from the second trumpet on plunger mute (above the first trumpet) is added to the final statement of the theme. Played by Albert Hinton, his intense vibrato adds to an intense wail or moan that is downright chilling. "Starvation Blues" is a startling arrangement that conveys a strong feeling for the blues. The other track from the session "Boot to Boot" is not as blues-informed but instead demonstrates the band's strength at playing up-tempo numbers. Unfortunately, the band fell apart due to mismanagement, and Stone went to work for George E. Lee.

A multi-instrumentalist, vocalist, and showman, Lee was among Moten's top competitors. His 1927 recordings are still ragtime-informed, but the presence of arranger Stone uplifts their 1929 recordings considerably as the music is more modern. Moreover, the band is strong, sounding inspired by Stone's sometimes complex arrangements. The instrumentals "Paseo Strut" and "Ruff Scufflin'" are gems of composition and arranging. Both songs feature extended forms and are through composed from start to finish. Throughout the performances, one gets the impression that nothing is orchestrated the same way twice, as Stone often adds small variations in texture (muted versus open trumpet) and timbre (breaks for the hi-hat and tuba). The music is sophisticated rhythmically, especially during the introduction and the C section of "Paseo Strut," which displaces the beat. The band pulls off the difficult music well, although they clearly sound more comfortable on the more straightforward arrangements heard on their vocal tracks.

Despite providing stiff local competition against Moten, Lee's recordings never had any national impact, and he remained in Kansas City. Stone, on the other hand, would enjoy a lengthy career as a performer, arranger, and bandleader through the Swing Era. He also played an important role in the birth of rock and roll, when, as Charles Calhoun, he composed a number of early rock and roll songs including a major hit for Big Joe Turner, "Shake, Rattle, and Roll."

WALTER PAGE AND HIS BLUE DEVILS

Moten's biggest nemesis may have been Walter Page's Blue Devils. Known originally as the Internationally Known Blue Devils, the band passed through Kansas City in 1922 where they hired the great bassist Walter Page (1900–1957). Born in Kansas City, Page studied at Lincoln High School under Major Nathaniel Smith who introduced him to the double bass. He toured with the Blue Devils for years and was based in Oklahoma. By 1925, he assumed leadership of the band, gathering a strong roster that included at various times Eddie Durham on trombone and guitar, Henry "Buster" Smith on alto saxophone, Oran "Hot Lips" Page on trumpet, Jimmy Rushing on vocals, and Bill "Count" Basie on piano. Following a successful audition for Brunswick, the group relocated to Kansas City with a public endorsement from Lee who dubbed them the "Syncopation Kings of the Southwest."[2]

Recording as Walter Page's Blue Devils, their output consists of two songs. Although the band sometimes sounds rushed, the seeds of the Kansas City sound are discernible. "Blue Devil Blues" features Rushing on vocals, but Page is on tuba and the song is firmly entrenched in the solid "two" feel that dominates early jazz. "Squabblin'," on the other hand, features Page on bass, and his robust sound greatly changes the feel of the music. The song features a head arrangement (an arrangement created on the spot and played by the musicians from memory), an emphasis on the ensemble, and individual solos by Page on trumpet and Smith on alto saxophone. There is also a feature for the rhythm section where there is no formal solo, just piano, guitar, bass and drums with the musicians playing their accompaniment parts. This would become a part of the Kansas City sound, as well as the use of riffs that would also be influential on Moten.

BENNIE MOTEN, 1927–1930

Moten's band lacked a frontman, and he was losing ground to Lee. His remedy was to change personnel and musical direction. He started by adding his nephew, "Bus" Moten, as the front man, leading the band on stage and playing piano and accordion. Moten's other tactic was to poach members of the Blue Devils away from the band beginning with Basie and Durham in 1929. Their influence is apparent on the group's next recording sessions in October 1929. Durham's arrangements accentuate a crisp ensemble sound, like on "Boot It" or "Small Black," while his guitar solos brightened the sound of the band. Basie, who was hired as second pianist, cowrote six of the eleven songs for the session. His solos further modernize the band with his stride-derived style and a stronger sense of swing. He is fluid, and his high-register fills during ensemble passages are particularly attractive, but he had not yet developed his minimalist approach.

The following year, Rushing and "Hot Lips" Page were brought in, and in 1931, the Blue Devils fell apart and the leader himself, Walter Page, relented and joined Moten. The combined forces of the two bands would result in a new Kansas City sound on the group's December 1932 recordings that would announce the arrival of the Swing Era.

MARY LOU WILLIAMS AND ANDY KIRK

The big three bands in Kansas City circa 1929 and 1930 were Moten, Lee, and Andy Kirk and His Twelve Clouds of Joy. A popular and successful band primarily associated with the Swing Era, Kirk's band emerged from Kansas City during the early jazz period and is perhaps best remembered today for its pianist Mary Lou Williams (1910–1981), whose arrangements helped catapult the group to mainstream success.

Born Mary Elfrieda Scruggs in Atlanta, Williams was raised in Pittsburgh. Her mother played piano and organ in church, and Williams began to show musical talent at an early age. Later, her interest in piano was cultivated by her stepfather, Fletcher Burley, who purchased a player piano for her along with the rolls of Jelly Roll Morton and James P. Johnson while encouraging her to play blues and boogie-woogie. Burley also took Williams to play at rent parties, dances, and tea parties. Local pianist Jack Howard was an early influence as was Lovie Austin, who passed through town accompanying shows and singers. But the support and encouragement Williams received from her family and friends was unusual for the time, as women, black or white, were discouraged from entering the entertainment industry. But Williams forged ahead and began touring in 1925.

While on tour, she met baritone saxophonist John Williams, and they married in 1926. Couples partnering together on tour was a practical decision due to difficult touring conditions and meager salaries. It also ensured that female performers would have protection from physical and sexual assault. The following year, the pair settled in Memphis and formed a band that recorded as John Williams Synco Jazzers in 1927 with Mary Lou taking her first recorded solo on "Now Cut Loose." John was called to join Terrence Holder's Dark Clouds of Joy, an Oklahoma-based band. It was a strong band with a high standard of musicianship, but Holder was kicked out for holding back money, and leadership was turned over to the tubist Andy Kirk, the eldest member of the band.

Andy Kirk (1898–1989) was born in Kentucky but was raised in Denver where he studied music at school with Wilberforce J. Whiteman, the father of the bandleader Paul Whiteman. In 1919, his formal training led him to work with George Morrison, a violinist who led a society band who specialized in playing classy arrangements of popular songs. The great Swing Era bandleader Jimmie Lunceford, incidentally, also passed through Morrison's band and, like Kirk, also studied with the elder Whiteman in Denver. Kirk started on tenor saxophone, then learned bass and sousaphone before settling on tuba. In 1925 he joined Holder and, having studied music theory in school, began writing arrangements. After taking over leadership of the Dark Clouds of Joy, and renaming them "Andy Kirk and His Twelve Clouds of Joy," he guided them to a successful audition at the Pla-Mor in Kansas City, where the band relocated, in 1929.

Though Williams was not formally a member of the band, she relished her time in Kansas City soaking in the city's vibrant music scene and participating in jam sessions, meeting Coleman Hawkins, Lester Young, Ben Webster, and others. Under the guidance of Kirk, she also developed as an arranger, learning by trial and error. The Pla-Mor engagement led to an audition to record for Brunswick Records in 1929. However, when the band's pianist failed to show, Williams filled in. She impressed the music executives and was immediately enlisted to write original arrangements to record, though she was still not officially a part of the band. This marked a turning point in the band as her arrangements would provide the basis for Kirk's mature sound.

Until this point, Kirk's sound was "sweet," but Williams's arrangements were imbued with an emphasis on blues, hot rhythms, and riffs. "Mess-A-Stomp," from November 7, 1929, stands out as by far the band's most advanced chart with rich chords, syncopated riffs, individual solos, and features for the saxophones and the full ensemble. But at a fast tempo, the band barely makes it through. However, on Williams's "Froggy Bottom," recorded four days later, the band sounds more relaxed and results are stronger. The swing is distinctive, augmented, at times, by quarter notes on the tuba. Blues permeates the entire performance, including the main theme and the individual solos, which ends with New Orleans-style counterpoint. But Williams is, by far, the dominant force, opening the performance with a brilliant piano solo. Her style at this point is a mix of boogie-woogie and stride piano styles. Earl Hines's influential approach is evident with right-hand tremolos and a left-hand that deviates from the strict bass-note chord pattern (Williams drops "bass bombs," or sudden accents in the lower register of the piano, on "Mess-A-Stomp"). Otherwise, her playing is rhythmic at heart with syncopations, riff-style improvisation, and a propulsive groove.

OTHER FEMALE PIANISTS

Besides Lil Hardin Armstrong, Williams was the most visible female pianist of the era. Her idol, Lovie Austin, by contrast, preferred the background role. As house pianist for Paramount records, she led recording sessions and backed singers, often accompanied by her own jazz-oriented group, the Blues Serenaders. She recorded under her own name, and her earliest recordings are her best, such as "Traveling Blues" from

Listening Guide: "Traveling Blues" 1924 by Lovie Austin and Her Blues Serenaders
Lovie Austin: piano; Tommy Ladnier: cornet; Jimmy O'Bryant: clarinet.
Paramount 12255. Recorded November 1924 in Chicago.

Time	Section	Comments
0:00	Chorus 1 (A)	Four bars of stop time before collective improvisation between cornet and clarinet resume. Note the unison clarinet-piano line to lead in the time.
0:14	Chorus 2 (A)	Same as above.
0:27	Chorus 3 (B)	Cornet and clarinet play the melody in thirds with clarinet fills and responses from the piano.
0:41	Chorus 4 (B)	Same as above.
0:54	Chorus 5(A)	Same as chorus 1 and 2.
1:07	C	Modulation to the subdominant. Collective improvisation.
1:25	C	Riffs played by cornet and clarinet with a boogie-woogie-style bass line before ending with collective improvisation.
1:42	C	Same as above with variations on the riff.
2:00	D	Collective improvisation with break for clarinet at 2:06.
2:18	D	Lanier anticipates the new section with a growling note at 2:16. Collective improvisation continues with cornet-clarinet break at 2:24.

November 1924, with Tommy Ladnier on cornet and Jimmy O'Bryant on clarinet.

Except for a short modulation to the relative minor in the C section, "Traveling Blues" is harmonically simple, made up of tonic, subdominant, and dominant chords, but Austin's arrangement is clever. Though the A and B sections are blues choruses, she distinguishes each section with stop time for the A sections and cornet and clarinet in thirds for the B section. The C section begins with collective improvisation before the cornet and clarinet state the riff-styled theme (and its variation). Austin's left hand is prominent here playing a boogie-woogie-style bass line. The D section features collective improvisation with a break in the middle of the form. Ladnier's growling note at 2:16 anticipates the next section and is an early example of the Chicagoan device, flare-up. O'Bryant is particularly fluid moving around the clarinet with ease, but Ladnier by contrast relies on short riffs for his part. Riffs were not yet common as Austin's arrangement looks ahead to Kansas City–style arrangements.

Instrumental trio performances were uncommon in 1924. While aided by the strong performances of O'Bryant and Ladnier's Armstrong-influenced playing, it is Austin's piano playing that completes the picture. Informed by barrelhouse and boogie-woogie styles then prominent in Chicago, she does not even solo but is adequately represented, filling in the sparse instrumentation with bass lines, chords, and countermelodies. She plays confidently, providing a solid foundation for the collective improvisation, the call-and-response phrases played by trumpet and clarinet, and the short, repeated riff figures.

Many other female pianists were active but did not record while others had to wait. Sweet Emma Barrett (1897–1983) was a pianist and vocalist who performed with the Original Tuxedo Orchestra during the 1920s and 1930s but did not make her first record until 1961. A self-taught pianist, she led the Preservation Hall Jazz Band during the 1960s; a persistent woman, she continued to perform even after a stroke in 1967 left her paralyzed on her left side. Pianist-vocalist Billie Pierce (1907–1974) also made her first recordings late, recording with Emile Barnes in 1946 and on her own in 1953. Originally from Florida, she danced and accompanied blues queens who passed through the Pensacola area including Ma Rainey and Bessie Smith during the 1920s before settling in New Orleans in 1930. She worked with Armand J. Piron, Alphonse Picou, trumpeter Dede Pierce, who became her husband, and later with the Preservation Hall band.

St. Louis

St. Louis is an underrated center for jazz, the character of its music shaped by traveling bands from around the country and especially upriver from New Orleans via steamboats. In addition to once being a center of ragtime, St. Louis also boasted a tradition of brass-band playing that dates back to the nineteenth-century with many German-born teachers providing quality instruction as reflected in the excellent trumpeters and trombonists that emerged during the early jazz era.[3]

Trumpeter and bandleader Charlie Creath (1890–1951) was a lead-ing figure and mentor to many musicians in St. Louis. He is also part of a tradition of St. Louis blues trumpeters along with Clifford King and Dewey Jackson. Creath began on alto saxophone before switching to trumpet. He also played accordion and began his career playing in carnivals and the circus including a band led by P. G. Lowery. He moved to St. Louis around 1918 and established himself quickly, eventually sending out several bands for jobs under his own name. He also worked Mississippi riverboats, eventually working side-by-side with Fate Marable. Frequent visits to New Orleans may explain the New Orleans character of his music right down to his own King Oliver–inspired solos played with a mute, not to mention his many sidemen who originated from the Crescent City including Zutty Singleton, Pops Foster, Lonnie Johnson, and Albert Wynn, among others.

Creath recorded twelve sides between 1924 and 1927, and blues dominates. Four of ten songs recorded from 1924 to 1925 are slow blues, but the band was versatile enough to convincingly play a sweet song and "Crazy Quilt," a slick performance from 1927 that is more in the New York vein. The band is strong with many talented sidemen, including Thornton Blue on reeds, Charlie Lawson on trombone, Cranston Hamilton on piano, and Floyd Campbell on drums and vocals. Marge Creath, his sister, played with his band but was not allowed to record when the opportunity arose. Covers of songs by Sidney Bechet and Jelly Roll Morton further the New Orleans connection as does Lawson's recreation of Louis Armstrong's solo from "Chimes Blues" played mostly note-for-note on "Market St. Blues," an astonishing feat for a trombonist and an indication of how pervasive Armstrong's influence was even in late 1924. An underrated trombonist who only recorded a handful of sides, he possessed a clear tone, excellent intonation, and remarkable control. Blue, who would later play in New York with the Missourians and Cab Calloway, was already an excellent soloist, playing a strong clarinet solo on Bechet's "Pleasure Mad" and sounding Bechet-like on alto on "Market St. Blues."

Cranston Hamilton on piano is strong whether exhibiting the influence of stride on his piano solo on "Market St. Stomp," showing off his fine technique on "Grandpa's Spells," or enhancing his accompaniments with his wide blues vocabulary. His playing behind vocalist Floyd Campbell's second chorus on "I Woke Up Cold in Hand" is ill-advised but daring and demonstrates his capabilities. Campbell's singing is said to have had an influence on Jimmy Rushing, although Rushing would be more of a shouter. Still, Campbell's diction is clear with a slight nasal quality that he shares with Rushing.

Dewey Jackson was another great St. Louis bandleader and trumpeter, who also worked on the riverboats from the late 1920s through the 1930s. The quality of his band can be heard on his four recordings from June 1926. The personnel includes Pops Foster making his recording debut on tuba as well as ex-Creath sidemen Campbell and Blue. Born in Missouri, Blue (1902–1968) was the son of a trumpeter who was a legendary music teacher and leader of the Pythian Brass Band in St. Louis. The younger Blue, who played clarinet and alto saxophone, gained experience on the road in the circus with P. G. Lowery and then with blackface comedian, Billy King, whose orchestra included members of the Blue Devils. Blue takes excellent clarinet solos on "Capitol Blues" and "Go 'Won to Town." Pianist Burroughs Lovingood has limited right-hand vocabulary but is well-versed in barrelhouse and boogie-woogie blues styles, a common trait among St. Louis pianists including Hamilton and Deloise Searcy.

Texas

Many bands emerged from Texas, and Alphonso Trent's band from Dallas is one of the strongest and perhaps best known. Despite only leaving behind a recorded output of eight tracks between 1928 and 1933, Trent's band has been acknowledged by Jimmie Lunceford, Mary Lou Williams, Herschel Evans, Louis Jordan, Budd Johnson, and others as one of the greatest bands in the region.

Alphonso Trent (1905–1959) was born in Arkansas and began his musical career there before gaining engagements in Oklahoma and Texas including an eighteen-month contract at the Adolphus Hotel in Dallas in 1925 that included nightly broadcasts on the radio, making them the first African American band to broadcast regularly on the radio in the Southwest.[4] The band toured in 1927 before playing on the Streckfus riverboats. Along the way, there were many band battles including one with Floyd Campbell's band featuring Louis Armstrong that ended in a draw. The group entered the studio in 1928, and their recordings reveal a precise and polished band. Noteworthy are "Black and Blue" and "Nightmare." The arrangements are creative, and the band handles the material with ease, showcasing impeccable musicianship and flawless intonation. The tight ensemble passages are balanced with excellent solos by Leo "Snub" Mosely on trombone, James Jeter on saxophone, and Leroy "Stuff" Smith on violin.

Despite being based away from the major music centers, Trent's recordings from 1930 already foreshadow the Swing Era. Like other territory bands, they suffered enormous hardships but pulled through into the early years of the Depression. By this time, Trent was no longer in the band, having formed his own territory band, and soon left the music business.

All-Female Bands

During the early jazz era, there were all-female groups, most of whom were local, including the Melody Girls from Sioux City, Bobbie Grice's groups from Indiana, and in England, Edna Courson's Rhythm Girls, the Grey Ladies' Orchestra, and the Grosvenor Ladies' Quintette.[5] The Schmitz Sisters from Wisconsin featured Viola Smith (1912–2020) on drums who would have a long career in music. The California Jazz Brides were led by Violet McAfee and advertised themselves as the "Greatest All-American Female Jazz Team in the World."[6]

For women who could not find work with bands led by male musicians, playing with all-female bands was often the best option available. Such ensembles were viewed as novelties that ultimately isolated women rather than integrating them into the mainstream.[7] Photographic evidence of all-female groups goes back to the nineteenth century during the period after the Civil War until World War I when all-female marching and brass bands formed in schools and even the military.[8] All-women ensembles thrived in Southern California and included the Los Angeles Women's Philharmonic, established in 1893, the Long Beach Women's Symphony, founded in 1925, and all-women concert bands appearing in San Diego from 1899.[9] All-black "ladies orchestras" became established during the 1910s, although the first were led by male musicians.[10] The first women conductors were in New York including Hallie Anderson (1885–1927) and Marie Lucas (1880s–1947), daughter of the celebrated minstrel composer Sam Lucas. A trombonist, Marie Lucas led the Famous Ladies Orchestra at the Lafayette Theater in Harlem before playing in other cities. There were also all-women saxophone groups during the early twentieth century including the Darling Four, the Schuster Sisters Saxophone Quartette, and the Twenty Saxophone Girls.[11] The Six Musical Spillers, an African American group playing a mixture of ragtime and classical music, were unusual in that they were comprised of three women and three men.

Some all-female bands toured on the vaudeville circuit as "flash acts." Surviving film footage of two such groups, the Ingenues and Bobbie Grice's Parisian Bricktops, provide documentation of such acts. Appearing on a lavish set, the band would appear looking glamorous, smiling, wearing big, showy dresses, and playing a wide range of music. The Ingenues all sang and doubled on multiple instruments, able to segue into an all-banjo and even an all-accordion ensemble.[12] Grice's group featured her over-the-top dances and gestures around the band. Her band was considered the best all-female group of the era: "They were absolutely great . . . I mean they swung. They sounded just like any male band you ever heard. You could go out of the room and just listen to them. You wouldn't know they were male."[13] Their opening number, "Because My Baby Don't Mean 'Maybe' Now," was their lone jazz number on the Vitaphone short that they made in 1929, as the band played a wide range of styles. Still, Grice's band and other all-female bands provided a foundation for the more visible and successful all-female swing bands of the 1930s and 1940s.

Chapter 12

Vocal Jazz

Singing is an important aspect of jazz history. Considering the strong African American vocal traditions in spirituals, work songs, field hollers, and blues that informed the development of jazz, it is a natural outgrowth of the genre (see chapter 1). Moreover, singing was a part of everyday life, and many early African American jazz musicians received their first exposure to music by singing either in church or with street corner barbershop quartets. Many continued to sing in addition to playing their instrument. Buddy Bolden, widely considered the first jazz musician, played cornet but was known to sing as well, as did Jelly Roll Morton, Eddie Condon, Jack Teagarden, and Louis Armstrong; later generations of musicians who were instrumentalist-singers include Nat "King" Cole, Roy Eldridge, Chet Baker, George Benson, and Nicholas Peyton. Then there are the instrumentalists, from Oscar Peterson to Keith Jarrett to Kurt Rosenwinkel, who would sing along with their own solos. Although these are not formally "vocals," it highlights how central singing is to jazz performance. The notion of instrumentalists imitating vocal sounds has deep roots going back to Africa, and when one considers the opposite, vocalists imitating instrumentalists, or scatting, the line between vocal and instrumental is further blurred. However, when it comes to jazz *singers*, the story gets complicated.

Long-standing biases in the jazz community against singers, women (who tend to be vocalists), and popular music have led to vocal jazz being overlooked in most jazz histories. The emphasis on instrument over vocal performance is deeply rooted in the early jazz era, because the period's popular dance bands focused on group and solo instrumentalists. Paul Whiteman made a breakthrough by hiring a vocalist, Irish-style tenor Morton Downey in 1924. Noting the enthusiastic audience response to Downey, he maintained singers as part of his band. But even then, performances almost always began with an instrumental rendition of the song first *before* the vocalist sang, a practice that continued into the 1930s. Initially, Whiteman only hired male singers, although he later broke the gender barrier when he brought Mildred Bailey to sing in 1929.

The story of vocal jazz is also complex as it brings to light its racially charged history. Prior to Mamie Smith's "Crazy Blues" in 1920, the first record of an African American singing the blues, the public were only familiar with white female singers singing songs "negro-style." At the turn of the century, they adopted African American vocal styles, sang coon songs, and were known as "coon shouters."[1] In addition, they wore blackface and were among the most popular singers on the vaudeville circuit. Incidentally, many were Jewish, including Fanny Brice, Nora Bayes, Stella Mayhew, Belle Baker, and Sophie Tucker, who heard in or related to the blues the shared plight of their race with African Americans. Tucker (1886–1966), known as the "Last of the Red Hot Mamas," and Marion Harris (1896–1944), the leading interpreter of W. C. Handy songs, were praised as the most successful whites to emulate African American singers. Harris's recording of "It Had to Be You" from 1924 is notable for its second chorus, substantially differently than the first one, where she sticks more faithfully to the written melody. Along with the pianist who also varies his accompaniment with grander gestures, Harris's embellishment of the melody creates a dreamier mood. This manner of singing through two choruses is still common practice among jazz vocalists today.

The most popular male singer of the early twentieth century was Al Jolson (1886–1950). Today he is best remembered for performing in blackface in the first full-length motion picture with sound (or "talkie"), *The Jazz Singer*, released in 1927. Such racially insensitive practices are rightly condemned, but to ignore Jolson's contributions to entertainment and popular singing is to miss his massive influence and impact on American entertainment. His singing style drew on a wide range of influences including opera, comedy, theater, popular music, and blues as he seamlessly blends singing, speaking, and declamation. He focused on the sound of words, reframing them with clear enunciation on the consonant and endless variations on vowels or diphthongs: melody becoming "mel-o-dee" while "blue" became "be-lew."[2] With a wide vocal range, his musicianship was impeccable with a captivating sense of rhythm and phrasing and a strong flair for improvising and embellishing the written melody. "Blue Skies" from *The Jazz Singer* is a fine example as Jolson, singing without blackface, masterfully paraphrases the melody with slides, slurs, scoops, grace notes, and melismas as he never sings the melody the same way twice.

With a vast repertoire, singing ballads, sentimental songs, and a lot of comedic songs, Jolson was an entertainer first. Watching Jolson in *The Jazz Singer*, he is extraordinary, bubbling with energy and using his entire body as he dances, smiles, points, and winks while he sings. Such gestures are anathema in jazz, but his manner of vocalizing and manipulating a song's melody and text are what a jazz singer does. More than any other white singer of his generation, he strongly exhibited the influence of African Americans, and his legacy is deep as he affected every singer and entertainer that came after him, black or white, male or female.

Ethel Waters

Over the course of her extraordinary career, Ethel Waters (1896–1977) gained success as a popular singer in the 1920s–1930s, then as an actress, starring in musicals, films, and later becoming the first African American to star on television. Her acting career eventually eclipsed her singing career, and her pioneering accomplishments as a jazz singer are forgotten. She initially came into national prominence through vaudeville and recordings, having been lumped into the classic blues category. But her vocal style was not as deeply entrenched in Southern blues, instead there are echoes of her African American contemporaries as well as white vaudeville singers like Nora Bayes, Fanny Brice, Marion Harris, Sophie Tucker, and Al Jolson. Her flexibility as a vocalist made her successful with both African Americans and whites, establishing her as one of the great early jazz vocalists.

Waters was born in Chester, Pennsylvania, following the rape of her teenaged mother. She started singing in church, but grew up in poverty, marrying at age thirteen before leaving her abusive husband to live in Philadelphia. Around this time, she began working as a singer and entertainer, working her way up from amateur shows and saloons to vaudeville, later moving up to touring shows and musical revues by the time she settled in New York in 1917. By this time, she was a headliner on the T.O.B.A. circuit, performing as "Sweet Mama Stringbean." Although her first recordings in March 1921 for the tiny Cardinal label did not have much of an impact, "Oh Daddy!" and "Down Home Blues," recorded two months later for Black Swan Records, were a big success. She maintains the theatrical element on the verses, but her individuality shines on the choruses where she is more likely to take liberties with the rhythms and melodies. Her voice was not as big or as earthy as Bessie Smith's or Ma Rainey's, but it was pleasant without being sweet while still maintaining the blues nuances of her contemporaries and emphasizing clear diction. "Ethel Sings 'Em," an original composition, was recorded in June 1923 and best features her grasp of the blues and an improvisatory spirit.

Waters's fame grew steadily from the mid-1920s as she sought to gain success among white audiences, singing on white vaudeville circuits and becoming the first African American to headline at the Palace, a prestigious venue in New York. In 1925, she introduced a new song, "Dinah," and her recording for Columbia Records became a huge hit. It was a commercial production with a large orchestra, so Waters does not deviate that far from the melody, but she began to be more daring with her improvisations during the late 1920s, particularly on recordings backed by a single pianist. "Lonesome Swallow," recorded with the great stride pianist James P. Johnson from 1928, is a moving performance as Waters's emotional involvement builds from start to finish. On her rendition of "West End Blues," with Clarence Williams, her voice is richer and warmer. Although she occasionally overenunciates a word on purpose, particularly enjoying rolling her Rs, the melody is decorated with slides, slurs, and grace notes in a highly personalized performance that also includes a short but wonderfully intimate scat solo. Her scat solo on "Guess Who's in Town" is outstanding and foreshadows Ella Fitzgerald and Carmen McRae among others. Finally, "I Got Rhythm" from 1930 with a small band features more wonderful scat singing but is even more adventurous as Waters reinvents the melody during her final exciting chorus with a growly, bluesy rendition.

Bing Crosby

Bing Crosby (1903–1977) was a hugely successful popular singer and actor, but in his early career, he, along with Armstrong, pioneered and helped popularize a new performance practice for popular male singers.[3] During an era when popular male singer voices veered from very low basses, high tenors, to falsetto voices, Crosby's natural approach highlighting his deep, baritone voice stood out. He relied on the microphone to amplify his voice and to make him sound more personable, and his lyrical approach was influential. The final touch was a detached sense of phrasing, as Crosby developed a straightforward manner of singing that would be emulated by just about every popular singer after him.

Crosby was raised in Spokane, Washington, and was inspired by a live performance by Al Jolson to pursue a career in show business. At college, he began singing with another vocalist, Al Rinker, brother of vocalist Mildred Bailey. They moved to Los Angeles and were performing on vaudeville, stopping shows with their unison scat breaks in the spirit of the two-cornet breaks by King Oliver and Louis Armstrong. In 1926, billed as "Two Boys and a Piano: Singing Songs Their Own Way" at a the Metropolitan in Los Angeles, they were discovered and recruited by Paul Whiteman. They became a jazz trio with the addition of Harry Barris, known as the Rhythm Boys, and complemented the orchestra's pop trio. It was Whiteman's first step towards establishing a more authentic jazz sound in his music.[4]

On record, Crosby frequently sang lead on Whiteman's jazz material, delivering remarkable performances on "Because My Baby Don't Mean 'Maybe' Now," "You Took Advantage of Me," and "From Monday On," which showcases his rich tone and sophisticated phrasing. More importantly, he *swings*, an important lesson he absorbed from his friend Louis Armstrong. "Muddy Water" from 1927 is the first recording of Crosby singing a full chorus, and his backphrasing and rhythmic punctuation is already advanced. Two takes of "Mary" reveal his inventive rhythmic and melodic variations as he never sings the same melody twice. During an era when vocalists sang in the middle of the performance, Crosby begins "T'Ain't So, Honey, T'Ain't So" on his own right before the band enters, the first such record by any vocalist. One of his best performances, though, is on "Changes."

Listening Guide: "Changes," Paul Whiteman's Orchestra with Bing Crosby
Bing Crosby: vocals; Henry Busse, Charles Margolis: trumpet;
Jimmy Dorsey, Charles Strickfaden, Nye Mayhew: baritone and alto
saxophones; Tommy Dorsey, Wilbur Hall: trombone; Chet Hazlett,
Hal McLean: alto saxophone; Kurt Dieterle, Mischa Russell, Mario
Perry, Matty Nalneck: violin; Harry Perella: piano; Mike Pingitore:
banjo; Mike Trafficante: tuba; Steve Brown: bass; Harold McDonald:
drums; John Fulton, Charles Gaylord, Austin Young, Harry Barris,
Al Rinker: vocals; Bill Challis: arranger. Victor 21103. Recorded
November 23, 1927, in Chicago.

Time	Section	Comments
0:00	Introduction	
0:10	Chorus 1 A	Full band: saxophones play the melody above a string pad and brass rhythmic hits, over the rhythm section.
0:19	B	Strings take the melody.
0:28	C	Trumpets play the Charleston rhythm–infused melody with responses from first the saxophones, then the strings (0:36).
0:38	A	Recapitulation of A.
0:45	AB	Interlude with short violin solo; rhythm section drops out.
0:52	Verse: AA	Syncopated verse that is an extension of the interlude. A sections feature trumpets and strings playing a variation of B from the chorus.
1:01	Verse: BA	B section features saxophone pads, before recapitulation of A.
1:10	Chorus: AB	Rhythm section resumes two-feel with the pop vocal trio, with its sweet sound.
1:29	C	Jazz vocal trio, the Rhythm Boys, enter, preceded by a break by Barris mimicking a cymbal stroke (1:28), scatting for the break at 1:35.
1:38	A	Pop vocal trio resumes singing.
1:47	Verse: AB	Bing Crosby vocals.
2:05	AB	Trumpet solo by Bix Beiderbecke.
2:24	CA	Full band on the Charleston rhythm melody.
2:40	Coda	Free time with a short saxophone solo ending with single tone from a bell.

On "Changes," arranger Bill Challis strikes a balance with symphonic, pop, and jazz elements as his arrangement features the various parts of the Whiteman orchestra including the string section, woodwinds, brass, rhythm section, and two vocal trios. The pop vocal trio sang with a sweet sound while the jazz vocal trio, the Rhythm Boys, sang with detached rhythm, scatted, and mimicked other instruments. The jazz content is represented by a terrific trumpet solo by Bix Beiderbecke and Crosby's swinging vocal. Despite the intricate melody and the fast tempo, he sings with clear enunciation and manages to sound relaxed, ending his phrases with slurred trombone-like phrasing that falls behind the beat. Crosby was able to achieve such subtlety in sound and phrasing by singing softly and accurately, letting the microphone amplify his voice. It was an important step that would propel him into stardom.

During the acoustic era, high tenors dominated the live stage because their voices could be heard in the back row of the theater, but radio, which amplified the voice with a microphone, paved the way for "crooning," a quiet, less forceful, and more intimate manner of singing. In 1928, saxophonist and singer Rudy Vallée was the first crooner to become a radio star and was very popular with the ladies. Others followed suit including Russ Columbo, Will Osborne, and Crosby whose style was well-suited to the microphone, making him more personable and relatable. Although still part of the Whiteman organization, Crosby began freelancing on other record dates including his own in 1929 before establishing a solo career. The release of "Just One More Chance" in June 1931 would propel Crosby into stardom as he reinvents American popular singing.

Other Singers

During an era when song pluggers dominated the music scene, singers often gave neutral or detached performances to boost the popularity of the song and sales of sheet music.[5] However, the innovations of Al Jolson, Ethel Waters, Louis Armstrong, and Bing Crosby, all of whom had distinctive vocal styles, would shift the focus towards the singer rather than the song. They are towering names in vocal jazz history, but they were certainly not the only ones singing jazz during the 1920s. Among male vocalists in the 1920s, Jack Teagarden and his blues-tinged baritone voice helped reinforce the sound of vocal jazz in the late 1920s, but novelty performer Cliff Edwards, or "Ukulele Ike," also played an important role.

Edwards was an example of a pedestrian singer who stood out because of his scatting, or "eefin" as he called it. His emphasis on its novelty sound makes it sound like caricature, especially when using his falsetto voice. As a high tenor he has the wrong voice type for jazz singing, but he was among the first to scat on record.

Many popular white female singers sang occasional jazz songs. Ruth Etting (1896–1978), a major star who was a Ziegfeld headliner and appeared on film, delivered a definitive performance of "Love Me or Leave Me" in 1929. Singing two choruses of the song, she moves away from the melody for the second chorus creating a more personalized performance. But Etting was a popular singer first, and such performances were the exception rather than the rule.

Annette Hanshaw (1901–1985), on the other hand, had a more consistent jazz aesthetic in her work. Primarily a studio musician, she became known for her studio work on record and on radio, recording a wide range of music. Except for her novelty material, Hanshaw sang mostly long-forgotten songs with a sweet voice that was typical of the era and managed to capture the spirit of jazz through a sure sense of rhythm, back phrasing, and her ability to swing. This allowed her to interpret the melody in such a way that personalized the performance. Her best performances include "Six Feet of Papa" or "Don't Take That Black Bottom Away" and paired Hanshaw with top New York studio musicians. "I'm Somebody's Somebody Now" and "Under the Moon," featuring Eddie Lang on guitar, Joe Venuti on violin, Adrian Rollini on bass saxophone, and Vic Berton on "hot" timpani, are particularly strong performances. But she achieves the same effect on "Ain't He Sweet" or "It All Depends on You" singing with longtime accompanist Irving Brodsky or accompanying herself on piano on "Lay Me Down to Sleep in California." The blend of sweet and hot styles in instrumental music was also creeping into vocal styles and would develop further during the 1930s.

Chapter 13

Jazz around the World

During the early jazz era, there were many pioneering American musicians whose work abroad had a powerful impact on the dissemination and continued popularity of jazz around the world. African American artists had been traveling abroad since the mid-nineteenth century, including various minstrel shows, musical revues, the Fisk Jubilee Singers, and other popular acts. Ragtime was not just a national phenomenon but was also an international one through the distribution of sheet music in Britain and other countries.[1] By 1911, the Six Musical Spillers, the Six Brown Brothers, and Wilbur Sweatman had traveled to Canada, with the Spillers and the Browns in England by 1914.[2] Other musicians who brought ragtime and syncopated music to England and France during the 1910s include drummer Louis Mitchell (1885–1957) and pianist Dan Kildare (1879–1920). Both men worked together and even recorded overseas. They were also associated with James Reese Europe who made his own trip overseas with his 369th U.S. Infantry Regiment's "Hellfighters Band."

In 1919, two groups traveled to Europe that would have a significant impact on jazz overseas. The Original Dixieland Jazz Band (ODJB) received an invitation to perform in England and arrived in London in April. While their stateside recordings had filtered abroad, the group made new ones in London, some with British pianist Billy Jones, that further deepened their influence when these recordings were distributed throughout Europe.

The second group was Will Marion Cook's Southern Syncopated Orchestra, which arrived in June. Cook (1869–1944) is best remembered as a composer for black musical theater at the turn of the century that featured all–African American casts. In late 1918, he formed the New

189

York Syncopated Orchestra, and the success of the group's U.S. tours in early 1919 led to their appearances overseas. Renamed the Southern Syncopated Orchestra (SSO), the music was primarily concert music with little jazz content, but they were well received with significant acclaim reserved for their star soloist, Sidney Bechet on clarinet. Hired to play on the blues number "Characteristic Blues," Bechet's playing especially impressed the critics including Swiss conductor Ernest Ansermet who praised Bechet in the first documented positive review of jazz and the first as well to acknowledge its African American roots.

While the SSO continued to tour Europe through 1922, Bechet left the group in late 1919 and stayed in London, playing in city's top dancing venues before being deported in November 1922 following an altercation. Bechet bought his first soprano saxophone during that trip, an instrument he'd be associated with in jazz until John Coltrane. Bechet returned to Europe as part of Claude Hopkins's band supporting a revue featuring Josephine Baker in 1925, but he soon moved on and stayed busy overseas, touring and leading his own bands, freelancing with Noble Sissle, touring Russia with Benny Peyton, and appearing in different revues before returning to the U.S. in 1932.

Arthur Briggs

Trumpeter Arthur Briggs (1899–1991) was also a member of the SSO. Born and raised in Granada, Briggs came to the United States in 1917, and soon attracted the attention of Cook, who invited him to join his New York Syncopated Orchestra in late 1918. Following the group's tour in England, Briggs stayed in Europe and built a significant career for himself overseas.[3] For the next decade, he spent time in London, Norway (1921), Brussels (1922–1925), Paris (1924–1925), Vienna (1925–1926), Istanbul (1926), and Berlin (1926–1928). Briggs played with a myriad of musicians including locals and a wide selection of Americans and other foreigners coming from as far away as Haiti, Senegal, and the Belgian Congo. Often billed as the Savoy Syncops Orchestra, Briggs made a short appearance in the 1925 silent film *Das Spielzeug von Paris* (Red Heels). He began to work and record with the English singer Al Bowlly (1899–1941). Half-Greek and half-Lebanese, Bowlly was raised in South Africa, but like Briggs, spent most of the 1920s traveling all over the world, touring South Africa, Southern Rhodesia, East Africa, and the

Far East. Soon after working with Briggs, he went to London where he became a pop superstar singing with English bandleader Ray Noble.

Briggs, meanwhile, maintained a heavy schedule booking club dates all around the continent. In December 1929, he joined Noble Sissle for an engagement at Ciro's in London and appeared in a 1931 film clip with fellow globetrotters Tommy Ladnier on trumpet, Rudy Jackson on clarinet, and Jack Carter on drums. Paris became Briggs's home base through the 1960s, after surviving time in a Nazi prisoner of war camp in 1942.

Sam Wooding

Post-1920, jazz in Europe was further stimulated by appearances of traveling New York dance orchestras. Paul Whiteman's European tours of 1923 and 1926 were tremendously successful; his overseas tours further popularized his brand of jazz in Europe. However, Sam Wooding's two long tours between 1925 and 1932 were also important for spreading jazz as well as for his being the first significant African American bandleader to play jazz in Europe, paving the way for others to follow including Claude Hopkins in 1925, Noble Sissle in 1928, and later Louis Armstrong in 1932 and Duke Ellington in 1933.

Wooding (1895–1985) began as a ragtime pianist before a stint in the army during World War I landed him in the 807th Pioneer Infantry Band under the leadership of Will Vodery (1884–1951), an important composer and arranger in African American musical theater. When he returned in 1919, he was inspired to start his own band starting in Atlantic City before moving on to New York. In addition to leading his own bands, he played in shows, accompanied singers, recording with Lucille Hegamin and Alberta Hunter in 1922, and developed his own songs and arrangements. His band succeeded Fletcher Henderson's Orchestra at the Club Alabam when the latter moved on to the Roseland Ballroom in July 1924.[4]

However, Wooding's biggest break came when his orchestra was picked up to be part of *The Chocolate Kiddies*, a revue of African American entertainers, including singers (notably Adelaide Hall), acrobats, dancers, comedians, and musicians. The show opened in Germany in May 1925 and the was a huge success, ultimately extending its stay for another two years. Duke Ellington wrote the music for the revue, but ultimately Wooding had some freedom for what songs to present, and the repertoire was diverse:[5] Wooding's sound by this time was firmly entrenched in Paul Whiteman's symphonic jazz style.[6] By June, the reception was so good that the group was offered a contract by Vox Records and they entered the recording studio.

The recording session yielded four songs, and the music is well played and cleverly arranged. Trumpeter Tommy Ladnier's solos are the highlight, with his improvisatory spirit evident on his breaks from both takes of "Alabamy Bound" even as he was still adjusting to a new method of playing the trumpet.[7] Hired specifically for the tour, it is abundantly clear that the New Orleans–born trumpeter has had the most experience with the blues language as the band otherwise reflects the pre-Louis Armstrong days of the New York jazz scene. The execution is heavy and the feel is stiff; moreover, echoes of vaudeville and minstrelsy abound in the ODJB-informed barnyard sounds, train effects, slap-tongue saxophone, and the banjo's fancy chordal work.

Perhaps the most intriguing aspect of the session is the inclusion of two sweet arrangements, "O Katharina" and "By the Waters of Minnetonka." Recording in Germany, Wooding was not subject to racist stereotyping (for recording) imposed by American music executives who would have balked at an African American band recording "sweet" music.[8] Both pieces are well played and highlight his musicians' ability to play different styles convincingly. His arrangement of "O Katharina," a popular song, is creative and aimed to please German audiences with quotes from German children's songs and the Christmas carol "O Tannebaum." "By the Waters of Minnetonka" is devoid of any jazz content, and the solos are strictly eloquent melodic statements. It is gently played and features melodic playing from various members of the band including Garvin Bushell on oboe and George Sedric on bass saxophone that better showcase their talents.[9]

Bushell (1902–1991) was a journeyman multi-reeds player who had a long and successful career as a sideman. He had been working with Wooding since 1923, but he was already an experienced musician having performed in the circus, on tour with vocalists Ethel Waters and Mamie Smith, in the studios with Fletcher Henderson, and on the vaudeville circuit. Born and raised in Springfield, Ohio, he studied briefly at Wilberforce University and was initially a clarinetist, but Bushell soon learned the alto saxophone, and in addition to learning alto clarinet and bass clarinet, he added bassoon, oboe, and flute. Although he was not a great soloist, he was a valuable section man with a wide variety of reed instruments at his disposal. During his career, which stretched into the

1980s, he worked with James P. Johnson, Fats Waller, Bessie Smith, Fletcher Henderson, Cab Calloway, Chick Webb, Wilbur de Paris, and John Coltrane.

Sam Wooding's tour was a success, and he played for royalty including the Crown Prince of Sweden, the King and Queen of Spain, as well as the leader of Russia, and his band was well received. By the time the group finally sailed for the U.S. in March 1927, they had visited and played in Sweden, Holland, Czechoslovakia, Hungary, Spain, Switzerland, Russia, Latvia, Poland, England, Italy, and France. Wooding and the band stopped off at Argentina for three months where they met violinist Leon Abbey (1900–1975), who had brought his own group to play in Argentina and later Brazil. A former member of Harlem's Savoy Bearcats, Abbey was another jazz ambassador whose travels would take him all over Europe through 1939 including an engagement at the Taj Mahal Hotel in India in 1935.

Wooding returned to Europe in June 1928 for another long tour, this time lasting until 1931. He recorded extensively in 1929, mostly commercial-based material, with numerous references to current artists and styles including Fletcher Henderson, Duke Ellington, Bix Beiderbecke-era Paul Whiteman, a variety of singing styles (Al Jolson, sweet, crooning, trio, scat, etc.), gaspipe clarinetists, blues guitar or banjo stylings, and vaudeville-style dialogues. The focus is on ensemble playing more than solos; otherwise these recordings are a snapshot of the jazz scene in the late 1920s.

White jazz dominated the public eye in the U.S. and especially in Europe where records by African American jazz musicians would not be available until the 1930s, making Wooding's recordings all the more valuable for spreading the sound of jazz. Although he played symphonic jazz, perpetuating Whiteman's musical ideals, Wooding was still an important interpreter of the music who spread jazz around wherever he traveled. His musicians were well compensated, and they were also given the opportunity to escape racism in the U.S. and to lead a different life as African Americans in the world. After his band broke up, many of Wooding's sidemen stayed in Europe.

Jazz in Asia

The demand for Western style entertainment from homesick European and American administrators and businessmen prompted the biggest hotels in Asia to import dance bands from agencies in Australia and the U.S. With enormous ballrooms to fill, there was plenty of work for musicians, and the center of activities was in Shanghai, China, the biggest modern city in Asia at the time. The night life scene was plentiful with numerous large, extravagant ballrooms like the Astor Club, the Majestic Ballroom, and the Paramount Hotel to host overseas bands.[10] Incidentally, most of the musicians were not Chinese, but Russians, most of whom were refugees in the wake of the Bolshevik Revolution of 1917.[11] But visiting American musicians had been present since at least 1919.[12]

Whitey Smith (1897–1970) was a Danish American drummer and vocalist who was a leading bandleader in Shanghai until 1937.[13] His two recordings from 1928, "She Wonders Why" and "Chinese Wedding," are closer to the New York dance band sound. The former is pop music and the latter merges traditional Chinese music with modern dance band instruments, even beginning with an excerpt of Chinese song, and is a good example of how the musicians had to meet their audiences halfway to present their music. Canadian trumpeter Jimmy Lequime was also active on the Asian circuit, playing in Shanghai but later led a band at the Grand Hotel in Calcutta, India where he recorded two songs, "Soho Blues" and "The House Where the Shutters Are Green," in March or April 1926.[14] Like most bands in the Far East, the lineup was international with musicians from Russia, the Philippines, Austria, the U.S., and England. "Soho Blues" features the recording debut of banjoist-vocalist Al Bowlly.

Pianist Teddy Weatherford (1903–1945) was perhaps the biggest name to travel to Asia. Born in Virginia, he spent time in New Orleans before ending up in Chicago in 1922, playing with Jimmy Wade and recording with the group in 1923, along with future jazz traveler Eddie South on violin. By 1925, he was considered Chicago's best pianist and joined Erskine Tate's Vendome Orchestra in 1925 and appears on the group's 1926 recordings with Louis Armstrong, playing remarkable solos. Then in August 1926, he joined drummer Jack Carter's group, which also included Valaida Snow on trumpet and vocals and reedsmen Albert Nichols and Billy Paige, for a residency at the Plaza Hotel in Shanghai followed by a tour of the Dutch West Indies.[15]

Jack Carter would remain active on the global jazz circuit through the 1930s, later playing and recording with Noble Sissle. A film of the band from 1931 in London offers a glimpse at the group's show mixing a well-played song, "Little White Lies," with a novelty number, "Happy Feet" with Carter singing lead while tubist Edward Cole dances. The band also includes fellow globetrotters Tommy Ladnier and Arthur Briggs on trumpets, as well as Rudy Jackson (1901–1969) on clarinet and saxophones. Jackson had already played with Carroll Dickerson and King Oliver (1923–1924) in Chicago before briefly playing with Duke Ellington's band in New York. After playing with Sissle in Europe through 1933, Jackson went on to play in India and Ceylon (modern-day Sri Lanka) until returning to the U.S. after World War II.

Teddy Weatherford was a respected pianist, and sadly no overseas recordings exist from this era. He remained abroad, basing himself in Shanghai, and would spend practically the rest of his life in Asia, returning to the U.S. in 1934 only to recruit musicians, among them trumpeter Buck Clayton. In the 1940s, he was in India, where he recorded for Indian Columbia Records and became a focal point of the jazz scene. His best work are his solo performances from 1937 and his trio recordings from 1942. He sings on the trio sides, and his piano work is sparkling.

Notes

Introduction

1. See Gunther Schuller, *Early Jazz* (New York: Oxford University Press, 1968), 78.

Chapter 1

1. Court Carney, *Cuttin' Up: How Early Jazz Got America's Ear* (Lawrence: University Press of Kansas, 2009), 7.

2. Caroline Vezina, *Jazz à la Creole: French Creole Music and the Birth of Jazz* (Jackson: University of Mississippi, 2022), 64.

3. Rudi Blesh and Harriet Janis, *They All Played Ragtime*, 4th ed. (New York: Oak Publications: 1971), 7.

4. John Edward Hasse, "Ragtime: From the Top," in *Ragtime: Its History, Composers, and Music*, ed. John Edward Hasse, 66–70 (New York: Schirmer, 1985).

5. Hasse, "Ragtime: From the Top," 66–70.

6. "Maple Leaf Rag," track 3 on Joshua Rifkin, *Piano Rags*, Nonesuch H-71248, 1970, vinyl.

7. Carney, *Cuttin' Up*, 19.

8. Carney, 20.

9. Blesh and Janis, *They All Played Ragtime*, 54–55; and David A. Jasen and Gene Jones, *Black Bottom Stomp: Eight Masters of Ragtime and Early Jazz* (New York: Routledge, 2001), 17–19.

10. Edward Berlin, *King of Ragtime: Scott Joplin and His Era*, 2nd ed. (New York: Oxford University Press, 2016), 198.

11. This appeared for the first time on "Leola" published in 1905, see Berlin, *King of Ragtime*, 198, and Vera Brodsky Lawrence, ed., *Scott Joplin: Complete Piano Works* (New York: Alfred Music, 1971), 126.

12. Ted Gioia, *History of Jazz*, 3rd ed. (New York: Oxford University Press, 2021), 28.

13. Max Morath, "May Aufderheide and the Ragtime Women," in *Ragtime: Its History, Composers, and Music* (New York: Schirmer, 1985), 155–156; and Gioia, *History of Jazz*, 25.

14. Max Morath, liner notes for *The Ragtime Women*, Vanguard VSD-79402, Vinyl record, 1977.

15. Ingeborg Harer, "Ragtime," in *African American Music: An Introduction*, ed. Mellonee V. Burnim and Portia K. Maultsby (New York: Routledge, 2006), 136.

16. Jon Milan, *Detroit: Ragtime and the Jazz Age* (Charleston, NC: Arcadia Publishing, 2009), 18 and 38.

17. Morath, "May Aufderheide and The Ragtime Women," 159; and Blesh and Janis, *They All Played Ragtime*, 221.

18. Sally Placksin, *Jazzwomen: 1900 to the Present, Their Words, Lives, and Music* (London: Pluto Press, 1985), 41–43.

19. Eileen Southern, *The Music of Black Americans: A History*, 3rd ed. (New York: W. W. Norton & Company, 1997), 232.

20. Southern, *The Music of Black Americans*, 235.

21. Southern, 236.

22. Marshall and Jean Stearns, *Jazz Dance: The Story of American Vernacular Dance* (New York: Da Capo Press, 1994), 65.

23. Stearns, *Jazz Dance*, 69.

24. Thomas J. Hennessey, *From Jazz to Swing: African American Jazz Musicians and Their Music, 1890–1935* (Detroit: Wayne State University, 1994), 18.

25. Alyssa Menhert, "Reconsidering McKinney's Cotton Pickers, 1927–34: Performing Contexts, Radio Broadcasts, and Sound Recordings," PhD diss. (University of Cincinnati, 2018), 46; and Mark Berresford, liner notes for Wilbur Sweatman, *Recorded in New York, 1916–1935*, Jazz Oracle BDW 8046, 2005, CD, 9.

26. Outlined in Lynn Abbott and Doug Seroff, *The Original Blues: The Emergence of the Blues in African American Vaudeville* (Jackson: University Press of Mississippi, 2017), 7–55.

27. Douglas Gilbert, *American Vaudeville: Its Life and Times* (New York: Dover Publications, 1940), 32.

28. Theodore Dennis Brown, "A History and Analysis of Jazz Drumming to 1942 (Volumes I and II)," PhD diss. (University of Michigan, 1976), 95.

29. Steven Lewis, "'Untamed Music': Early Jazz in Vaudeville," undergraduate honors thesis (Florida State University, 2013), 26–27.

30. Joe Laurie Jr., *Vaudeville: From the Honky-Tonks to the Palace* (New York: Henry Holt and Company, 1953), 81.

31. Gilbert, *American Vaudeville*, 33.

32. Garvin Bushell, *Jazz from the Beginning* (New York: Da Capo Press, 1998), 17.

33. Ads are quoted in Lewis, "'Untamed Music,'" 30.

34. As a young man, alto saxophonist and future free jazz leader Ornette Coleman joined Silas Green from New Orleans in 1949, a minstrel show that originated in the early 1900s.

Chapter 2

1. Biographical information from Pat Cather, "Birmingham Blues," Sunday Blues, accessed December 31, 2022, https://sundayblues.org/wp-content/uploads/2018/05/birmingham.pdf.

2. Henry Pleasants, *The Great American Popular Singers* (New York: Simon and Schuster, 1974), 22.

3. Angela Y. Davis, *Blues Legacies and Black Feminism: Gertrude "Ma" Rainey, Bessie Smith, and Billie Holiday* (New York: Vintage Books, 1999), 11.

4. Davis, *Blues Legacies and Black Feminism*, 13.

5. This section is taken from Pamela Brown Lavitt, "First of the Red Hot Mamas: 'Coon Shouting' and the Jewish Ziegfeld Girl," *American Jewish History* 87, no. 4 (December 1999): 257–258.

6. Lynn Abbott and Doug Seroff, *The Original Blues: The Emergence of the Blues in African American Vaudeville* (Jackson: University Press of Mississippi, 2017), 162.

7. Abbott and Seroff, *The Original Blues*, 15.

8. Abbott and Seroff, 125–126.

9. Abbott and Seroff, 164.

10. Abbott and Seroff, 164–165.

11. Abbott and Seroff, 169.

12. Thomas Brothers, *Louis Armstrong's New Orleans* (New York: W. W. Norton and Company, 2006), 159.

Chapter 3

1. Thomas Brothers, *Louis Armstrong's New Orleans* (New York: W. W. Norton and Company, 2006), 178–179.

2. Brothers, *Louis Armstrong's New Orleans*, 29.

3. Samuel Charters, *A Trumpet around the Corner: The Story of New Orleans Jazz* (Jackson: University of Mississippi, 2008), 17–19.

4. Donald M. Marquis, *In Search of Buddy Bolden: First Man of Jazz* (Baton Rouge: Louisiana State University Press, 2005), 35.

5. Marquis, *In Search of Buddy Bolden*, 36.

6. Charles Edward Smith, "White New Orleans," in *Jazzmen,* ed. Frederick Ramsey Jr. and Charles Edward Smith (New York: Harcourt Brace Jovanovich, 1967), 44.

7. John McCusker, *Creole Trombone: Kid Ory and the Early Years of Jazz* (Jackson: University Press of Mississippi, 2012), 73.

8. See McCusker, *Creole Trombone,* 88, and Bruce Boyd Raeburn, "The Storyville Exodus, or Why Louis Armstrong Didn't Leave . . . ," *Southern Quarterly* 52, no. 2 (Winter 2015): 10–33.

9. Brothers, *Louis Armstrong's New Orleans,* 136.

10. Marquis, *In Search of Buddy Bolden,* 107–108, and Brothers, *Louis Armstrong's New Orleans,*141.

11. Lawrence Gushee, "The Nineteenth-Century Origins of Jazz," supplement: Best of BMRJ, *Black Music Research Journal* 22 (2002): 165.

12. See discussion in Caroline Vezina, *Jazz à la Creole: French Creole Music and the Birth of Jazz* (Jackson: University of Mississippi, 2022), 104–120.

13. Tom Stoddard, *The Autobiography of Pops Foster* (San Francisco: Backbeat Books, 2005), 54.

14. Vic Hobson, *Creating Jazz Counterpoint: New Orleans, Barbershop Harmony, and the Blues* (Jackson: University of Mississippi Press, 2014), 88–92.

15. Raeburn, "Stars of David and Sons of Sicily," 128–129.

16. Garry Boulard, "Blacks, Italians, and the Making of New Orleans Jazz," *Journal of Ethnic Studies* 16, no. 1 (Spring 1988): 53 and Joshua Berrett, "Louis Armstrong and Opera," *Musical Quarterly* 76, no. 2 (Summer 1992): 240.

17. Boulard ("Blacks, Italians, and the Making of New Orleans Jazz," 54–55) and De Stefano discuss Italian lynching by white southern Americans in the early 1890s. George De Stefano, "Sonic Affinities: Sicilian and African American Musical Encounters in New Orleans," *Italian American Review* 9, no. 1 (2019): 70.

18. Raeburn, "Stars of David and Sons of Sicily," 138–139.

19. Raeburn, 147–148.

20. Charters, *A Trumpet around the Corner,* 100.

21. Lawrence Gushee, *Pioneers of Jazz: The Story of The Creole Band* (New York: Oxford University, 2005), 288–290.

22. Thomas Brothers, *Louis Armstrong: Master of Modernism* (New York: W. W. Norton and Company, 2014), 26.

23. McCusker, *Creole Trombone,* 117.

24. Lewis Porter, "Where Did the Word *Jazz* Come From?," *Jazz: A Century of Changes, Readings and New Essays* (New York: Schirmer Books, 1997), 10.

25. Alyn Shipton, *A New History of Jazz,* rev. and updated (New York: Continuum, 2010), 74.

26. Richard M. Sudhalter, *Lost Chords: White Musicians and Their Contributions to Jazz, 1915–1945* (Oxford University Press: New York, 1999), 41–42.

27. See chapter 9.

Chapter 4

1. Louis Armstrong is another, but he will be further profiled in chapter 8.
2. John McCusker. *Creole Trombone: Kid Ory and the Early Years of Jazz* (Jackson: University Press of Mississippi, 2012), 113.
3. Thomas Brothers. *Louis Armstrong's New Orleans*. New York: W. W. Norton and Company, 2006, 122.

Chapter 5

1. Rick Kennedy, *Jelly Roll, Bix, and Hoagy: Gennett Records and the Rise of America's Musical Grassroots*, revised and updated (Bloomington: Indiana University Press, 2013), 69.
2. For more Tarto and Berton, see chapter 10.
3. Chicagoans are profiled in chapter 9.
4. Albert McCarthy, *Big Band Jazz* (New York: G. P. Putnam's Sons, 1974), 183–184.

Chapter 6

1. Tom Davin, "Conversation with James P. Johnson," in *Jazz Panorama*, ed. Martin Williams (New York: Collier Books, 1964), 50.
2. Dick Wellstood with Willa Rouder, liner notes to *James P. Johnson*, Time-Life Records, TL-J18 P315521, 1981, vinyl box set, 16.
3. Richard Carlin and Ken Bloom, *Eubie Blake: Rags, Rhythm, And Race* (New York: Oxford University Press, 2020), 26.
4. David A. Jasen and Gene Jones, "Willie 'The Lion' Smith," in *Black Bottom Stomp: Eight Masters of Ragtime and Early Jazz* (New York: Routledge, 2002), 91.
5. Thomas Cunniffe, "Fats Waller at the Pipe Organ," March 5, 2019, https://jazzhistoryonline.com/fats-waller/, accessed August 18, 2022.

Chapter 7

1. Reid Badger, *A Life in Ragtime: A Biography of James Reese Europe* (New York: Oxford University Press, 1995), 82–83.
2. Morgan Howland, "1910s Pop Trend: The Ragtime Dance Craze," *Pop Song History*, June 10, 2014, https://popsonghistory.wordpress.com/2014/06/10/1910s-pop-trend-the-ragtime-dance-craze/. Accessed July 28, 2022.
3. Reid Badger, *A Life in Ragtime*, 64.

4. Gunther Schuller, *Early Jazz: Its Roots and Musical Development* (Oxford University Press: New York, 1968), 248.

5. See Christopher J. Wells, "'Go Harlem!' Chick Webb and His Dancing Audience during the Great Depression," PhD Diss. (University of North Carolina Chapel Hill, 2014) and Brian Harker, "Louis Armstrong, Eccentric Dance, and the Evolution of Jazz on the Eve of Swing," in *Journal of the American Musicological Society* 61, no. 1 (Spring 2008), 67–121.

6. Joshua Berrett, *Louis Armstrong and Paul Whiteman: Two Kings of Jazz* (New Haven, CT: Yale University Press, 2004), 19–20.

7. Berrett, *Louis Armstrong and Paul Whiteman,* 20.

8. Wooding is further profiled in chapter 13.

9. See Court Carney, *Cuttin' Up: How Early Jazz Got America's Ear* (Lawrence: University Press of Kansas, 2009), 128–137.

10. Whiteman is further profiled in chapters 9 and 12.

11. Samuel B. Charters and Leonard Kunstadt, *Jazz: A History of the New York Scene* (New York: Da Capo Press, 1962), 102 and 105.

12. Jeffrey Magee, *The Uncrowned King of Swing: Fletcher Henderson and Big Band Jazz* (New York: Oxford University Press, 2005), 36.

13. A theme heavily explored in Karl Hagstrom Miller, *Segregating Sound: Inventing Folk and Pop Music in the Age of Jim Crow* (Durham, NC: Duke University Press, 2010).

14. Rex Stewart, "Smack! Memories of Fletcher Henderson," In *Jazz Masters of the Thirties,* edited by Rex Stewart (New York: Macmillan, 1972), 26.

15. Magee, *The Uncrowned King of Swing,* 86.

16. Alyssa Mehnert, "Reconsidering McKinney's Cotton Pickers, 1927–34: Performing Contexts, Radio Broadcasts, and Sound Recordings," PhD. Diss. (University of Cincinnati, 2018), 85 and 92.

17. Mehnert, "Reconsidering McKinney's Cotton Pickers," 84.

18. Frank Driggs, "Don Redman, Jazz Composer-Arranger," in *Jazz Panorama,* ed. Martin Williams (New York: Collier Books, 1964), 99.

19. John Howland, "Artful Entertainment: Ellington's Formative Years in Context," in *The Cambridge Companion to Duke Ellington,* ed. Edward Green (Cambridge: Cambridge University Press, 2014), 25.

20. Jeffrey Magee, "Ellington's Afro-Modernist Vision in the 1920s," in *The Cambridge Companion to Duke Ellington,* ed. Edward Green (Cambridge: Cambridge University Press, 2014), 86.

21. Carney, *Cuttin' Up,* 91.

Chapter 8

1. Thomas Brothers, *Louis Armstrong's New Orleans* (New York: W. W. Norton and Company, 2006), 103.

2. Garvin Bushell as told to Mark Tucker, *Jazz from the Beginning* (New York: Da Capo Press, 1998), 22.

3. See chapter 7 for more about Armstrong's tenure with Fletcher Henderson.

4. Thomas Brothers, *Louis Armstrong: Master of Modernism* (New York: W. W. Norton and Company, 2014), 159.

5. Bob Wilber, Liner Notes to *Johnny Dodds*, Time Life STL-J26, Vinyl Box Set, 1982.

6. Brothers, *Louis Armstrong's New Orleans*, 94–95.

7. Brothers, *Louis Armstrong: Master of Modernism*, 248 and Brian Harker, *Louis Armstrong's Hot Five and Hot Seven Recordings* (New York: Oxford University Press, 2011), 61.

8. William Howland Kenney, *Chicago Jazz, A Cultural History 1904–1930* (New York: Oxford University Press, 1993), 59.

9. Brothers, *Louis Armstrong: Master of Modernism*, 190.

10. Harker, *Louis Armstrong's Hot Five and Hot Seven Recordings*, 89–90.

11. Harker, 97–100.

12. Harker, 126.

13. Harker, 140–142.

14. Lewis Porter, "She Wiped All the Men Out," *Music Educators Journal* 71, no. 1 (September 1984), 44.

15. Placksin, Sally, *Jazzwomen: 1900 to the Present: Their Words, Lives, and Music* (London: Pluto Press, 1985), 64.

16. Placksin, *Jazzwomen*, 64.

17. Will Friedwald, *A Biographical Guide to the Great Jazz and Pop Singers* (New York: Pantheon Books, 2010), 192–193 and Andre Hodeir, *Jazz: Its Evolution and Essence*, updated ed. (New York: Grove Press, 1956), 162–168.

18. Harker, 169–170.

Chapter 9

1. Eddie Condon with Thomas Sugrue, *We Called It Music: A Generation of Jazz* (New York: Da Capo Press, 1992), 152.

2. Information on Thelma Terry from Brian Scott McKenzie, "Thelma Terry, Jazz Bandleader of the 20s," *Brian Scott McKenzie* (blog), December 20, 2015, https://brianscottmackenzie.medium.com/thelma-terry-jazz-bandleader-of-the-20s-dd28130c7239, accessed July 13, 2022 and Marquis Howell, "Thelma Terry, a Bassist to Remember," *Art of Slap Bass*, September 30, 2019, https://www.artofslapbass.com/thelma-terry/, accessed July 13, 2022.

3. Marty Grosz, "Frank Teschemacher: Biography and Notes on the Music," liner notes for *Frank Teschemacher*, Time-Life Records STL-J23, 1982, Vinyl box set, 30.

4. The Chicagoans' story continues in chapter 5.

5. Richard M. Sudhalter, *Lost Chords: White Musicians and Their Contributions to Jazz, 1915–1945* (Oxford University Press: New York, 1999), 448.

6. Ate Van Delden, "Jean Goldkette (1893–1962)," liner notes for *Jean Goldkette Bands 1924–1929*, Timeless Records CBC 1-084, CD, 2003.

7. Mike Peters, liner notes for Joe Venuti and Eddie Lang, *The Classic Columbia and Okeh Joe Venuti and Eddie Lang Sessions*, Mosaic MD8-213, 2002, 1.

Chapter 10

1. Bob Wilber, liner notes to *Johnny Dodds*, Time-Life Records, TL-J26, Vinyl box set, 1982, 23.

2. Joel B. O'Sickey, "Fess Williams: Showman, Bandleader, & Clarinetist," Liner notes for Fess Williams, *1926–1930*, Jazz Oracle DBW 8041, 2003, CD, 14.

3. Mark Berresford, *That's Got 'Em! The Life and Music of Wilbur C. Sweatman* (Jackson: University Press of Mississippi, 2010), 50–52.

4. For more on "tailgate" trombone and Kid Ory, see chapter 3.

5. Rex Stewart, "The Father of Swing Trombone (Jimmy Harrison)," in *Jazz Masters of the Thirties* (New York: MacMillan, 1972), 52.

6. Richard Hadlock, "Jack Teagarden," in *Jazz Masters of the Twenties* (New York: Macmillan, 1965), 178.

7. Hadlock, "Jack Teagarden," 182.

8. For more on Eddie Lang and race, see Michael O'Malley "Dark Enough as It Is: Eddie Lang and the Minstrel Cycle," *Journal of Social History* 52, no. 2 (Winter 2018): 234–259.

9. For more information on Walter Page see chapter 11.

10. David Chevan, "The Double Bass as a Solo Instrument in Early Jazz," *The Black Perspective in Music* 17, no. 1/2 (1989): 76 and Donald Marquis, *In Search of Buddy Bolden: First Man of Jazz* (Baton Rouge: Louisiana State University Press, 2005), 80.

11. Danny Barker, *A Life in Jazz* (New York: Oxford University Press, 1986), 64. Approximate birth year and Marrero family history from "Eddie Marrero 1961-10-11," interview by William Russell, October 11, 1961, interview 1, William Ransom Hogan Archive of New Orleans Jazz Oral History Database, https://musicrising.tulane.edu/listen/interviews/eddie-marrero-1961-10-11/, accessed July 7, 2022.

12. Theodore Dennis Brown, "A History and Analysis of Jazz Drumming to 1942 (Volumes I and II)," PhD. diss., University of Michigan, 1976, 82.

13. Nick Jaina, "The Birth of the Drum Set," *Smithsonian Folkways Magazine*, Winter/Spring 2015, https://folkways.si.edu/magazine-winter-spring-2015-the-birth-of-the-drum-set/article/smithsonian, accessed July 9, 2022 and "Louis

Cottrell Jr.," interview by William Russell, August 25, 1961, Reel 1, William Ransom Hogan Archive of New Orleans Jazz Oral History Database, https://music rising.tulane.edu/wp-content/uploads/sites/383/2018/07/cottrell_louis_19610825. pdf, accessed July 8, 2022.

14. For more on "traps" including origins of the term see Brown, "A History and Analysis of Jazz Drumming to 1942," 95–98.

15. Matt Brennan, *Kick It* (New York: Oxford University Press, 2020), 63.

16. Brown, "A History and Analysis of Jazz Drumming to 1942," 216.

17. Brown, 236.

18. For more on Conselman and Kettler, see Brown, 310–316.

19. Anatol Schenker, liner notes to *Eddie South 1923–1937*, Chronological Classics 707, Compact Disc, 1993.

20. John Chilton, *Who's Who in Jazz*, rev. ed. (New York: Da Capo, 1985), 216.

Chapter 11

1. Gunther Schuller, *Early Jazz: Its Roots and Development* (New York: Oxford University Press, 1968), 289.

2. Frank Driggs and Chuck Haddix, *Kansas City Jazz: From Ragtime to Bebop—A History* (New York: Oxford University Press, 2005), 82–83.

3. Schuller, 310.

4. Henry Q. Rinne, "A Short History of the Alphonso Trent Orchestra," *Arkansas Historical Quarterly* 45, no. 3 (Autumn, 1986): 230.

5. John Cunningham, "All-Women Orchestras: A Big Band for the Girls in the Band," in *The Guardian*, November 4, 1983, https://www.theguardian. com/music/2016/nov/04/all-women-orchestras-archive?CMP=gu_com, accessed July 14, 2022.

6. Jon Milan, *Detroit: Ragtime and the Jazz Age* (Charleston, NC: Arcadia Publishing, 2009), 14.

7. Art Napoleon, liner notes to *Women in Jazz: All Women Groups*, Stash Records ST-111, Vinyl record, 1978.

8. Jill M. Sullivan, "A Century of Women's Bands in America," in *Music Educators Journal* 95, no. 1 (September 2008): 33.

9. Jeannie Gayle Pool, *Peggy Gilbert and Her All-Girl Band* (Los Angeles: Jaygayle Music Press, 2020), 28–29.

10. Eileen Southern, *The Music of Black Americans: A History*, 3rd edition (New York: Norton, 1997), 349.

11. Stephen Cottrell, "Early Twentieth-Century Light and Popular Music," in *The Saxophone* (New Haven, CT: Yale University Press, 2012), 149–150.

12. See Bobbie Grice's Parisian Bricktops, "1929 Bobbie Grice's Parisian Bricktops—Corrected Title," December 1, 1921, https://www.youtube.

com/watch?v=3KWSJ_AJgZ0, accessed August 1, 2022 and the Ingenues "The Ingenues-Band Beautiful (1928)," October 12, 2007, https://www.youtube.com/watch?v=8ACtACBX0gM, accessed August 1, 2022.

13. Sally Placksin, *Jazzwomen: 1900 to the Present: Their Words, Lives, And Music* (London: Pluto Press, 1985), 70.

Chapter 12

1. The history of the "coon" songs and "coon shouters" are discussed in more detail in chapter 2.

2. Henry Pleasants, *The Great American Popular Singers: Their Lives, Careers & Art* (New York: Simon and Schuster, 1974), 57.

3. See chapter 8 for more on Louis Armstrong and his contributions to vocal jazz.

4. Gary Giddins, *Bing Crosby: A Pocketful of Dreams, The Early Years 1903–1940* (New York: Little, Brown and Company, 2001), 143–145.

5. Giddins, *Bing Crosby*, 239.

Chapter 13

1. Catherine Parsonage, "A Critical Reassessment of the Reception of Early Jazz in Britain," in *Popular Music* 22, no. 3 (October 2003): 319–321.

2. Mark Miller, *Some Hustling This! Taking Jazz to the World 1914–1929* (Toronto: The Mercury Press, 2005), 11.

3. Biographical information from Horst P. J. Bergmeier and Rainer E. Lotz, "James Arthur Briggs," *Black Music Research Journal* 30, no. 1 (Spring 2010); 93–181.

4. Chip Deffaa, "Sam Wooding" in *Voices of the Jazz Age* (Urbana and Chicago: University of Illinois Press, 1992), 13.

5. Deffaa, "Sam Wooding," 15–16 and Bergmeier and Lotz, "James Arthur Briggs," 10.

6. Garvin Bushell as told to Mark Tucker, "On the Road with the Chocolate Kiddies in Europe and South America, 1925–1927, Part One" in *Storyville*, 131 (September 1, 1987), 184, https://nationaljazzarchive.org.uk/explore/journals/storyville/storyville-132/1264323, accessed July 26, 2022.

7. Bergmeier and Lotz, "James Arthur Briggs," 12.

8. Wooding had a diverse repertoire when he appeared at the Alabam, see Deffaa, "Sam Wooding," 13. On racist stereotyping see Rex Stewart, "Smack! Memories of Fletcher Henderson," *Jazz Masters of the Thirties* (New York: Mac-

millan, 1972), 26, and Karl Hagstrom Miller, *Segregating Sound: Inventing Folk and Pop Music in the Age of Jim Crow* (Durham, NC: Duke University Press, 2010).

9. By contrast, Paul Whiteman's version from 1924 is decidedly more in the hot jazz vein. The song was also in Fletcher Henderson's book, see Thomas Brothers, *Louis Armstrong: Master of Modernism* (New York: W. W. Norton and Company, 2014), 122.

10. Edward S. Walker, "Can't We Talk It Over?," *Storyville* 146 (June 1, 1991), 66–67, https://nationaljazzarchive.org.uk/explore/journals/storyville/storyville-146/1264161, accessed July 26, 2022.

11. Andrew F. Jones, "Notes on the Chinese Age," in *Jazz Planet*, edited by E. Taylor Atkins (Jackson: University of Mississippi Press, 2003), 231.

12. Miller, *Some Hustling This!*, 128, 137.

13. Andrew David Field, "Jazz Bandleader Whitey Smith, 'The Man Who Taught China to Dance' in Shanghai, 1920s–1930s," *Shanghai Sojourns: The Website of Andrew David Field*, May 19, 2017, http://shanghaisojourns.net/blog/2017/5/19/the-story-and-the-songs-of-jazz-bandleader-whitey-smith-the-man-who-taught-china-to-dance-in-shanghai-1920s-1930s., accessed July 27, 2022.

14. Henry A. Stonor, "They Played at Raffles," in *Storyville* 42 (August 1, 1972), 217–223, https://nationaljazzarchive.org.uk/explore/journals/storyville/storyville-042/1267220-storyville-042-0010?q=Al%20Bowlly, accessed July 27, 2022.

15. Peter Darke and Ralph Gulliver, "Teddy Weatherford," *Storyville* 65 (June–July 1976), 177–178, https://nationaljazzarchive.org.uk/explore/journals/storyville/storyville-065/1265207, accessed July 27, 2022.

Bibliography

Abbott, Lynn, and Doug Seroff. *Ragged But Right: Black Traveling Shows, "Coon Songs," and the Dark Pathway to Blues and Jazz*. Jackson: University Press of Mississippi, 2012.

Abbott, Lynn, and Doug Seroff. *The Original Blues: The Emergence of the Blues in African American Vaudeville*. Jackson: University Press of Mississippi, 2017.

Ake, David. *Jazz Cultures*. Berkeley: University of California Press, 2002.

Albertson, Chris. Liner notes for *Jelly Roll Morton*. Time-Life Records STL-J07, 1979. Vinyl box set.

Albertson, Chris. Liner notes for *Bessie Smith*. Time-Life Records STL-J28, 1982. Vinyl box set.

Albertson, Chris. *Bessie*. Revised and expanded edition. New Haven, CT: Yale University Press, 2005.

Anderson, Gene. "The Genesis of King Oliver's Creole Jazz Band." *American Music* 12, no. 3 (Autumn 1994): 283–303.

Armstrong, Louis. *Satchmo: My Life in New Orleans*. New York: Prentice-Hall, 1954.

Atkins, E. Taylor, ed. *Jazz Planet*. Jackson: University of Mississippi Press, 2003.

Badger, Reid. *A Life in Ragtime: A Biography of James Reese Europe*. New York: Oxford University Press, 1995.

Barker, Danny. *A Life in Jazz*. New York: Oxford University Press, 1986.

Bergmeier, Horst P. J., and Rainer E. Lotz. "James Arthur Briggs." *Black Music Research Journal* 30, no. 1 (Spring 2010): 93–181.

Berlin, Edward A. *King of Ragtime: Scott Joplin and His Era*, 2nd. ed. New York: Oxford University Press, 2016.

Berlin, Edward A. *Ragtime: A Musical and Cultural History*. New York: Open Road Distribution, 2016.

Berresford, Mark. Liner notes for Wilbur Sweatman, *Recorded In New York, 1916–1935*. Jazz Oracle BDW 8046, 2005. Compact disc.

Berresford, Mark. Liner notes *The Jazzworthy Ted Lewis*. Retrieval 79014, 2006. Compact disc.

Berresford, Mark. *That's Got 'Em! The Life and Music of Wilbur C. Sweatman.* Jackson: University Press of Mississippi, 2010.

Berrett, Joshua. "Louis Armstrong and Opera." *Musical Quarterly* 76, no. 2 (Summer, 1992): 216–241.

Berrett, Joshua. *Louis Armstrong and Paul Whiteman: Two Kings of Jazz.* New Haven, CT: Yale University Press, 2004.

Blesh, Rudi, and Harriet Janis. *They All Played Ragtime.* 4th ed. New York: Oak Publications, 1971.

Bough, Thomas. "The Role of the Tuba in Early Jazz Music from 1917 to the Present: A Historical, Pedagogical, and Aural Perspective." PhD diss. Arizona State University, 1999.

Boulard, Garry. "Blacks, Italians, and the Making of New Orleans Jazz." *Journal of Ethnic Studies* 16, no. 1 (Spring 1988): 54–55.

Brennan, Matt. *Kick It.* New York: Oxford University Press, 2020.

Brooks, Tim. *Lost Sounds: Blacks and the Birth of the Recording Industry.* Urbana and Chicago: University of Illinois Press, 2005. Kindle.

Brothers, Thomas. *Louis Armstrong's New Orleans.* New York: W. W. Norton and Company, 2006.

Brothers, Thomas. *Louis Armstrong: Master of Modernism.* New York: W. W. Norton and Company, 2014.

Brown, Theodore Dennis. "A History and Analysis of Jazz Drumming to 1942 (Volumes I and II)." PhD diss., University of Michigan, 1976.

Burnim, Mellonee V., and Portia K. Maultsby, eds. *African American Music: An Introduction.* 2nd ed. New York: Routledge, 2015.

Burrows, George. *The Recordings of Andy Kirk and His Clouds of Joy.* New York: Oxford University Press, 2019.

Bushell, Garvin. *Jazz from the Beginning.* New York: Da Capo Press, 1998.

Bushell, Garvin, as told to Mark Tucker. "On the Road with the Chocolate Kiddies in Europe and South America, 1925–1927, Part One." *Storyville* 131 (September 1, 1987), 184, https://nationaljazzarchive.org.uk/explore/journals/storyville/storyville-132/1264323, accessed July 26, 2022.

Calt, Stephen, Woody Mann, and John Miller. Liner notes for *Pioneers of the Jazz Guitar.* Yazoo, L-1057, 1977. Vinyl.

Capes, John. Liner notes for *"Hot Notes": New York—Volume 1.* Frog DGF8, 1996. Compact disc.

Carlin, Richard, and Ken Bloom. *Eubie Blake: Rags, Rhythm, and Race.* New York: Oxford University Press, 2020.

Carney, Court. *Cuttin' Up: How Early Jazz Got America's Ear.* Lawrence: University Press of Kansas, 2009.

Cather, Pat. "Birmingham Blues." accessed December 31, 2022. https://sunday-blues.org/wp-content/uploads/2018/05/birmingham.pdf.

Chapman, Con. *Rabbit's Blues.* New York: Oxford University Press, 2019.

Charters, Samuel B., and Leonard Kunstadt. *Jazz: A History of the New York Scene*. New York: Da Capo Press, 1962.

Charters, Samuel. *A Trumpet around the Corner: The Story of New Orleans Jazz*. Jackson: University of Mississippi Press, 2008.

Chevan, David. "The Double Bass as a Solo Instrument in Early Jazz." *The Black Perspective in Music* 17, no. ½, 1989: 73–92.

Chilton, John. *Who's Who in Jazz*. Rev. ed. New York: Da Capo Press, 1985.

Collier, James Lincoln. *Louis Armstrong: An American Genius*. New York: Oxford University Press, 1983.

Condon, Eddie, with Thomas Sugrue. *We Called It Music: A Generation of Jazz*. New York: Da Capo Press, 1992.

Cottrell Jr., Louis. "Louis Cottrell Jr. 1961-08-25" interview with William Russell. Musicrising.tulane.edu. August 25, 1961. https://musicrising.tulane.edu/wpcontent/uploads/sites/383/2018/07/cottrell_louis_19610 825.pdf.

Cottrell, Stephen. *The Saxophone*. New Haven, CT: Yale University Press, 2012.

Cunniffe, Thomas. "Fats Waller at the Pipe Organ." Last modified March 5, 2019. https://jazzhistoryonline.com/fats-waller/.

Cunningham, John. "All-Women Orchestras: A Big Band for the Girls in the Band." *The Guardian*. November 4, 1983. https://www.theguardian.com/music/2016/nov/04/all-women-orchestras-archive?CMP=gu_com.

Dance, Stanley. Liner notes for *Earl Hines*. Time-Life Records, STL-J11, 1980. Vinyl box set.

Dance, Stanley. Liner notes for *Johnny Hodges*. Time-Life Records, STL-J19, 1981. Vinyl box set.

Darke, Peter, and Ralph Gulliver. "Teddy Weatherford." *Storyville* 65 (June–July 1976), 175–190. https://nationaljazzarchive.org.uk/explore/journals/storyville/storyville-065/1265207.

Davin, Tom. "Conversation with James P. Johnson." In *Jazz Panorama*, edited by Martin Williams. New York: Collier Books, 1964.

Davis, Angela Y. *Blues Legacies and Black Feminism: Gertrude "Ma" Rainey, Bessie Smith, and Billie Holiday*. New York: Vintage Books, 1999.

Deffaa, Chip. *Voices of the Jazz Age*. Urbana and Chicago: University of Illinois Press, 1992.

DeLong, Thomas A. *Pops: Paul Whiteman, King of Jazz*. Piscataway, NJ: New Century Publishers, 1983.

De Stefano, George. "Sonic Affinities: Sicilian and African American Musical Encounters in New Orleans." *Italian American Review* 9, no. 1 (2019): 68–86.

DeVeaux, Scott, and Gary Giddins. *Jazz*. 2nd ed. New York: W. W. Norton and Company, 2015.

Driggs, Frank. "Don Redman, Jazz Composer-Arranger." In *Jazz Panorama*, edited by Martin Williams. New York: Collier Books, 1964.

Driggs, Frank. "Good-Bye Fess." *Storyville* 67 (October–November 1976): 14–23.

Driggs, Frank. Liner notes to *Sweet and Low Blues: Big Bands and Territory Bands of the 20s*. New World Records, NW 256, 1977. Vinyl.

Driggs, Frank, and Bertrand Demeusy. "Leon Abbey." *Storyville* 73 (October–November 1977), 4–28. https://nationaljazzarchive.org.uk/explore/journals/storyville/storyville-073/1263835.

Driggs, Frank, and Chuck Haddix. *Kansas City Jazz: From Ragtime to Bebop—A History*. New York: Oxford University Press, 2005.

Driggs, Frank, and Harris Lewine. *1920–1950 Black Beauty, White Heat: A Pictorial History of Classic Jazz*. New York: William Morrow and Company, 1982.

DuPage, Richard, and Frank Driggs. Liner notes for *Thesaurus of Classic Jazz*. Columbia, C4L 18, 1959. Vinyl box set.

Edwards, Bill. "Adolph Eugene Victor Maximilian 'Max' Hoffman," ragpiano.com. Accessed January 8, 2023. http://ragpiano.com/comps/mhoffmann.shtml.

Englund, Björn. "Chocolate Kiddies: The Show That Brought Jazz to Europe and Russia in 1925." *Storyville* 62 (December 1975–January 1976), 44–50. https://nationaljazzarchive.org.uk/explore/journals/storyville/storyville-062?.

Fell, John L., and Terkild Vinding. *Stride! Fats, Jimmy, Lion, Lamb, and All the Other Ticklers*. Lanham, MD: Scarecrow Press, 1999.

Field, Andrew David. "Jazz Bandleader Whitey Smith, 'The Man Who Taught China to Dance' in Shanghai, 1920s–1930s." *Shanghai Sojourns: The Website of Andrew David Field* (blog). May 19, 2017. http://shanghaisojourns.net/blog/2017/5/19/the-story-and-the-songs-of-jazz-bandleader-whitey-smith-the-man-who-taught-china-to-dance-in-shanghai-1920s-1930s.

Friedwald, Will. *A Biographical Guide to the Great Jazz and Pop Singers*. New York: Pantheon Books, 2010.

Gara, Larry. *The Baby Dodds Story*. Rev. ed. Alma, MI: Rebeats Publications, 2002.

Garner, David, and Mary Caton Lingold. "Banjo and Jazz." *Banjology*. Accessed July 8, 2023. https://sites.duke.edu/banjology/banjo-and-jazz/.

Gilbert, Douglas. *American Vaudeville: Its Life and Times*. New York: Dover Publications, 1940.

Giddins, Gary. *Bing Crosby: A Pocketful of Dreams, The Early Years 1903–1940*. New York: Little, Brown, and Company, 2001.

Gioia, Ted. *History of Jazz*. 3rd ed. New York: Oxford University Press, 2021.

Givan, Ben. "Duets for One: Louis Armstrong's Vocal Recordings." *Musical Quarterly* 87, no. 2 (Summer, 2004): 188–218.

Green, Edward, ed., *The Cambridge Companion to Duke Ellington*. Cambridge: Cambridge University Press, 2014.

Gridley, Mark. "The Time-Life 'Giants of Jazz' Series: An Essay Review." *Black Music Research Journal* 3 (1983), 70–82.

Grosz, Marty. Liner notes for *The Guitarists*. Time-Life Records STL-J12, 1980. Vinyl box set.

Grosz, Marty. Liner notes for *Frank Teschemacher*. Time-Life Records STL-J23, 1982. Vinyl box set.

Gushee, Lawrence. Liner notes for *King Oliver's Jazz Band—1923*. Smithsonian Collection R 001, 1975. Vinyl.

Gushee, Lawrence. Liner notes for *Steppin' on the Gas: Rags to Jazz 1913–1927*. New World Records, NW 269, 1977. Vinyl.

Gushee, Lawrence. "The Nineteenth-Century Origins of Jazz." Supplement: Best of BMRJ, *Black Music Research Journal* 22 (2002): 151–174.

Gushee, Lawrence. *Pioneers of Jazz: The Story of The Creole Band*. New York: Oxford University, 2005.

Hadlock, Richard, ed. *Jazz Masters of the Twenties*. New York: Macmillan, 1965.

Handy, D. Antoinette. *Black Women in American Bands and Orchestras*. New York: Scarecrow Press, 1981.

Handy, W. C. *Father of the Blues*. New York: Collier Books, 1941.

Harer, Ingeborg. "Ragtime." In *African American Music: An Introduction*, edited by Mellonee V. Burnim and Portia K. Maultsby. New York: Routledge, 2006.

Harker, Brian. "Louis Armstrong, Eccentric Dance, and the Evolution of Jazz on the Eve of Swing." *Journal of the American Musicological Society* 61, no. 1 (Spring 2008): 67–121.

Harker, Brian. *Louis Armstrong's Hot Five and Hot Seven Recordings*. New York: Oxford University Press, 2011.

Harrison, Max, ed. *Jazz Retrospect*. Boston: Crescendo Publishing Co., 1976.

Harrison, Max, Charles Fox, and Eric Thacker. *The Essential Jazz Records: Ragtime to Swing Volume 1*. London: Mansell, 1984.

Hasse, John Edward, ed. *Ragtime: Its History, Composers, and Music*. New York: Schirmer, 1985.

Hasse, John Edward. "Ragtime: From the Top." In *Ragtime: Its History, Composers, and Music*, edited by John Edward Hasse. New York: Schirmer, 1985.

Hasse, John Edward. *Beyond Category: The Life and Genius of Duke Ellington*. New York: Da Capo Press, 1993.

Hennessey, Thomas J. *From Jazz to Swing: African American Jazz Musicians and Their Music, 1890–1935*. Detroit, MI: Wayne State University, 1994.

Hentoff, Nat, and Albert J. McCarthy, eds. *Jazz: New Perspectives on the History of Jazz by Twelve of the World's Foremost Jazz Critics and Scholars*. New York: Da Capo Press, 1975.

Hobson, Vic. *Creating Jazz Counterpoint: New Orleans, Barbershop Harmony, and the Blues*. Jackson: University of Mississippi Press, 2014.

Hodeir, Andre. *Jazz: Its Evolution and Essence*. Updated edition. New York: Grove Press, 1956.

Holly, Ellistine Perkins. "Black Concert Music in Chicago, 1890 to the 1930s." *Black Music Research Journal* 10, no. 1 (Spring 1990): 141–149.

Homzy, Andrew. "Jazz-Style and Theory: From Its Origin in Ragtime and Blues to the Beginning of the Big Band Era." Master's Thesis. McGill University, 1971.

Howell, Marquis. "Thelma Terry, A Bassist to Remember." *Art of Slap Bass* (blog). September 30, 2019. https://www.artofslapbass.com/thelma-terry/.

Howland, John. "Artful Entertainment: Ellington's Formative Years in Context." In *The Cambridge Companion to Duke Ellington*, edited by Edward Green. Cambridge: Cambridge University Press, 2014.

Howland, Morgan. "1910s Pop Trend: The Ragtime Dance Craze." Last modified June 10, 2014. *Pop Song History*. https://popsonghistory.wordpress.com/2014/06/10/1910s-pop-trend-the-ragtime-dance-craze/.

Jaina, Nick. "The Birth of the Drum Set." *Smithsonian Folkways Magazine* (Winter/Spring 2015). https://folkways.si.edu/magazine-winter-spring-2015-the-birth-of-the-drum-set/article/smithsonian.

Jasen, David A., and Gene Jones. *Black Bottom Stomp: Eight Masters of Ragtime and Early Jazz*. New York: Routledge, 2001.

Johnson, Jerah. "Jim Crow Laws of the 1890s and the Origins of New Orleans Jazz: Correction of an Error." *Popular Music* 19, no. 2 (April 2000): 243–251.

Jones, Andrew F. "Notes on the Chinese Age." In *Jazz Planet*, edited by E. Taylor Atkins. Jackson: University of Mississippi Press, 2003.

Keepnews, Orrin. Liner notes for *Riverside History of Classic Jazz*. Riverside Records, SDP II, 1956. Vinyl box set.

Kennedy, Rick. *Jelly Roll, Bix, and Hoagy: Gennett Records and the Rise of America's Musical Grassroots*. Rev. and updated. Bloomington: Indiana University Press, 2013.

Kenney, William Howland. "The Influence of Black Vaudeville on Early Jazz." *The Black Perspective in Music* 14, no. 3 (Autumn, 1986): 233–248.

Kenney, William Howland. *Chicago Jazz: A Cultural History 1904–1930*. New York: Oxford University Press, 1993.

Kenney, William Howland. *Jazz on the River*. Chicago: University of Chicago Press, 2013.

Kernodle, Tammy L. *Soul on Soul: The Life and Music of Mary Lou Williams*. Urbana: University of Illinois Press, 2020.

Kinzer, Charles E. "The Tios of New Orleans and Their Pedagogical Influence on the Early Jazz Clarinet Style." Educational Philosophy and Pedagogy, *Black Music Research* 16, no. 2 (Autumn, 1996): 279–302.

Kmen, Henry. *Music in New Orleans: The Formative Years, 1791–1841*. Baton Rouge: Louisiana State University Press, 1966.

Lange, Horst H. *The Fabulous Fives*. Revised by Ron Jewson, Derek Hamilton-Smith, and Ray Webb. Essex: Storyville Publications, 1978.

Laurie, Joe, Jr. *Vaudeville: From the Honky-Tonks to the Palace*. New York: Henry Holt and Company, 1953.

Lavitt, Pamela Brown. "First of the Red Hot Mamas: 'Coon Shouting' and the Jewish Ziegfeld Girl." *American Jewish History* 87, no. 4 (December 1999): 253–290.

Lawrence, Vera Brodsky, ed. *Scott Joplin: Complete Piano Works.* New York: Alfred Music, 1971.

Levin, Floyd. *Classic Jazz: A Personal View of the Music and the Musicians.* Berkeley: University of California Press, 2002.

Lewis, Steven. "'Untamed Music': Early Jazz in Vaudeville." Undergraduate honors thesis. Florida State University, 2013.

Lotz, Rainer. Liner notes for *The Earliest Black String Bands, Vol. 1 1914–1917.* Document DOCD-5622, 1998. Compact disc.

Lowe, Allen. *That Devlin' Tune: A Jazz History, 1900–1950.* Berkley, CA: Music and Arts Programs of America, Inc., 2001.

Magee, Jeffrey. *The Uncrowned King of Swing: Fletcher Henderson and Big Band Jazz.* New York: Oxford University Press, 2005.

Magee, Jeffrey. "Ellington's Afro-Modernist Vision in the 1920s." In *The Cambridge Companion to Duke Ellington,* edited by Edward Green. Cambridge: Cambridge University Press, 2014.

Marquis, Donald M. *In Search of Buddy Bolden: First Man of Jazz.* Baton Rouge: Louisiana State University Press, 2005.

Marrero, Eddie, "Eddie Marrero 1961-10-11," interview with William Russell. Musicrising.tulane.edu. October 11, 1961. https://musicrising.tulane.edu/listen/interviews/eddie-marrero-1961-10-11/.

Martinelli, Francesco, ed. *The History of European Jazz: The Music, Musicians, and Audience in Context.* Bristol, CT: Equinox, 2018.

McCarthy, Albert. *Big Band Jazz.* New York: G. P. Putnam's Sons, 1974.

McCusker, John. *Creole Trombone: Kid Ory and the Early Years of Jazz.* Jackson: University Press of Mississippi, 2012.

McDonough, John. Liner notes for *Pee Wee Russell.* Time-Life Records, ST-J17, 1981. Vinyl box set.

McKenzie, Brian Scott. "Thelma Terry, Jazz Bandleader of the 20s." *Brian Scott McKenzie* (blog). December 20, 2015. https://brianscottmackenzie.medium.com/thelma-terry-jazz-bandleader-of-the-20s-dd28130c7239.

Menhert, Alyssa. "Reconsidering McKinney's Cotton Pickers, 1927–34: Performing Contexts, Radio Broadcasts, and Sound Recordings." PhD diss. University of Cincinnati, 2018.

Milan, Jon. *Detroit: Ragtime and the Jazz Age.* Charleston, NC: Arcadia Publishing, 2009.

Miller, Karl Hagstrom. *Segregating Sound: Inventing Folk and Pop Music in the Age of Jim Crow.* Durham, NC: Duke University Press, 2010.

Miller, Mark. *Some Hustling This! Taking Jazz to the World 1914–1929.* Toronto: The Mercury Press, 2005.

Morath, Max. Liner notes for *The Ragtime Women*. Vanguard VSD-79402, 1977. Vinyl.

Morath, Max. "May Aufderheide and the Ragtime Women." In *Ragtime: Its History, Composers, and Music*. New York: Schirmer, 1985.

Morgenstern, Dan. Liner notes for *Duke Ellington*. Time-Life Records ST-J02, 1979. Vinyl box set.

Morton, Jelly Roll. *Library of Congress Recordings by Alan Lomax*. Rounder Records, 1166-1888-2, 2006, Compact disc.

Napoleon, Art. Liner notes for *Women in Jazz: All Women Groups*. Stash Records ST-111, 1978. Vinyl.

Odell, Jay Scott, and Robert B. Winans. "Banjo." *Grove Music Online*. Edited by Deane Root. January 31, 2014. http://www.oxfordmusiconline.com.

O'Malley, Michael. "Dark Enough as It Is: Eddie Lang and the Minstrel Cycle." *Journal of Social History* 52, no. 2 (Winter 2018): 234–259.

O'Meally, Robert G. Liner notes for *The Jazz Singers*. Smithsonian Collection RD 113, 1998. Compact disc.

O'Sickey, Joel B. "Fess Williams: Showman, Bandleader, & Clarinetist." Liner notes for Williams, Fess. *1926–1930*. Jazz Oracle DBW 8041, 2003. Compact |disc.

Parsonage, Catherine. "A Critical Reassessment of the Reception of Early Jazz in Britain." *Popular Music* 22, no. 3 (October 2003): 315–336.

Perhonis, John Paul. "The Bix Beiderbecke Story: The Jazz Musician in Legend, Fiction, and Fact: A Study of the Images of Jazz in the National Culture: 1930–the Present." PhD diss. University of Minnesota, 1978.

Peters, Mike. "Joe Venuti and Eddie Lang." Liner notes for *The Classic Columbia and Okeh Joe Venuti and Eddie Lang Sessions*. Mosaic MD8-13, 2002. Box set.

Placksin, Sally. *Jazzwomen: 1900 to the Present: Their Words, Lives, And Music*. London: Pluto Press, 1985.

Pleasants, Henry. *The Great American Popular Singers*. New York: Simon and Schuster, 1974.

Pool, Jeannie Gayle. *Peggy Gilbert and Her All-Girl Band*. Los Angeles: Jaygayle Music Press, 2020.

Porter, Lewis. "She Wiped All the Men Out." *Music Educators Journal* 71, no. 1 (September 1984): 42–52.

Porter, Lewis, ed. *Jazz: A Century of Changes, Readings and New Essays*. New York: Schirmer Books, 1997.

Porter, Lewis. "Where Did the Word *Jazz* Come From?" In *Jazz: A Century of Changes, Readings and New Essays*. New York: Schirmer Books, 1997.

Priestley, Brian. Liner notes for *Classic Earl Hines Sessions 1928–1945*. Mosaic MD7-254, 2012. Compact disc.

Raeburn, Bruce Boyd. "Stars of David and Sons of Sicily: Constellations beyond the Canon in Early New Orleans Jazz." *Jazz Perspective* 3, no. 2 (August 2009): 123–152.

Raeburn, Bruce Boyd. "The Storyville Exodus, or Why Louis Armstrong Didn't Leave." *Southern Quarterly* 52, no. 2 (Winter 2015): 10–33.

Ramsey, Frederic, Jr., and Charles Edward Smith, ed. *Jazzmen*. New York: Harcourt Brace Jovanovich, 1967.

Rayno, Don. *Paul Whiteman: Pioneer in American Music Volume I: 1890–1930* (Lanham, Maryland, and Oxford: Scarecrow Press, 2003).

Reich, Howard, and William Gaines. *Jelly's Blues: The Life, Music, and Redemption of Jelly Roll Morton*. New York: Da Capo Press, 2002.

Rice, Marc. "The 1923 Recordings of the Bennie Moten Orchestra." *Musical Quarterly* 86, no. 2 (Summer 2002): 282–306.

Rinne, Henry Q. "A Short History of the Alphonso Trent Orchestra." *Arkansas Historical Quarterly* 45, no. 3 (Autumn 1986): 228–249.

Roth, Russell. "On the Instrumental Origins of Jazz." *American Quarterly* 4, no. 4 (Winter, 1952): 305–316.

Rust, Brian. Liner notes for *The Georgians 1922–1923*. Retrieval RTR79003, 2006. Compact disc.

Rustin, Nichole T., and Sherrie Tucker. *Big Ears: Listening for Gender in Jazz Studies*. Durham, NC: Duke University Press, 2008.

Rye, Howard. "Southern Syncopated Orchestra." *Black Music Research Journal* 29, no. 2 (Fall 2009): 153–228.

Rye, Howard. "The Jazz Kings and Other Spin-Off Groups." *Black Music Research Journal* 30, no. 1 (Spring 2010): 85–92.

Sandke, Randy. *Where the Dark and Light Folks Meet: Race and the Mythology, Politics, and Business of Jazz*. Lanham, MD: Scarecrow Press, 2010.

Schuller, Gunther. *Early Jazz: Its Roots and Musical Development*. New York: Oxford University Press, 1968.

Schuller, Gunther. *The Swing Era: The Development of Jazz, 1930–1945*. New York: Oxford University Press, 1989.

Schenker, Anatol. Liner notes for *Eddie South 1923–1937*. Chronological Classics 707, 1993. Compact disc.

Shapiro, Nat, and Nat Hentoff. *Hear Me Talkin' to Ya: The Story of Jazz as Told by the Men Who Made It*. New York: Dover, 1955.

Shipton, Alyn. *A New History of Jazz*. Revised and updated. New York: Continuum, 2010.

Simon, George T. Liner notes for *Benny Goodman*. Time-Life Records, TL-J05, 1979. Box set.

Smith, Charles Edward. Liner notes for *Riverside History of Classic Jazz*. Riverside Records, SDP II, 1956. Box set.

Smith, Charles Edward. "White New Orleans." In *Jazzmen*, edited by Frederick Ramsey Jr. and Charles Edward Smith. New York: Harcourt Brace Jovanovich, 1967.

Southern, Eileen. *The Music of Black Americans: A History*. 3rd ed. New York: W. W. Norton and Company, 1997.

Stearns, Marshall and Jean. *Jazz Dance: The Story of American Vernacular Dance.* New York: Da Capo Press, 1994.

Stewart, Rex, ed. *Jazz Masters of the Thirties.* New York: Macmillan, 1972.

Stoddard, Tom. *The Autobiography of Pops Foster: New Orleans Jazzman.* San Francisco: Backbeat Books, 2005.

Stonor, Henry A. "They Played at Raffles." *Storyville* 42 (August 1, 1972): 217–229. https://nationaljazzarchive.org.uk/explore/journals/storyville/storyville-042/1267220-storyville-042-0010?q=Al%20Bowlly.

Sudhalter, Richard M. Liner notes for *Bix Beiderbecke.* Time-Life Records, ST-J04. 1979. Box set.

Sudhalter, Richard M. *Lost Chords: White Musicians and Their Contributions to Jazz, 1915–1945.* New York: Oxford University Press, 1999.

Sudhalter, Richard M. Liner notes for *The Complete Okeh and Brunswick Bix Beiderbecke, Frank Trumbauer, and Jack Teagarden Session (1924–36).* Mosaic MD7-211, 2001. Compact disc.

Sudhalter, Richard M., and Philip B. Evans, with William Dean-Myatt. *Bix: Man and Legend.* New Rochelle, NY: Arlington House Publishers, 1974.

Sullivan, Jill M. "A Century of Women's Bands in America," *Music Educators Journal* 95, no. 1 (September 2008): 33–40.

Szwed, John. "Doctor Jazz." Liner notes for *The Complete Library of Congress Recordings by Alan Lomax.* Rounder 11661-1888-2 BK01, 2005. Compact disc box set.

Teachout, Terry. *Pops: A Life of Louis Armstrong.* New York: Houghton Mifflin Harcourt, 2009.

Teachout, Terry. *Duke: A Life of Duke Ellington.* New York: Gotham Books, 2013.

Thomson, David. Liner notes for *Fats Waller.* Time-Life Records ST-J15. 1980. box set.

Toll, Robert C. *Blacking Up: The Minstrel Show in Nineteenth-Century America.* New York: Oxford University Press, 1974.

Van Delden, Ate. "Jean Goldkette (1893–1962)." Liner notes for *Jean Goldkette Bands 1924–1929.* Timeless Records CBC 1-084, 2003. Compact disc.

Van Delden, Ate. *Adrian Rollini: The Life and Music of a Jazz Rambler.* Jackson: University of Mississippi, 2020.

Vezina, Caroline. *Jazz à la Creole: French Creole Music and the Birth of Jazz.* Jackson: University of Mississippi, 2022.

Walker, Edward S. "Can't We Talk It Over?" *Storyville* 146 (June 1, 1991), 64–68. https://nationaljazzarchive.org.uk/explore/journals/storyville/storyville-146/1264161.

Webb, Ray. Liner notes for *Lovie Austin And Her Blues Serenaders.* Fountain Records FJ 105, 1972. Vinyl.

Wells, Christopher J. " 'Go Harlem!' Chick Webb and His Dancing Audience during the Great Depression." PhD diss. University of North Carolina Chapel Hill, 2014.

Wellstood, Dick, with Willa Rouder. Liner notes for *James P. Johnson*. Time-Life Records, TL-J18, 1981. Box Set.

White, Shane, and Graham White. *The Sounds of Slavery: Discovering African American History through Songs, Sermons, and Speech*. Boston: Beacon Press, 2005.

Wilber, Bob. Liner notes for *Johnny Dodds*. Time-Life Records, TL-J26, 1982. Box set.

Wilber, Bob, and Richard M. Sudhalter. Liner notes for *Sidney Bechet*. Time Life Records, TL-J09, 1980. Box set.

Wilby, John. "Red Nichols." Liner notes for *The Complete 1926 to May, 1932 Brunswick Recordings of Red Nichols, Including the Wabash Dance Orchestra*. Jazz Oracle BDW 8062, 2011. Compact disc.

Williams, Martin. *King Oliver*. New York: A. S. Barnes and Company, 1961.

Williams, Martin, ed. *Jazz Panorama*. New York: Collier Books, 1964.

Williams, Martin, ed. *Jazz Masters of New Orleans*. New York: Macmillan, 1967.

Williams, Martin. Liner notes for *The Smithsonian Collection of Classic Jazz*. Smithsonian P6 11891, 1973. Box set.

Wilson, John S. Liner notes for *Louis Armstrong*. Time-Life Records, TL-J01, 1979. Box set.

Wilson, John S. Liner notes for *Jack Teagarden*. Time-Life Records, TL-J06, 1979. Box set.

Index